Observing the Economy

Observing the Economy: Historical Perspectives

Annual Supplement to Volume 44
History of Political Economy

**Edited by Harro Maas
and Mary S. Morgan**

Duke University Press
Durham and London 2012

Contents

Observation and Observing
in Economics

Harro Maas and Mary S. Morgan

The Question:
Observation as a Process and a Result

How do economists observe the world? For colleagues in the economics department, the question is almost automatically transformed into another with a seemingly easier answer: What are economic observations? "My statistical data, of course."

This change of question, from asking about a process to answering with an outcome, from *observing* as a verb to *observation* as a noun, has enormous consequences for economics and so for our histories. It hides the multitudinous practices of both *looking*—how economists of the past have focused their attention, have found out places, peoples, and practices in which economic behavior might be manifest, and of different perspectives that might be taken to these; and of *seeing*—of describing, typifying, mapping, and maybe measuring those things that had been observed in appropriate recordings.

But observation is no more identical with quantification than observing is with measuring. This conflation can be historically situated. After the rise of statistical thinking in the nineteenth century, and the econometric revolution in the 1930s, economists (and also their methodologists and historians) came to identify "observations" with statistical data sets gathered by statistical bureaus all over the world. These data sets— prerecorded by others and for other purposes—are commonly considered

History of Political Economy 44 (annual suppl.) DOI 10.1215/00182702-1631761

to serve as inputs for models and the testing ground for theories, and so these measurements came to be considered the "observations" economists work with. It is only comparatively recently that economists have generated their own observations through controlled experiments, yet retain that sense of outputs despite the attention to the process involved. Such observations tend to remain attached to their site of scientific observation and so not obviously freely available to the profession at large. Both genres of observations, the senior statistical and junior experimental, fit well with the mid-twentieth-century emphasis in the philosophy of science on observational statements, rather than on the process of observing, just as they fit contemporary economists' emphasis on measurement, quantification, and testing.

When questioned historically, these tenets in economics and philosophy of science lose their self-evidence. In *Representing and Intervening*, Ian Hacking (1983, 167) argued that much of twentieth-century philosophy of science was premised on two "philosophical fashions" that distorted our views on observation. The first was what Willard Quine called semantic assent: focus the analysis on observational *statements* rather than on observing as a process and as a practice. The second was turning experiment active and observing passive, well expressed by the nineteenth-century physiologist Claude Bernard, who degraded the observer into an "untrained and unprejudiced assistant" whose only work was to "patiently record nature's answers verbatim." As shown in detail in *Histories of Scientific Observation*, the outcome of an interdisciplinary project at the Max Planck Institute for the History of Science in Berlin, early modern philosophers had theorized observation as the "fusion of perception, judgment, memory, and reason," but for Bernard, "The observer no longer reasons; he registers" (quoted in Daston and Lunbeck 2011, 4).[1]

Turning the observer into a passive registering device left little of interest in the notion of observation for philosophers in the logical empiricist tradition over and above what could be expressed linguistically and preferably in "protocol sentences." Debates on the observability of theoretical concepts or the theory-ladenness of observational statements, spurred by Norwood Russell Hanson's and Thomas Kuhn's groundbreaking works, focused on the contributions of theory to observation, not on the process of

---

1. For references to literature in the history and philosophy of observation, we refer to this volume. References in this introduction are limited to literature cited.

observing as actively enriching scientific knowledge.[2] So philosophers of science tended and still tend to see observing, even when loaded with theory, as the mere registration of and reporting on facts in the world. The debate in the 1950s between Milton Friedman and Paul Samuelson on the status of modeling assumptions and the virtues and vices of operationalism in economics equally effectively confined the interest of economists and methodologists to the observability of the economist's theoretical constructs, understood in terms of their measurements and predictive values.

Yet observation "suggestively ambiguously" keeps the middle between process and result, as Lorraine Daston and Elizabeth Lunbeck (2011, 7) write. By insisting on the ambiguous seat of observation between doings and outcomes, this volume traces a history of sites, practices, and techniques of observing that shaped—and still shape—the economics discipline.

Observing Economic Observers:
A Casual Historical Tour

From a historical point of view, the idea that the observations made by political economists can be identified with quantified data outcomes is less than obvious. Rather the opposite, in fact. It is well known, for instance, that Adam Smith and other classical economists were highly critical of the work of so-called political arithmeticians, or "statists." In contrast, reference was made to the "common sense" of mankind as a source for observation in preference to the "false statistics" of political arithmeticians. Most famous perhaps are Adam Smith's observations on the workings of the pin factory (probably taken from secondary sources such as the French *Encyclopédie*) that informed his analysis of the division of labor. Perhaps equally famous is Smith's paradoxical comparison between the wealth of an African prince and an ordinary workman in Scotland, which can be traced to correspondence of John Locke with the administration in the Carolinas on the social and economic conditions of the indigenous Americans (Maas 2011).

In the nineteenth century, observations were made at different sites and reported in different formats, ranging from the writer's desk to the settings of parliamentary committees, and from official reports to novels. In the nineteenth century, references to "evidence" in British parliamentary

2. For a recent overview and critical discussion of this literature, see Radder 2006.

reports (on agriculture, monetary reform, etc.) were not to the numerical tables included in appendixes but to reports and examination of eyewitnesses. The observations of Thomas Carlyle in *Past and Present*, of Henry Mayhew in *London Labour and London Poor*, and the fictional narratives of Elizabeth Gaskell, Charles Dickens, Honoré de Balzac, Émile Zola, and many other novelists functioned in public debate on a par with the observations of political economists. At the turn of the twentieth century, the massive investigation into the behavior of "trusts," monopolies and cartels in the United States, both included the observations of economists and provided observational resources for them. Governmental inquiries, particularly at the state level, offered a wealth of observational details about the behavior of railroads, the conditions of labor, housing, and so forth. American economists were well known to be both contributors to these exercises and users of them.

The tools and instruments of the economists also varied widely. In that same late nineteenth and early twentieth-century period, we find Ernest Engel, triggered by Frédéric Le Play's studies in household budgets, investigating the cost of living of Belgium working-class families (Hacking 1987, 1990) and the French engineer and economist Émile Cheysson investigating family budgets using Le Play's method of monographs (Desrosières 1986). At the beginning of the twentieth century John R. Commons instructed and employed his students in the famous Pittsburgh Survey of 1907 (Rutherford 2011), and the Men and Religion Forward Movement transformed the self-image of America by embarking on a series of local social and economic surveys to advocate the Social Gospel, gathering observations that were to be significant for American institutionalism (Bateman 2001).

Observations were made at home and on the move. Turgot wrote his posthumously published "Lettres sur le commerce des grain" traveling through the French province of the Limousin during the famine of 1770 (Rothschild 2001, 74). The marquis de Condorcet's *Réflexions sur le commerce des blés* appeared in the same year as Smith's *Wealth of Nations* and was heavily informed by his conversations with his friend Turgot on the Limousin experience. In the interwar period Ronald Coase made historical studies on gas, water, and electricity supply in Britain before journeying to America where he visited, among others, large-scale production plants of Union Carbide in Cleveland and Ford Motor Company in Detroit, plants that vastly surpassed any scale he knew of. These informed his foundational paper on the nature of the firm in the 1930s, in which he questioned the validity of established theories (Coase 1988). Reading Joan Robinson's papers on imperfect competition of the same period, he was curious to find out if her theory was the result of introspection or firsthand observations, and he wrote to her—so the story goes—asking about which firms she had visited in developing her theory.[3]

Problems at the desk could also prompt economists to leave the office to make firsthand observations. Because of the difficulties economists such as Phyllis Deane and Wolfgang Stolper experienced in forcing statistical data from colonial and postcolonial Africa in the mold of Richard Stone's system of national accounts, they traveled there to observe and ask local inhabitants about their economic ways of doing (Morgan 2011). Even today, members of the Monetary Policy Committee of the Bank of England travel through the country to listen and learn "firsthand" of economic conditions in Britain, while the Federal Reserve Board retains local governors in its process of policymaking as a way to discover local economic variations.

Economists also use casual modes of observation, although not all economists warm up to such "armchair observations" (Gibbard and Varian 1978; Simon and Bartel 1986). The Nobel laureate Robert Lucas wrote that his "earlier papers" on business cycles were concerned with "coffee-break facts" that he obtained "second-hand," or "common knowledge around Chicago and Carnegie Mellon" (Boumans 2005, 92). Others refer to personal experiences at airports (Sutton 2000) as the kind of observation that needs to be explained by their models.

However and wherever made, observations were never simply reported; it was a process of combining and thinking in which personal experiences mixed with other sources. After the Great War, John Maynard Keynes left the delegacy of the British Treasury in a burst of outrage to pen his observations on and frustrations with the Versailles peace treaty negotiations in his best-selling *Economic Consequences of the Peace* (1919). Keynes proceeded synthetically, as a novelist constructing a plot. He combined his intimate experience of the "micro-cosmos" of Versailles with observations taken from a wide variety of sources into a magisterial epic that spanned the past "economic Utopia" abruptly ended by the war, the present peace treaty negotiations, and their grim future prospects. This melding of personal experiences with his wide reading in history and political economy and intimate knowledge of British state finances created his

---

3. We would like to thank Steve Medema for providing information on this episode.

vision on the economic consequences of the treaty and fit his view of the business of economists as inherently "introspective" and "moral" (Maas 2011; see also Skidelsky 2004).

In a similar vein Paul Krugman wrote in *The Return of Depression Economics and the Crisis of 2008*, an extension of his earlier book on the Asian crisis, that his "spine chilled" when crisis struck Asia at the end of the 1990s, and it "should have . . . anyone with a sense of history." For him, the world no longer needed economists who used the "scaffolding" of "equations and diagrams" to construct an "intellectual edifice" but economists who constructed a "narrative," a "story line," connecting such disparate events as "what Prime Minister Mahathir said in Kuala Lumpur in August 1997 and relates it to what Donald Tsang ended up doing in Hong Kong a year later" (Krugman 2009, 4–7). Thus, Krugman suggested, the tools, instruments, and strategies of observing that Keynes had used to great effect in earlier days should replace the modeling strategies of contemporary economists. But as argued in the present volume, the models Krugman takes distance from may serve to flesh out narratives that first make things visible.

This short and nonsystematic journey through the history of economics shows that observations of things economic were made in the confines of the private study, while traveling as a government delegate or on private journeys, at official sites for hearings by select committees, at research departments, think tanks, and policy institutes, as well as in conversations with friends and colleagues. Observations were made by political economists in person or came to them second- or thirdhand. They were reported in many different formats, in book-length tracts and histories, in sermons, narratives, letters, and pamphlets, in secret and public minutes, reports, and documents. Nowadays, they are reported in statistical and accounting reports, graphical representations, editorial comments, blogs, tweets, and newspaper columns, testimonies of experts to parliamentary committees, model simulations produced in research departments of central banks and economic research laboratories, country studies of the Organisation for Economic Co-operation and Development, and in papers and articles on field or laboratory experiments. They appear in economic forecasts, "now-casts," and "stress-tests" that all, one way or another, report "observations" on the economy that are used by economists for theorizing, by governments and business to prepare economic interventions, and by the general public to brace itself for a default of countries or banks that will have consequences for social security and pension payments. All these different modes of reporting things observed reflected, and reflect, a process of different connected steps that defy the idea of simple representations or measurements.

Observing, Registering, and Thinking

Our examples of observation certainly did not and do not all have the format of quantified statistical evidence, and even if they do, this does not mean they naturally follow the laws of probability. As Theodore Porter (1994, 2011) points out, quantified (statistical) data are better considered a particular *kind* of observation. Quantification in economics does not always imply the locating of means and variances, but may follow the classificatory grid of national accounting, the peculiarities of an exemplary case study, or the disciplined recording of observations in the field. These methods may not be highlighted by the economics profession in its public utterances, but they are well-established research methods, each with a logic that does not reduce to statistics and yet often found hidden in the base of statistical evidence used by economists (as we see in some of the essays in this volume). Contemporary discussions about the importance of "real-time data" for modeling and policy purposes, and the renewed interest in questionnaires and field research, show the economist's awareness both that there is a gap between the recorded measurement and what the measurement intends to express, and that such measurements do not capture all that may be observable.

So, in many fields nowadays, we find a reverse process, in which quantitative measurement is a stepping-stone in constructing an observation rather than observations leading to quantitative measurements. For example, both a supernova explosion and an fMRI-scan showing that emotions are involved in choice behavior depend on complex computations transgressing disciplinary boundaries before anything can be seen, and both what can be computed and what is seen involve trajectories of learning and socialization for the scientist.[4] The many different technical elements and the human processes of explicit and tacit knowledge acquisition that lie behind the observation offered in a GNP figure are just as daunting to unpack, not least because they, too, transgress disciplinary boundaries.

Our historical examples also show how far we have been led astray by the idea that observing is a mere registering of "facts." To make

4. See, for example, Alač 2004 and Pasveer 1989.

observations is far from passive, but involves the hard work of scientists, individually and as a collective. It involves thinking and conjecturing, tools and instruments, and the acquisition of skills. It is no coincidence that economic tracts of the seventeenth and eighteenth century—perhaps the heyday of *observations* as a genre of writing—interchangeably had *Observations* and *Reflections* in their titles, bearing witness to the close connection in the educated mind between observing and thinking.[5] Although sometimes concerned with the special and the peculiar, observations of economic phenomena were often made in a process that stretched over time and was a collective effort, as in William Petty's massive Down Survey, in which he enlisted one thousand soldiers to chart Ireland so that the English government could meet the land demands of claimants who had financed the bloody suppression of Ireland's rebellion of 1641. The survey provided Petty with a wealth of observations he used for his comparative studies into the causes of richness of the Dutch and the Irish (Aspromourgos 1996; Petty and Larcom 1851). One can find equally time-consuming and large-scale comparisons in the collection of information on the state (the original meaning of statistics) made in the cameralist tradition (Nikolow 2001; Tribe 1988).

Even a paradoxical observation such as that of Smith on an African prince and a common workman in Scotland was premised on a previous history of observing. And even after observing became associated with numbers, it remained an open question at what point such observations were made. Did Phyllis Deane start observing when she sat down to look at data from the Colonial Office at her desk in London, or when she realized that those data did not fit the classifications of Stone's accounting grid, or did she observe only once she was in Africa using Stone's accounting system as a measuring rod, or when she gave up on the possibility of making a coherent set of national accounts for Rhodesia (see Morgan 2011; Speich 2008, 2011)? As that case, and those in this volume attest, there are just as many not quite closed links that take the economist from raw observations to final ones in such a process as Bruno Latour (1999, 58) found in his account of how information about soil quality traveled

---

5. See, for example, the responses of Tench Coxe, assistant to Secretary of Treasury Alexander Hamilton, on the *Observations on the Commerce of the American States with Europe and the West Indies* (first published 1783) of the Irish peer Lord John Sheffield. Coxe published his replies, "Examination of Lord Sheffield's Observations on Commerce of the United States" and "Reflexions on the State of the Union" in the *American Museum* in 1791 and 1792, respectively. See Meardon 2011.

from Latin America to Paris via a "long chain of translations" involving scientists, institutions, and instruments that needed to be developed and put to work.

Once we realize that there is more to observation (the noun) in economics than statistics, and more to observing (the verb) than the passive registration of given facts, we find a rich history of both in economics. The purpose of the present volume is to uncover enough elements of that history to broaden our understanding of how economists observe the world and so change the way historians, philosophers, and economists think about this basic activity of science.

Histories of Scientific Observation

The following collection of essays results from the annual *HOPE* conference held April 16–18, 2011, at Duke University. This conference, which was funded by Duke University Press and the Netherlands Organisation for Scientific Research, would not have been possible without the earlier participation of the two guest editors in the project on histories of scientific observation of the Max Planck Institute for the History of Science in Berlin. As can be witnessed from this introduction, we are heavily indebted to this project, which extended over four years. Before we talk in more detail about the present volume, we would like to highlight two outcomes of the Berlin project that have particular relevance for our history here.

The first pertains to the word *observation* itself that, as said, ambiguously refers to a process and a result. As a process, observing was from ancient times not so much related to what, following Ernst Mach, became almost emblematic, an impression of the senses, but to the notion of observance—the careful and repeated following of rules closely associated with religious practices. The astronomical observations of monks obeyed standards of "goodness" captured in disciplined behavior performed not just on an individual basis but in fact over different generations and geographic spheres. Although individuals could be "good" or "bad" observers, it was not so much the individual acumen that was valued, because those individual capacities tended to vanish behind the rules observed. New astronomical observations built on and added to the fund of astronomical observations collected over centuries (Park 2011). Much has changed since then, but regimentation of the observer has become more rather than less important.

The second issue pertains to observation—as a process and in outcomes—as a collective endeavor. When physicians in the early modern period began to write *observationes* on their patients, these observations were collected and collated in compendia that trained the individual physician in turn to recognize specific diseases to which he could add observations from his own patient histories (Pomata 2010, 2011; on the notion of historia, see Pomata and Siraisi 2005). Natural historians formed corresponding networks, of which that of Carolus Linnaeus perhaps is the most famous, in which observations (with or without the specimen observed) circulated with extensive descriptions and drawings of the place where the specimen was found (Bleichmar 2011; Müller-Wille 2003; Roberts 2009).

Collective observation posed questions about the reliability of the individual observer, whether in the past or in the present, and so helped create criteria of "goodness" of observations. But the rapidly increasing number of observations posed challenges to technologies of compression and synthesizing as well, to which standardized questionnaires, schemata, maps, taxonomies, tables, but also folded paper or clever clips to facilitate counting, became answers (Mendelsohn 2011; Didier, this volume). These tools and instruments in their turn created objects that themselves became the subject of observation, such as a world map of the tides or the winds, the *Carte du ciel* map of the heavens (Daston 1994), cadastral maps showing patterns in tithe payments (Snyder 2011) and in farming and pasturage (D'Onofrio 2010), an agricultural map of the United States (Didier, this volume), or tables of national income accounts of UN countries. These objects could not possibly have been observed by isolated single observers but depended on a host of single observers as well as teams and institutes. Such tables and maps were and still are the result of large-scale observing operations that could extend over decades and involved a great many devoted observers with different skills and qualities (Daston 2011b).

Such operations never were a neutral endeavor but were intimately related to the power of states and enterprises (Aubin, Bigg, and Sibum 2010; Daston 2011a; Scott 1999). Dutch businessmen resisting the establishment of a national bureau of statistics in the early twentieth century were perfectly aware of what Alain Desrosières (1998) analyzed so thoroughly, that the numerical was political (see also Klep, van Maarseveen, and Stamhuis 2006; Tooze 2001). Think again of Petty's Down Survey, the cameralists' statistical observations, geodetic and mining expeditions in nineteenth-century Russia (Barnett, this volume; Gordin 2004), the expeditions of the Dutch Republic's East India Company that combined commercial and scientific interests (Cook 2007), or the cadastral maps that served taxing purposes (D'Onofrio 2010). Francis Bacon's "Merchants of Light" sailed the seas as spies to supply "knowledge of affairs . . . and especially of the sciences, arts, manufactures, and inventions of all the world"—as Daston (2011a, 88) notes, a "neat and prescient conflation of diplomatic, mercantile, and scientific models of early modern collective observation" that are still with us today.

Dimensions of the Observation Process

The essays in the volume that resulted from the Berlin project span the dizzying time line from the early Middle Ages until after the Second World War and cover disciplines ranging from astronomy via natural history, medicine, and chemistry, to economics and psychoanalysis. The present volume is much more modest in scope, not just in its limitation to one discipline—economics—but also in terms of the time frame covered. With two essays stretching the time line back into the eighteenth and forward to the last decade of the twentieth century, most essays concentrate on the first half of the previous century, which, not incidentally, is the period in which economics became a well-established academic discipline with increasingly stabilized methods of research, but which was also the period that saw the bureaucratic collection of data starting on scales that vastly surpassed the "avalanche of numbers" of the early nineteenth century (Hacking 1990).

We have organized the essays under three themes or dimensions of the observation process that emerged as the most salient from our conference: (1) articulating the space of observation; (2) questions of trust; (3) the configuring role of instruments. These three themes suggest how histories of scientific observation might be expanded with special attention to the social sciences.

Articulating the Space of Observation

How to define the space of observation is by no means obvious. "Articulation"—as used by Latour (1999)—usefully points to the mediating steps that are involved in creating not only the observed but also the observer. It moves away from notions of representation that—one way or another—presuppose that the object to be observed is "out there" and simply waiting for tools and a language that a skilled scientist will use to report what it is. Scholarship in the history of statistics has repeatedly pointed out how administrative categories work to create the thing observed (e.g., Hacking 1990; Porter 1986, 1994; Power 1999). Emmanuel Didier introduces in his essay the fiction of a "plasma"—a messy, opaque field of actors and information within which a statistician starts looking for information and distilling numbers. Didier's fiction helps trace the mediating steps that transformed widely heterogeneous observations into a connected numerical image of rural America.[6] It helps in rethinking the problem of numbering the social, but of course numbers and cunning ways to contrive them have been associated with states and commerce from ancient times.

Articulating a space of observation is rule and tool bound, as well as perspectively determined by the direction and focus of the gaze (Morgan 2011). It is a thoroughly contingent process, depending on found possibilities and constraints, such as existing institutional settings that can be fruitfully mobilized for another purpose, the ingenuity and credibility of the actors involved not only on the side of the investigators but also on the side of the investigated. Actors on both sides—the observer and the observed—will have different interests and purposes. It is more likely than not that the purposes with which, for example, an agricultural survey was started were multiple and change en route. The US Department of Agriculture not only intended to fight speculation but also wanted to gain better knowledge of the composition and total agricultural production in America. As Barnett (this volume) shows us, in surveys of Russian *zemstvo* statisticians, the different goals of assessing the value of landholdings for tax and data collection to improve rural living conditions coexisted. It would therefore be a shortcut to think of the resulting statistics as a representation of something "out there." What becomes the space of observation is rather something that emerges in the process and depends on the mixtures of different goals.

Possibilities to mobilize networks may be crucial for success or failure, or even for producing a result in the first place (Charles and Théré, this volume). To counter criticism that physiocratic concepts were void of content, François Quesnay and his collaborator Etienne Marivetz tried to gather empirical support by setting up an informational network outside the existing institutional framework of the French administration. But their laundry list of questions that the marquis de Mirabeau included in his *Ami des hommes* (1758) as a sort of "manual for the countrymen" received not one single answer, partly because of its inordinate length and

---

6. On the concept of mediation, see also Morrison and Morgan 1999.

complexity but also because of its unclear provenance and purposes. Was this list made by state functionaries? Was it for taxing? It needed more of a physical effort to collect data than to send out a questionnaire with an unclear status from Quesnay's premises at the court of Versailles. Just like Didier's statisticians used the existing grid of highways and byways in rural America to situate themselves in the midst of their object of inquiry, so the efforts of the physiocrats to mold rural France in the grid of their concepts became more effective when mobilizing existing social networks or when they traveled the province themselves armed with Quesnay's guidelines for making observations.

Equally contingent in any particular science's history of observational practice are questions about the relevant units of observation. In the history of economics, searching for typologies or for statistical laws, writing monographs or collecting family budgets, were all as important as taking surveys. But the choice of these was not self-evident. Scale mattered, as did ethnographic differences that themselves were constructed, but no less real. Standardization of questionnaires was not the obvious answer in countries such as the United States, Italy, or Russia, where socioeconomic conditions were so visibly different that it did not even seem feasible to think of different parts of the same country as part of the same economy. In the Russian case, seeing differences in complex wholes seemed a more viable way to proceed than smoothing them out, and the choice of Russian economists and statisticians for Le Play's method of monographs seemed a better fit to produce reliable and useful knowledge of the country than random sampling, producing distributions with random meaning. Gathering and collating numbers do not necessarily end in statistical distributions governed by the laws of probability, but may for good reasons lead to classifications that highlight the typical and serve as norms. This sometimes, as Barnett notes, had devastating consequences, as in the case of the statistical category of the kulaks, which an administration gone wild decided to physically exterminate.

The Fragile Dynamics of Trust

If there is a relevant difference between the natural and the social sciences, it is situated in the interaction of the observer and the observed. The four contributions that we collect under this label given to us by Federico D'Onofrio's contribution all show how statistical institutes, economists, and psychologists struggled with the issue that the making of social observations is an inherently collaborative effort between the observer and the observed. The social observer is better thought of as a broker trying to compromise between different interests than someone fitting the image of the detached observer of the natural world. Friedrich Engels's *Condition of the Working Class in Britain* (1844) relied heavily on the evidence given to parliamentary committees on child labor and factory conditions. But Engels relied no less on a source of information that middle-class enthusiasts for statistics in Lancashire found too close for comfort, namely, the first-person access that his Irish girlfriend gave him to the slums of Little Ireland in Manchester. This may be the most far-reaching way to bring a frightening world indoors and into the ambit of the observer, but no social observation is possible without some sort of participation of the observed in the process. This holds as much in economics as in any of the other social sciences, and there may be good reasons to consider this issue of wider significance, as most saliently in the study of primates.

Observers had to invent ways to gain access to their primary sources of information. In D'Onofrio's study, those inquiring into the conditions of Sicilian peasants appeared with a "panoply of revolvers and rifles," perhaps to enforce honesty on those observed who preferred to keep their affairs hidden or lie about them, perhaps out of mere self-defense. They observed largely illiterate farmers who talked in dialects the observers did not understand but who, in fact, possessed the expert knowledge the observers eagerly sought. In Thomas Stapleford's study we find the bureaucrats at the US Bureau of Labor Statistics struggling with different formats to enlist their respondents—initially housewives—so that those observed would provide trustworthy answers to questionnaires. The bureau's strategy zoomed in first on the communicative character and skills of the interviewer, thence to questions of standardization of questionnaires, and finally to the construction of a composite respondent. These strategies of course lead to very different outcomes with very different meanings, but all, at root, had to deal with how economists, as investigators, imprint categories on their subject and how the subject contributes productively to their creation, as well as how investigators prevent subjects from determining their own categories of observation while still ensuring their collaboration. Preestablished categories and classifications make sense only if the observer succeeds in co-opting the observed into them. If illiterate Italian farmers, American housewives, or any public at large refuses to recognize a social scientist's category as relevant, the social scientist must devise new categories or must look for different things to

observe. Ian Hacking's (1992) notion of the "self-vindication" of laboratory research is more fragile outside the laboratory—in the field and in the
social realm—where the thing and the concept are coproduced and depend
on the consent of subjects.[7]

The implication of this is that social statistics and classifications are
always the outcome of strategic interactions that are politically loaded.
Acknowledging, and even highlighting, this strategic nature means that
social observations are normally made in a "hostile environment"—not in
the sense of needing a weapon to protect oneself but in the scientific sense
of an environment of people and places that are radically uncontrolled,
ever changing, and not to be trusted. One of the problems Oskar Morgenstern saw was that social science observations were not made by scientists
and so necessarily fell short of standards of scientific accuracy—they were
the product of ignorance, falsehood, or deliberate fraud. Another problem
was the unique and dynamic nature of economic phenomena themselves.
Morgenstern sought for the solution neither in an engagement or dialogue
with the social realm, nor in washing out errors by treating them all as
part of a probability distribution, but in attempting to characterize, and so
tame the "error" in, those unruly and untrustworthy observations through
"scientific observers" who would rely heavily on theory in their expert
judgments (Boumans, this volume). Despite these differences, Morgenstern's strategy parallels an older one found in other scientific domains
(Swijtink 1987), namely, an uncertainty measured is an uncertainty tamed
and no longer so threatening. Morgenstern's strategies for accurate observation show us the processes of detachment from their subject matter
that social scientists came to practice across many domains in the mid-
twentieth century as they fought to establish their credibility as scientists
(see also Renwick 2011).

Thus, during the twentieth century, the economist became a consumer
of data sets for modeling purposes in the space of his or her office. He or
she might be concerned about the quality of the data, just as we are concerned about the quality of our food in a restaurant, but would stay out

7. We also think this situation is different from Latour's notion that the object of study
actively contributes to its scientific articulation. Whatever the commonalities are between the
natural and the social, a difference (which may go back to Wilhelm Dilthey if not to Giambat-
tista Vico) is that in the social sciences, the self-understanding of the subject plays a part.
Human individuals can protest against being labeled in such and such way, and they do. The
consequences of this simple point for the stability of "evidence" are, in our view, substantially
underrated, at least in economics.

of the kitchen and concentrate on theory. Observation being made passive, trust became invested in the rigor of mathematical theory, statistical models, and the promises of the computer (Weintraub 2002; Morgan 2003, 2012b).

The idea that theory could fill the gap between the economist and his or her data became increasingly problematic in the later twentieth century. It is indicative that when economics turned to experiments in these last decades, discussions around the formation of a new society of economists did not center on the experiment as a defining characteristic but on the perceived failure of the econometric project as a nonexperimental science and the felt need for economists to take responsibility again for their own data production. What became the Economic Science Association was not limited to experimental economists but embraced all economists who considered economics an observational science. Reflecting on the famous "measurement without theory debate" between Tjalling Koopmans and Jacob Viner just after the Second World War about the appropriate road forward in economics, the experimental economist Vernon Smith argued that the promises of the 1950s had remained unfulfilled and had, in fact, turned into "theory without measurement." As Smith, who won a Nobel Prize for his pioneering work in experimental economics, expressed the mission of this new society in a luncheon address in 1986 that became foundational: "The battle is not for experimentalism. The battle is for a way of thinking that emphasizes the integrity and primacy of observation" (quoted in Svorencik 2011).

Those who in the 1950s had challenged the high hopes of economists had a hard time finding a sympathetic hearing. Thus when George Katona, the Gestalt psychologist, turned to consumer research during the Second World War, he questioned the possibility of extracting causal mechanisms from statistical data sets (Edwards, this volume). Statistical data, he argued, did not express a mute mechanism the economist could guess at; rather, individuals (and populations) could take different lines of action on a given statistics, depending on their understanding of the social complex. As a consequence, economists could not use statistics to build economic models that somewhat mechanically would pour out predictions. In contrast, they should engage in a game of trust; they should engage with their subject pool—the public—and policymakers to flesh out a shared understanding of the economy in relation to possible lines of action. Statistics did not predict but should be seen as an "announcer" awaiting interpretation.

For economists who had just found a possible way out of their lack of control by utilizing econometrics, the computer, and theoretical models, such a program was just too vague and far off the scientific standards that were propagated by logical empiricism to fit what by then was becoming an established symmetry between explanation and prediction in econometric modeling. For such economists, like James Tobin, Katona's project of surveys of intentions seemed to fit ill with both the observations on consumption that they already had on hand and the various theoretical elements (theories of inflation, of household consumption, of life cycles, etc.) through which they made sense of those observations and tested their theories.

The Configuring Role of Instruments

It has become a convention in the recent history of science to see instruments as critical partners in scientific knowledge production. Instruments of observation are no longer seen as "mere registering devices" but complex objects embodying scientific knowledge in their construction that matters to their use and interpretation of the observations they produce. Instruments reconfigure vision. That is, instruments configure the relation of the observer to the observed and to observations in very different ways. Whether these instruments remain black-boxed or their workings are revealed for the reader, they are largely conceived of as physical and so understood as part of the material culture of science. In the social and human sciences, such instruments may well be human, and this is especially true in the processes of observing. The empathy of the psychoanalyst is perhaps the most well-studied of such human instruments (see Lunbeck 2011), but the ways in which the scientist as human acts as its own instrument of scientific observation has also been discussed in the history of field sciences such as ecology and geology. Such experiential observation links both methodologically and historically with how social scientists work in the field, as in the social/human science ethnographies of anthropology (see Kuklick and Kohler 1996). Here, in Malcolm Rutherford's essay, we see how economists too have followed this ethnographic path as a way of getting close enough to their subjects in order to observe firsthand through participant observation in their activities. There is an inevitable trade-off—between the observer going undercover to observe the subject in a way that keeps the observed person and group honest, and getting so involved with those subjects that detached, objective observation on the part of the economist-observer is compromised. That trade-off varies with the degree of engagement: as the economist becomes more of the detached observer, his or her observations may become less fruitful, and the observees may become less willing to share their experiences.

Many instruments of observation in science in more recent times have been designed to observe and record the observations simultaneously. The moves from early and simple telescopes and microscopes to the modern generations of these instruments are good examples of this tendency (Schickore 2007). We find the same shared characteristic of observing and recording in the laboratory and computer-based experiments of economics, but equally in a much older instrument in economics although operating in a much wider public place, namely, in narrative writings. Craufurd Goodwin's essay takes up two different examples of this. First, Frank Norris's own participant observation and journalistic investigations parallel much of the experiential observing of the economists discussed by Rutherford. Norris embeds his own economic observations into fictional narratives about the American economy of that same period. This fictional shell allows Norris to repeat that eighteenth-century writer's trick that we noted earlier of both recording his observations and reflecting on them, implicitly judging them, at the same time.

In contrast, and in a way that forms a neat link to the final essay in the volume, Goodwin investigates how E. M. Forster uses his narrative observations on the economic characteristics and events that beset the different classes in early twentieth-century England to probe the economic understandings of this same world offered by his contemporary economists. He uses his narrative to observe the economists as much as to observe the economy. Narrative fiction, conceived as an instrument that brings observation into the public gaze, has a tremendous ability to reveal both detail and the wider picture, to make descriptions along with judgments, and to communicate both in a way that has no pretense to science but that lays strong claim to the closely associated modes of observing and reporting found in the humanities such as anthropology and history.

While it might seem odd to pair fictional narratives with econometric models, both, by this account, offer instruments that synthesize observation of the economy with ways to understand the economy. The notion that econometrics is a mode of observation (Hoover 1994) and that econometric models are instruments that enable economists to find their ways to economic observations that are hidden in raw data numbers (Boumans

2005) may still be an unusual way to think of econometrics, but is well established in the historical and philosophical writings on that subfield of economics. The econometric model operates as an instrument that both turns raw data into numeric relations and works to seek out hidden numbers. It is not so much an observation and recording device but an observation and revealing device rather like the modern fMRI scans, which produce sophisticated versions of the traditional X-rays. Yet, as Pedro Duarte and Kevin Hoover explain, models can flip between functioning as the device that shows the random elements as background noise while keeping the economic observations in the foreground to the reverse, showing the random elements as data or important evidence about phenomena. The history of random elements in modern macroeconomics, from the early work of Ragnar Frisch in which they played a theoretical role as innovations but were not directly observable to the recent central place as observable entities, either as data or as phenomena, is characteristic of the changing relationships between modeling and observing in twentieth-century economics.

Like other instruments and modes of observing, modeling invites both trust and distrust. The models of the economist are artificial constructions. They may be reliable instruments of observation, but as all such instruments, they have to be proved so by testing their performance in the field. A similar trust-distrust relation, with a testing-out process between observer and observed, occurs in the undercover fieldwork of the institutionalist economists. For the latter, those trust-distrust issues reside in the personal relationships that form the heart of participant observation, rather than in the technical relations between models and observations in econometrics (see Morgan 2012a for a broader discussion of the participant observation problem). Each observing setup has to be tried and tested, even where the basic rules and constraints of such a mode of observation are well understood by the observers.

Observing the Economy

The essays collected in this volume allow us to regain sight of practices of observation that had seemed lost in the identification of observations with statistics. Taking the double meaning of observation as a process and as a result as the key to unlock that history has revealed practices of observation that are far richer than merely purchasing time-series data sets over the Internet for modeling purposes. Through much of the earlier history, the economist was not just a passive consumer of data found elsewhere but actively contributed to their making. In doing so, he or she was not only observing a world found "out there" but actively constructing that world to be subsequently theorized. We have seen this creation of the space of observation in contributions that all, interestingly, related to one of the major concerns of political economists over the centuries: grain and agriculture. But it is easy to see the message of these essays extended to other domains, most obviously to national accounting and so to macroeconomics and macroeconomic policy (Morgan 2011; Comim 2001; Speich 2011), and to the field of (international) finance that recently has come under close and stimulating scrutiny by economic sociologists such as Donald MacKenzie and Michel Callon. These scholars prefer to think of the relation of the economist to the world in terms of performativity, that is, as a one-way movement from theory to the world. Our contributions give evidence that coproduction may be the better way to think about this relation.

The coproduction of observational knowledge is not unique to economics. What we do think unique to the social sciences, including economics, is that coproduction depends on a form of collaboration with the subject of study that can be distinguished from that in the natural sciences—even though this may be a gradual rather than categorical difference. In the social realm, subjects can actively disagree with typologies, classifications, and measurements that are proposed by the economist, and act on their disagreement to change them. This turns any observation, including measurements, in the social realm into a dialogue between observer and observed. If traders on the Chicago mercantile exchange had not found the small charts of trading prices Fisher Black distributed (for pay) on the trading floor useful, they would not have bought into the categories of option price theory. There are interests on both sides of the observation process in ways different from the natural sciences, and this makes observing the social a dialogue, or a game of strategy, in which the observed may seek to hide or misreport its own activities while the observer seeks to see behind the superficial or the reported elements.

These interactions, in which interests on both sides may be hidden from view, almost disappeared in much of the twentieth-century project in which economists became not passive recording devices but passive as consumers while active as manipulators rather than coproducers. For the health of economics, it is reassuring that, at present, economists show a renewed interest in methods of research that were long scorned by the profession. The reemergence of field research, questionnaires, and surveys, as well as the explosion of experimental research in economics and the new foray into field trials, shows observational practices are changing rapidly. This is not just a return to forlorn practices, and old-methods-in-new-jackets are not without their problems, but it does mean that economists are becoming aware, again, of the multifarious ways in which they can explore their subject. That they do so consciously is all for the better, because behind their backs, as witnessed by the essays in this collection, these other methods shaped—and shape—the data the economist took as "given." Thus the present volume may serve as a reminder and an encouragement to rethink what it means to observe the economy, as a practice and in its results.

References

Alač, Morana. 2004. "Negotiating Pictures of Numbers." *Social Epistemology* 18 (2–3): 199–214.

Aspromourgos, Tony. 1996. *On the Origins of Classical Economics: Distribution and Value from William Petty to Adam Smith*. London: Routledge.

Aubin, David, Charlotte Bigg, and H. Otto Sibum. 2010. *The Heavens on Earth: Observatories and Astronomy in Nineteenth-Century Science and Culture*. Durham, N.C.: Duke University Press.

Bateman, Bradley. 2001. "The Men and Religion Forward Movement." In *The Age of Economic Measurement*, edited by Judy L. Klein and Mary S. Morgan. *HOPE* 33 (supplement): 57–85.

Bleichmar, Daniella. 2011. "The Geography of Observation: Distance and Visibility in Eighteenth-Century Botanical Travel." In *Histories of Scientific Observation*, edited by Lorraine Daston and Elizabeth Lunbeck, 373–95. Chicago: University of Chicago Press.

Boumans, Marcel J. 2005. *How Economists Model the World into Numbers*. New York: Routledge.

Coase, Ronald H. 1988. "The Nature of the Firm: Origin." *Journal of Law, Economics, and Organization* 4 (1): 3–17.

Comim, Flavio. 2001. "Richard Stone and Measurement Criteria for National Accounts." In *The Age of Economic Measurement*, edited by Judy L. Klein and Mary S. Morgan. *HOPE* 33 (supplement): 213–34.

Cook, Harold J. 2007. *Matters of Exchange: Commerce, Medicine, and Science in the Dutch Golden Age*. New Haven: Yale University Press.

Daston, Lorraine. 1994. "Enlightenment Calculations." *Critical Inquiry* 21 (1): 182–202.

———. 2011a. "The Empire of Observation, 1600–1800." In *Histories of Scientific Observation*, edited by Lorraine Daston and Elizabeth Lunbeck, 81–115. Chicago: University of Chicago Press.

———. 2011b. "Observation as a Way of Life: Time, Attention, Allegory." Hans Rausing Lecture 2010, Uppsala University.

Daston, Lorraine, and Elizabeth Lunbeck. 2011. *Histories of Scientific Observation*. Chicago: University of Chicago Press.

Desrosières, Alain. 1986. "L'ingénieur d'état et le père de famille." *Annales des
mines: Gérer et comprendre*, 66–81.

———. 1998. *The Politics of Large Numbers: A History of Statistical Reasoning*.
Cambridge: Harvard University Press.

D'Onofrio, Federico. 2010. "The Renovation of Italian Agrarian Statistics
(1905–1915)." Paper presented to the annual conference of the European Society
for the History of Economic Thought, Amsterdam, March.

Gibbard, Allan, and Hal R. Varian. 1978. "Economic Models." *Journal of Philosophy* 75 (11): 664–77.

Gordin, Michael D. 2004. *A Well-Ordered Thing: Dmitrii Mendeleev and the Shadow
of the Periodic Table*. New York: Basic Books.

Hacking, Ian. 1983. *Representing and Intervening*. Cambridge: Cambridge University Press.

———. 1987. "Prussian Numbers, 1860–1882." In *The Probabilistic Revolution*.
Vol. 1 of *Ideas in History*, edited by Lorenz Krüger, Lorraine J. Daston, and
Michael Heidelberger, 377–94. Cambridge: MIT Press.

———. 1990. *The Taming of Chance*. Cambridge: Cambridge University Press.

———. 1992. "The Self-Vindication of the Laboratory Sciences." In *Science as
Practice and Culture*, edited by Andrew Pickering, 29–64. Chicago: University
of Chicago Press.

Hoover, Kevin. 1994. "Econometrics as Observation: The Lucas Critique and the
Nature of Econometric Inference." *Journal of Economic Methodology* 1 (1): 65–80.

Klep, Paul M. M., Jacques G. S. J. van Maarseveen, and Ida H. Stamhuis. 2006. *The
Statistical Mind in Modern Society: The Netherlands, 1850–1940*. Amsterdam:
Amsterdam University Press.

Krugman, Paul. 2009. *The Return of Depression Economics and the Crisis of 2008*.
New York: Norton.

Kuklick, Henrika, and Robert E. Kohler. 1996. Introduction to "Science in the
Field," special issue, *Osiris*, 2nd ser., 11:1–14.

Latour, Bruno. 1999. *Pandora's Hope: Essays on the Reality of Science Studies*.
Cambridge: Harvard University Press.

Lunbeck, Elizabeth. 2011. "Empathy as a Psychoanalytical Mode of Observation:
Between Sentiment and Science." In *Histories of Scientific Observation*, edited
by Lorraine Daston and Elizabeth Lunbeck, 255–75. Chicago: University of Chicago Press.

Maas, Harro. 2011. "Sorting Things Out: The Economist as an Armchair Observer."
In *Histories of Scientific Observation*, edited by Lorraine Daston and Elizabeth
Lunbeck, 206–29. Chicago: University of Chicago Press.

Meardon, Stephen. 2011. "'A Reciprocity of Advantages': Mathew Carey and the
Growth of the Protective Doctrine." Paper presented at the conference "Ireland,
America, and the Worlds of Mathew Carey," Philadelphia, October 27–29.

Mendelsohn, J. Andrew. 2011. "The World on a Page: Making a General Observation in the Eighteenth Century." In *Histories of Scientific Observation*, edited by Lorraine Daston and Elizabeth Lunbeck, 396–420. Chicago: University of Chicago Press.

Morgan, Mary S. 2003. "Economics." In *The Modern Social Sciences*, edited by T. Porter and D. Ross, 275–305. Vol. 7 of *The Cambridge History of Science*. Cambridge: Cambridge University Press.

———. 2011. "Seeking Parts, Looking for Wholes." In *Histories of Scientific Observation*, edited by Lorraine Daston and Elizabeth Lunbeck, 303–25. Chicago: University of Chicago Press.

———. 2012a. "*Chorizo* Reporting, Virtual Witnessing, and the Role of the 'Stranger': Going into the Social Field, and Bringing It Back Inside." Working paper, London School of Economics.

———. 2012b. *The World in the Model*. Cambridge: Cambridge University Press.

Morrison, Margaret, and Mary S. Morgan. 1999. *Models as Mediators: Perspectives on Natural and Social Science*. Cambridge: Cambridge University Press.

Müller-Wille, Staffan. 2003. "Joining Lapland and the Topinambes in Flourishing Holland: Center and Periphery in Linnaean Botany." *Science in Context* 16:461–88.

Nikolow, Sybilla. 2001. "A. F. W. Crome's Measurements of the 'Strength of the State': Statistical Representations in Central Europe around 1800." In *The Age of Economic Measurement*, edited by Judy L. Klein and Mary S. Morgan. *HOPE* 33 (supplement): 23–56.

Park, Katherine. 2011. "Observation in the Margins, 500–1500." In *Histories of Scientific Observation*, edited by Lorraine Daston and Elizabeth Lunbeck, 15–44. Chicago: University of Chicago Press.

Pasveer, Bernike. 1989. "Knowledge of Shadows: The Introduction of X-Ray Images in Medicine." *Sociology of Health and Illness* 11 (4): 360–81.

Petty, William, and Thomas A. Larcom. 1851. *The History of the Survey of Ireland: Commonly Called the Down Survey, A.D. 1655–6*. Dublin: For the Irish Archaeological Society.

Pomata, Gianna. 2010. "Sharing Cases: The *Observationes* in Early Modern Medicine." *Early Science and Medicine* 15 (3): 193–236.

———. 2011. "Observation Rising: Birth of an Epistemic Genre, 1500–1650." In *Histories of Scientific Observation*, edited by Lorraine Daston and Elizabeth Lunbeck, 45–80. Chicago: University of Chicago Press.

Pomata, Gianna, and Nancy G. Siraisi. 2005. *Historia: Empiricism and Erudition in Early Modern Europe*. Cambridge: MIT Press.

Porter, Theodore M. 1986. *The Rise of Statistical Thinking, 1820–1900*. Princeton: Princeton University Press.

———. 1994. "Making Things Quantitative." *Science in Context* 7:389–407.

———. 2011. "Reforming Vision: The Engineer Le Play Learns to Observe Society Sagely." In *Histories of Scientific Observation*, edited by Lorraine Daston and Elizabeth Lunbeck, 281–302. Chicago: University of Chicago Press.

Power, Michael. 1999. *The Audit Society: Rituals of Verification*. Oxford: Oxford University Press.

Radder, Hans. 2006. *The World Observed/The World Conceived*. Pittsburgh: University of Pittsburgh Press.

Renwick, Chris. 2011. "Observation and Detachment: William Beveridge and 'The Natural Bases of Social Science.'" University of York (UK), mimeo.

Roberts, Lissa. 2009. "Science and Global History, 1750–1850: Local Encounters and Global Circulation Encounters." Special issue, *Itinerario* 33 (1).

Rothschild, Emma. 2001. *Economic Sentiments: Adam Smith, Condorcet, and the Enlightenment*. Cambridge: Harvard University Press.

Rutherford, Malcolm. 2011. *The Institutionalist Movement in American Economics, 1918–1947: Science and Social Control*. Cambridge: Cambridge University Press.

Schickore, Jutta. 2007. *The Microscope and the Eye: A History of Reflections, 1740–1870*. Chicago: University of Chicago Press.

Scott, James C. 1999. *Seeing like a State: How Certain Schemes to Improve the Human Condition Have Failed*. New Haven: Yale University Press.

Simon, Herbert A., and Richard D. Bartel. 1986. "The Failure of Armchair Economics." *Challenge* 29 (5): 18–25.

Skidelsky, Robert. 2004. *John Maynard Keynes: Philosopher, Economist, Statesman*. London: Palgrave.

Snyder, Laura J. 2011. *The Philosophical Breakfast Club: Four Remarkable Friends Who Transformed Science and Changed the World*. New York: Broadway Books.

Speich, Daniel. 2008. "Travelling with the GDP through Early Development Economics' History." Working paper 08/33, Department of Economic History, London School of Economics.

———. 2011. "The Use of Global Abstractions: National Income Accounting in the Period of Imperial Decline." Special issue, *Journal of Global History* 6:7–28.

Sutton, John. 2000. *Marshall's Tendencies: What Can Economists Know?* Cambridge: MIT Press.

Svorencik, Andrej. 2011. "Twenty Five Years of the Economic Science Association." Working paper, Utrecht School of Economics.

Swijtink, Zeno. 1987. "The Objectification of Observation: Measurement and Statistical Methods in the Nineteenth Century." In *The Probabilistic Revolution*, 261–85. Vol. 1 of *Ideas in History*, edited by Lorenz Krüger, Lorraine J. Daston, and Michael Heidelberger. Cambridge: MIT Press.

Tooze, Adam. 2001. *Statistics and the German State, 1900–1945: The Making of Modern Economic Knowledge*. Cambridge: Cambridge University Press.

Tribe, Keith. 1988. *Governing Economy: The Reformation of German Economic Discourse, 1750–1840*. Cambridge: Cambridge University Press.

Weintraub, E. Roy. 2002. *How Economics Became a Mathematical Science*. Durham, N.C.: Duke University Press.

Part 1
The Space of Observation

Cunning Observation:
US Agricultural Statistics
in the Time of Laissez-Faire

Emmanuel Didier

When the agricultural market began to expand nationally during the nine-teenth century in the United States, it gave rise to its evil twin: specula-tion. As early as 1863, the Lincoln administration, through its newly born Department of Agriculture, decided to intervene against that ill effect. The antidote that it developed was a statistical measurement of the nation's agricultural production copied from the Prussian example (USDA 1863, 576).[1] Its publication was intended to prevent the circulation of false or misleading reports produced by speculators whose primary interest was to control and manipulate prices (Estabrook 1915). In so doing, the admin-istration rendered the task of speculators much more complicated because they did, of course, continue to manipulate demand (which depended mainly on them), but stage-managing supply became much more difficult. To counter market distortions, the administration realized that *objectivity* was a most effective weapon. In what was generally considered a laissez-faire economy, it turned out that the federal government played a crucial role, and a political one, in producing public objectivity to fight against what we would today call an asymmetry of information.

This essay was supported by the French National Agency for Research, project number ANR-09–SSOC-054–01. I first drafted this essay in French; Priya Vari Sen translated my draft into English, and what is presented here is a substantially modified version of the translation.

1. The Prussian agricultural statistics were thoroughly described by Max Weber (Pollak 1986).

History of Political Economy 44 (annual suppl.) DOI 10.1215/00182702-1631770

But how were those agricultural statistics generated? The task was all the more difficult, as the area covered was vast and varied: a single standard for tropical Florida and snow-covered Montana, separated by thousands of miles, was impractical, especially to comply with the same rule to produce data. The overall translation, several times a year, of the diversity of American agriculture into statistical data aggregated to the national level created many problems.

This essay describes the new method of observation that was developed between 1890 and 1930, epitomized in 1914 when the US Department of Agriculture (USDA) organized for the first time a network of full-time civil service statistical agents, one in every state, to perform this task (Taylor and Taylor 1952, 231).[2] It was the time when statistical expertise took shape in the department. The essay proposes to explain how these new statisticians, professionals, yes, but human beings nonetheless who, like all human beings, brought their own idiosyncrasies to the task, aggregated their local observations into data about an entire state and even about the United States "as a whole," to use a formula that appeared at the time. And we will insist on the fact that, aside from the virtues of temperance, patience, and precision, which are often associated with good scientific observation, a certain amount of cunning intelligence, less frequently pointed out, was also essential to the task.

We know, as Lorraine Daston (2010) has so brilliantly shown, that observation creates time. Thus it is not surprising that it also creates space. Indeed, to quantify the agriculture of the entire nation, statisticians had to express—in a statistical sense—what "agricultural America" meant. The things and geographic areas the statistician was supposed to gather data on were far from given.[3] We will thus explore here what the concrete task of transforming local observations of agriculture into figures expressing agricultural America as a whole consisted of.

To begin with, an agency had to be created to take charge of personnel and operations. Today this institution is called the National Agricultural Statistical Service, but it is difficult to say what it was called then, as it

2. Prior to this date, the federal government relied on marshals, tax assessors, and representatives of the state's agricultural departments. The hiring of federal agents in 1914 aimed at avoiding the biases provoked by these interviewers. In the small East Coast states, a single statistician was assigned to several states.

3. For example, the list of crops that fit into their inquiry was not clear-cut and changed during the twentieth century (for a discussion about the interest of quantifying pickles, see Didier 2007). In addition, the status of subsistence farming was initially not clear: given that its products remained on the farm and did not enter the market, should it be counted?

changed names frequently. In 1917 it was the Bureau of Crop Estimates; in 1921 it became the Division of Crop Estimates; in 1922 it was renamed the Division of Markets and Crop Estimates; toward the end of the period covered here, it was called the Division of Crop and Livestock Estimates (Taylor and Taylor 1952). In view of this litany of titles, for the purpose of the present essay, I will call it "the division," because during the period under scrutiny it remained mainly a division of the USDA. The statistics discussed below were created by the division.

When I opened the division archives, I found a massive jumble of documents—dozens of cartons, in-house notes, letters, drafts, question-naires, lists of names, pay slips, rulers, tables of numbers, soil samples, mathematical formulas.[4] The most striking characteristic of this moun-tain of archives was its diversity. How were items so different in nature combined to constitute a single and unique entity, an agricultural statistic? One of the lessons of childhood is the impossibility of comparing apples and oranges. But the administrative machinery responsible for these cal-culations was composed not only of apples and oranges but also of thou-sands of other ingredients. As paradoxical as it may seem, the creation of homogeneous numbers (e.g., the overall quantity of wheat produced by the United States at a given date) boiled down to amalgamating a multi-tude of perfectly heterogeneous elements. How is it possible to change heterogeneity into homogeneity?

To understand this operation, we will start from the time when every-thing constituted a challenge for statistics, and we will advance step by step toward the construction of the final figure. In this way, we discover concretely, on a human scale, as it were, the observational methods of the agricultural statisticians in the time of laissez-faire.

The Plasma

To understand the process by which the statisticians in our story finally managed to generate numerical figures, it helps to ask when that first began: at what point did a statistical act take place? When the statisti-cians learned the theory of statistics at school? When during breakfast they reflected on unsolved problems encountered the day before? When they took up their pens to do the first calculations? All these answers have

---

4. The division as a government institution had the immense advantage of having its archives preserved in the American National Archives, Washington, DC, Record Group 83. Hereafter cited as RG 83.

some justification and are of some interest. To avoid a long discussion I will peremptorily impose, as in fiction, the stage at which for us statistics began. This stage I call *plasma*.

This term comes from the Greek verb *plassō*, which originally designated Prometheus's task of sculpting man and Hephaestus's act of creating Pandora with wet clay (Cassin 1995). The linguistic root of *plasma* is thus a verb whose meaning denotes "modeling." Substantively, plasma is the raw material that the person modeling, shaping, has in hand—which makes the activity of conformation possible. It is something that has its own specific characteristics, but insofar as it presents itself for shaping and modifying. Plasma is what was available to our statisticians when they wanted to initiate something but had not yet started.

The plasma is thus something open to human manipulation; apart from the statisticians in our story, others manipulated it too, but the manipulation that it underwent at the hands of those others was not statistical. Thus a sheet of paper is produced by diverse artisans and skilled laborers— from the woodcutter to the papermaker—and has its own specific characteristics (it is perhaps white or cream, A4 or US Letter in size, etc.), but as long as the question of printing a questionnaire on it does not arise, the sheet is still plasma. It ceases to be plasma once it becomes part of a statistical project. The plasma was the entire panoply of elements available to the division or to one of its representatives when it (or they) decided to transform those elements into statistics. It was the elements that interested the division because it suspected that the elements would have been interesting when transformed into statistics, although no one had bothered to transform them into statistics before.

Aside from plasma, there were already statistical elements. Prior practices left former routines, tools, mathematical formulas, and so forth that already belonged to the statistical realm. But when a survey was launched, it necessarily responded to something that had escaped those initial elements (otherwise the survey would have been pointless). It is this unknown—but interesting—element that I call plasma.

Reporters

In the winter of 1913, after having worked in the regional meteorology offices of the Department of Agriculture, Verne H. Church was hired by the division as one of the first statisticians and was put in charge of Michigan. Excited by this new challenge, he immediately set out to explore the countryside, seeking direct contact with the area under his charge. This is how the plasma appeared to this novice:

> In keeping with my instructions, I then shut my office and left for one week's excursion in the country. My apprenticeship was both painful and disappointing. Thanks to the directories and a personal survey, I located the grain, fruit and vegetable marketers. I found that some were cooperative while others were not. Most criticized statistical results and methods. Because of my lack of experience and sketchy knowledge of the subject, I did not have the results in my head and very few in my brief case. I found that the greater part of the criticism was levelled against State statistics, which at that time I didn't know much about. Those who were satisfied with the reports published by the State thought that the federal invasion of the countryside was a waste of effort and expenditure. . . . The first few weeks of roaming around was the only period during which I had regrets about leaving the meteorological service. (Church 1943, 213–14)[5]

The initial experience of the statistician was disappointing—he left full of enthusiasm, but met mostly unhelpful interlocutors. His role was to produce statistics, but statistics did not appear to be popular among farmers. The way out of this embarrassing situation was a list, a simple list of names, first standardized in the 1910s and afterward regularly kept. Indeed, rather than weaken the morale of its agents, the division began to retain the names of those interlocutors who, once they understood the purpose of the questionnaires, agreed to fill them out regularly. All that was needed was to convince some farmers just once of the utility of the approach. Recruitment was never easy: "Making long lists of addresses was quite difficult and progress slow" (Church 1943, 9). But occasionally it succeeded. Thus each time a survey was initiated, the division posted a questionnaire to each farmer listed, always the same ones, and asked them to complete and send it within the given time. These interlocutors the division called *voluntary crop reporters*, because they were like agricultural information volunteers.

As these reporters were a rare commodity, the division turned them into loyal allies and tried to forge as lasting a link as possible with them. It used to send them, for example, *Crops and Markets*, a monthly report

---

5. Church 1943 is the unpublished autobiography of Verne H. Church. It was very kindly made available to me by his descendant Gregg Wager.

of the survey results. It also sent them guidelines for filling out the questionnaires and for using the published figures, and even Christmas greetings at the end of each year. In short, the division made efforts to remain in close and enduring contact with its sympathetic interlocutors.

But was any person who was willing to cooperate a suitable person? It seems that two additional directives guided the choice of reporters. First, the division tried to have them well scattered over the entire territory. The objective was more or less achieved, as in 1926, for example, the list contained no less than forty thousand names (USDA 1933, 4), which greatly exceeded the number of rural townships.

Second, the farmers who agreed to become reporters seemed to have been intellectually superior to the others. Indeed, unlike the representative surveys of today, the reporters' task was not to share their feelings or their experiences but to inform the division about the state of agriculture in the entire neighborhood. They had to conduct a personal investigation, observe neighboring agriculture, and not be influenced by their personal results (which could differ from those of others); only after this work had been accomplished did they send a memorandum to the division on the growth condition of the crops. Thanks to their own inspection of the neighborhood and to their public spirit, reporters were able to discover the truth of local production, and they were "known for their intelligence and their discernment" (USDA 1933, 186).

The questions asked were based on a simple principle of estimation that had been established during the nineteenth century. As the goal was to estimate the total production of different cereals in volume, the division asked informants to evaluate two variables per cereal: the area cultivated and the yield per acre. Area was expressed in acres (and thus statisticians called this variable "crop acreage"), and yield was termed "condition of growth" (informants were asked what the plants' conditions of growth had been during the period surveyed). The multiplication of one by the other gave the volume of production.

These two estimates were requested in the form of a percentage of variation compared with a norm. In fact, with the help of a certain number of studies that the division claimed to have conducted on people in general, it had come to the conclusion that it was difficult to estimate absolute values, whereas it was easier to estimate percentages (Becker 1928). For example, when it asked for an estimate of the number of acres under wheat cultivation, the reporter tended to give a somewhat inaccurate answer, whereas if it asked for a comparison with, say, past observations, the response was much more precise. So, with reference to a specific crop, the division asked the reporters to compare the area under cultivation in the current year with the previous one. A similar detour was done with the condition of growth. The division then simply had to translate these percentages of variation into an absolute value (which was done with reference to the decennial census) and then multiply the area by the yield to obtain an estimate of production (for details, see Didier 2007).

Thus these two indicators resulted from the composition of a great number of elements extracted from the plasma: the lists containing the names of the reporters; the "theory" according to which they were better able to estimate percentages than absolute values; the mountains of letters on the basis of which the division tried to establish a relationship of trust with them; and so forth. Before the survey all these elements were separated; they were not necessarily linked. The act of surveying consisted in establishing the list of reporters, dispatching questionnaires to them, and writing out and transmitting the instructions; the reporters conducted their own inquiry and translated their observations into figures. The statisticians identified these elements, reorganized them, and reconstituted them into the one little number recorded by the reporters in the box intended for this purpose. The number contained and summarized this multitude statistically, and thus gave a texture—still unfinished—to what the United States would become at the end of the process. At this stage, however, it was itself only a minuscule element, only valid for a ridiculously small area. Let us now see the fate reserved for these first components.

Touring on the Job

The task of the statistician was to prepare reports on the agriculture of his state based on data that the reporters had communicated to him. But reports were not his sole and unique source of information. He also accumulated intimate knowledge of his territory. This personal knowledge helped him interpret and study the percentages passed on by the reporters in the most constructive way possible. Hence the initial processing of the questionnaires, paradoxically, consisted of setting them aside while he went out to survey the land directly. As I have already shown through Church's example, accumulating detailed observations of the terrain was not easy. Let us review some of the additional difficulties that the statistician encountered and see how he resolved them.

First and foremost, observation necessitated great mobility, and in fact, it appears that this was one of the profession's chief attractions. Church (1943, 5) explains that the most attractive characteristic he saw in the profession of statistician before he was hired was that it "would take [him] out of his office" and on "to the field."

However, these trips posed a thousand difficulties. The first was that the means of transport were often nonexistent in the 1910s. "To interview farmers and inspect crops, it was necessary to use horse and automobile liveries for trips into the country. Because the cost of this type of transportation was usually based on distance and time, interviews had to be brief, and the return trip often made over the same route as the outgoing one" (19).

The statisticians wanted to increase their mobility, like sales representatives, and get an automobile of their own. They asked the division to supply one, but it was much too expensive. Finally, in 1921, they got the right to be reimbursed for the use of their own automobiles at work (222).

The second constraint, related to the first, was the administrative boundaries, which further complicated the statistician's task. Emerson M. Brooks (1977, 29), the statistician of Kentucky in the 1920s, explains that "the topography and shape of the State were not conducive to efficient operations as it stretched 700 miles from east to west, but averaged less than a third of that north and south. The road system radiated out from Louisville with few intersticing roads, making cross state travel a round about, time-consuming, jaunt."

Hence even if the statistician had a car, the physical shape of the state further complicated his movements. And this on top of the fact that local roads and highways were far from being surfaced and suffered from mud holes and ruts created by the wheels on horse-drawn carts and the like. In addition, it was not until 1926 that the federal system of numbering highways was formally adopted—before which maps were rare and often reduced to simple route books that were extremely misleading (Akerman 1993, 81). All these difficulties, however, make it possible to understand how the surveys should ideally proceed: the statistician should do long interviews and travel easily over many roads to inspect different crops.

To reach this goal, statisticians benefited from a series of resources, the first of which was a districting of the territory. In the 1910s the division had obtained from the Post Office Department (as it was then known) a map of its "postal routes" and had transformed them into "crop reporting districts" into which the states "had been divided on the basis of agricultural and geographical homogeneity" (Brooks 1977, 13). (See figure 1.)

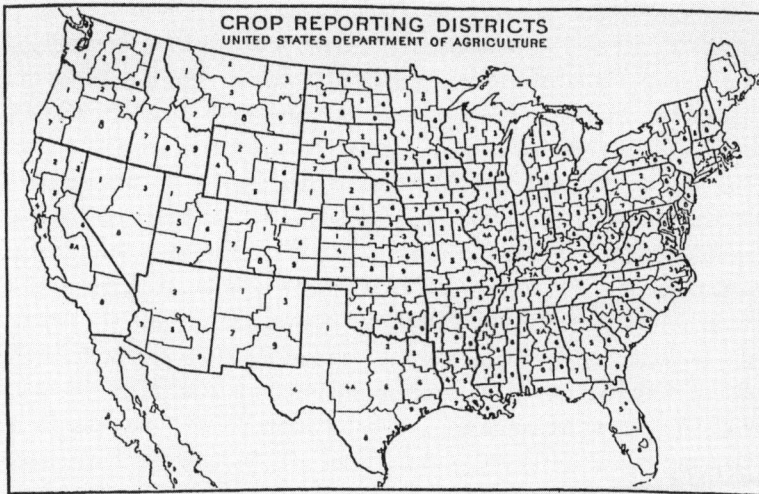

CROP REPORTING DISTRICTS
UNITED STATES DEPARTMENT OF AGRICULTURE

FIGURE 2.—Districting of States for crop-reporting purposes is a modification of the system used by the Post Office Department in handling the mails. The district boundaries follow county lines and include those contiguous counties which together make up the most homogeneous agricultural producing areas possible under the limitations of location. Shifts in the boundaries have been made from time to time, especially in the Western States. This map shows the present lines

Figure 1 Map of the crop-reporting districts (USDA 1933, 28)

The division of a territory into crop-reporting districts was made with gathering agricultural statistics in mind. Its advantage was that, as each district was homogenous, any information pertaining to a given crop was valid for the entire district.

Apart from the divisions, another crucial resource was what statisticians called "Area Confabs." Let Church (1943, 215) remind us of their first occurrence sometime between 1917 and 1920: "Bryant, Cochran and I immediately agreed that we could meet together occasionally near the common boundary of our three states, not only to collect information at that point, but to exchange ideas and experiences concerning the work and the problems involved."

Brooks (1977, 215) explains that this experience "inaugurated the practice of Area Confabs where Stats in adjoining or nearby states, get together once a year or so at a convenient time and place to mull over their difficulties, check on the 'grapevine' and get better acquainted." For the statisticians the area confab was thus an opportunity to share their experiences and synthesize their methods. It was an opportunity given to officials to reflect on the matters at hand.

Lastly, equipped with all these resources, the statistician directly questioned the farmers he had managed to identify as right for the questionnaire. These interactions were generally quite friendly, but could also turn out to be incredibly complex. Here is an example narrated by Church, about a survey on the quantity of potatoes to be put on the market. It was a difficult exercise, for it involved a cash crop, that is, a product grown to bring some hard cash to farmers (as opposed, e.g., to corn for feeding pigs) and therefore susceptible to market prices: "Most farmers felt the estimates influenced the market prices, which made them reluctant to give unbiased information" (Church 1943, 223). Despite the difficulty, Church went, as usual, to Greenville, the capital of Montcalm County, where he had discovered a farmers' cooperative and three wholesalers, of whom the most important was Sam Metzger. Church describes his interaction with Metzger:

> While he pretended to be co-operative in supplying information to me, his talk was mostly generalities about the potato situation and the big things he was doing in a business way. The real information I was seeking, he carefully concealed, or it was suspiciously unreliable. I always called on him merely to satisfy his egotism and minimize his criticism of our estimates, although I obtained my best information from the other Greenville dealers. (223)

Church and Metzger thus found themselves in a complex situation where they talked to each other each time they met, but to lie all the better both indulged in half-truths and manipulation. Church knew that Metzger "concealed" pertinent information, but listened to him nevertheless, not for what he said but to defuse in advance his interlocutor's criticism (insofar as the latter had participated in producing the final figure, he could not say that it was bogus, unless he confessed that he had lied). Inversely, Metzger cooperated because he knew that if he did not meet Church, he had no way to influence the numbers that the latter would produce. For the statistician, learning about agriculture required mastery as much of manipulation as of agronomy.

Building a personal observation of a state's agricultural situation required that the statistician master a series of resources: means of transportation, physical geography, communication abilities. With these resources, he could build a second point of view on state agriculture, apart from that of the reporters and of their method of reporting. He was now ready to compare his own observations with those of the reporters.

Editing

Exhausted by his travels, the statistician finally returned to his office. His first task was to sort out the questionnaires that had piled up in his absence. To preserve hundreds of loose sheets without letting disorder and its correlate, error, reign was not a trivial task. He secured them in ordinary envelopes in which he could separate the questionnaires on the various ongoing surveys (one for wheat, one for corn, one for pigs, etc.).

Once the date for the fact-gathering phase had passed, the task of processing the questionnaires could commence. He opened the envelopes and systematically discovered that . . . many of the reporters had made obvious mistakes. What could he do about these errors? Editing helped repair the damage.

In some cases, editing was carried out directly on the questionnaire to correct the most obvious mistakes made by the reporters. A typical error was to confuse the boxes meant for cattle with the ones for grains (heads of cattle were not written down as a percentage but counted) and consequently to record figures much greater than one hundred in those boxes where, normally, this was impossible. When the error was identifiable, editing consisted of transferring the information to the appropriate boxes.

In other cases, editing involved eliminating some questionnaires from the calculations. There was apparently initially no general rule about editing, but only individual practices. Leslie Carl, at the time the Iowa statistician, explained, for example, with respect to a survey of March 1932 on falling land prices, that he edited (i.e., eliminated) the questionnaires where the variations in the price of land in one year as compared with the price of land in another exceeded 35 percent. Carl did not offer a justification for choosing this limit, but he decided to disregard the questionnaires that exceeded it, probably for being too extreme. This operation enabled him to "bring into line" the results obtained that year with those of the previous year. The decrease, which became 19 percent after the editing, was comparable, on the one hand, with the 15.6 percent obtained from the "paired reports," that is, with the reports of the reporters who had replied in two consecutive years and which the statistician had collated two by two, and on the other, with the aggregated results of the previous year. The figure obtained after editing was thus "aligned" with the earlier results.[6] Editing thus had the advantage of rendering a

6. "Comments on Crop Reports," Iowa report, March 1, 1932, RG 83.

survey compatible with the totality of the results already produced, among which it came to take its place.

There was also one enormous drawback. Selectively eliminating questionnaires implied lack of faith in the authenticity of the information provided by the reporters who had filled them out. However, as the latter were in fact the division's principal informers, it seemed highly paradoxical to disqualify them. On what logical basis did the statisticians choose to doubt the data from the year's faithful informers rather than the data from the preceding year? The answer is straightforward: when the different sets of data were contradictory, it was necessary to exclude the weakest ones, which might be the reporters' answer. "In our editing out of extreme reports, it is possible to rely on first hand knowledge of local conditions. Extreme reports which other information does not substantiate, are brought into line or rejected. We do not feel warranted in accepting extreme reports which first hand knowledge of local conditions would discount."[7]

The statistician did not always go by his own gut feeling though, preferring sometimes to give priority to the assessments made by the reporters when they differed from his. C. J. West, the Ohio statistician in 1923, gives us an example of this type of dilemma during one of his surveys. He says that, according to his own travel observations of the number of breeding sows kept on a farm, he could have increased the answers of the reporters slightly compared with the preceding year. But here he felt that his own judgment had to give way to the "average recorded by the Reporters," which was the same as the previous year. The reason, he explained, was that, according to a general rule he had formulated, a sort of raw social theory he had constructed, farmers tend carry on as in the previous year when they are short on enthusiasm. Being pessimistic, they tend not to be innovative and repeat their decisions of the preceding year. Now, according to him, the reporters seemed that year to have effectively shown little enthusiasm. As a result, West recommended that this theory and the reporters' responses be given priority over his own observations.

Thus, contrary to what one might imagine, the statistical work performed by the division's statisticians was not governed solely by mechanical rules and procedures. Editing, which was an essential step, was one example of this. In fact, the data were nearly always self-contradictory. As

7. Entry 83, "Comments on Crop Reports," Leslie Carl's letter to W. Callander, May 27, 1932, RG 83.

a result, the statistician had no other option but to do a personal nonstandardized evaluation aimed at tallying the data as best he could. This evaluation consisted of asking which data could be eliminated and, after that, of reorganizing the remainder into a *coherent* whole, one that contained the *maximum number of elements*. To try to include more agricultural data (personal knowledge accumulated by the statistician, some theories on the farmers, etc.), Leslie Carl, like C. J. West, first sought to incorporate contradictory data in such a way as to sacrifice as little as possible. Editing was thus a delicate operation that *had to be carried out* (mutually exclusive information could not be retained), but it deprived the statistician of all his anchor points (all sources of information could be called into question). Hence it was left to the sole *discretion* of the statistician.

Adding

Once edited, the questionnaires were ready for the task of calculating the average. There is nothing more mechanical than an average: all it requires is to add all the observations and then divide the total by their number. Everyone knows this. But in practice is it that easy? Has the reader ever taken a hundred loose sheets of paper (approximately the number of questionnaires that the statistician received from each agricultural district), select just one of the several columns, and add the numbers that it contained without ever repeating or forgetting any entry? Although the formula may be simple, accurately computing a hundred questionnaires is far from foolproof.

Hence an ingenious mechanism was developed in the beginning of the 1920s that resolved the difficulties: "The schedules were sorted by crop-reporting districts and 'shingled,' one district at a time, without reference to counties within the districts. . . . A blank schedule was placed at the bottom on which the number of reports, sums and averages for each item were entered" (Church 1943, 6).

Prior to totaling the entries and calculating the average, the questionnaires for each district had to be *physically* rearranged. *Shingling* meant that the statistician had to take all the questionnaires of one district and make them overlap each other, just like roof tiles, so that only the numbers were visible. After the last questionnaire, he added a blank one, then he used a long wooden ruler—the peg strip—which resembled a skirt-peg wire hanger (except that it was more than a meter in length), that tightly clipped together the entire lot of questionnaires (see figure 2).

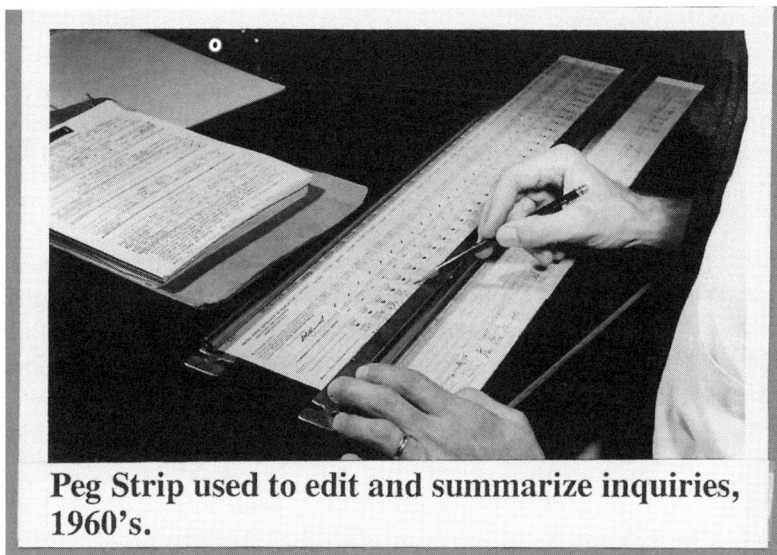

Peg Strip used to edit and summarize inquiries, 1960's.

Figure 2 The peg strip in use in 1960. Photograph courtesy of National Agricultural Statistical Service–USDA, Rich Allen's archives

The calculations could thus be done directly, without having to copy the reports and without the risk of forgetting some or counting them twice. The totals and the number of reporters were directly noted in the boxes of the blank questionnaire found at the end of the lot.

A further complication could arise when statisticians wanted to "weight" the sample, that is, give more importance to some observations than to others. This could be worthwhile, for example, when the townships in one reporter's district were larger than those in another. In this case, the statistician did not divide the sum by the number of questionnaires but by a set of weights. Once again, this meant that he had to decide which ones to choose, and why.

Hence initially every individual questionnaire was related to the neighborhood of the reporter who had filled it out, but through the shingling method, the integrated and reorganized schedules now constituted together the district on which the average bore. Thanks to this special concrete organization of questionnaires, the total was a new element extracted from the plasma that characterized the district. Thus, little by little, the state's elements were starting to "take." Editing had helped collate certain elements, and shingling had completed the process and produced districts. State by state, the United States was also in the process of taking concrete shape. But there was still work to be done before consolidating it for good.

Smoothing

Once the averages had been calculated, the statisticians noticed that sometimes, even in neighboring districts, the averages varied considerably, so much so that at times the variation did not seem plausible. To resolve this problem, the statisticians carried out an operation called smoothing, which required a geographic base map.

On the map, only the district or county boundaries were shown. Inside each of them, the statistician noted the corresponding average. This step thus highlighted the distribution of the growth condition—if we take this variable as an example—in the subelements of the state. He could now see how the growth condition had evolved when he looked from left to right or from top to bottom. If he observed excessive differences between neighboring districts, he could minimize them, which is to say, "smooth" them. This procedure rested on the principle that if two neighboring districts had very different results, it was possible that the difference was the result of an error that needed to be corrected. On the map of Kansas (figure 3), we can see that the statistician has circled an odd-shaped zone that is consistent in itself (wheat had reached close to 70 percent of its maturity), but not with the zones surrounding it (where it was closer to 90 percent). The statistician had to decide whether to "smooth" this peculiar variation or leave it as it was. But then he had to provide an explanation.

During the smoothing process, the state in its entirety began to emerge. But it is remarkable that this step, which is a kind of generalization, was *not* an induction, that is, the whole inferred from its parts. It used elements from the totality (the form of the state) as well as from the localities (the values ascribed to the counties), and even certain other factors that fit inside each other like the famous nesting Russian dolls (the principle according to which one had to be wary of marked variations). On the contrary, the totality was used to calculate local values, as much as local values helped construct the totality. The emergence of the state was an add-on and an overlapping of the extra elements and not an induction. It is in this way that the observation of the United States was consolidated much more than it was induced.

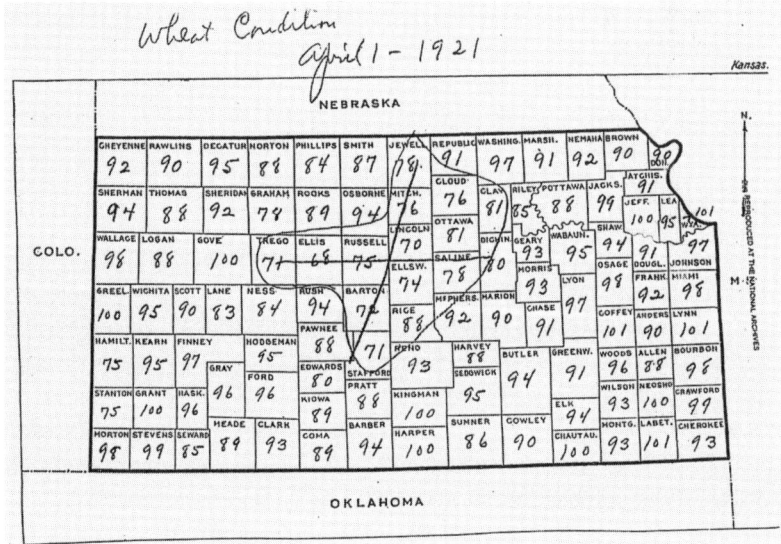

Figure 3 Smoothing carried out on the growth condition of wheat in Kansas in April 1921. The statistician has highlighted the central depression by circling it (US National Archives, RG 83).

Sending the Results

Once the percentages had been smoothed out, they were reported on a "summary sheet" that contained all the thousand and one elements extracted from the plasma by the reporters and the statistician (the administrative boundaries, trust between a person and an institution, a car, discussions between colleagues, letters, skirt-peg hangers, base maps, etc.) once they had been edited, totaled, smoothed out, weighted, and organized. It was itself an element in the general tallying process, incorporating all the partial elements and all the meticulous operations that could, finally, be sent to the central office in Washington, DC.

But first the summary sheet was transformed into a new document, which contained only the principal results and was immediately dispatched by telegram. These results were telegraphed to ensure that they reached Washington, DC, rapidly. They were, moreover, coded: each number from 1 to 120 (for the percentages) was replaced by a common name, which ensured the confidentiality of the data, which, at this stage, attracted the interest of potential speculators.

And after sending the figures to Washington, the statistician had to write "comments on crop reports," whose purpose was to mention all the elements mobilized during the processing of the answers. During the 1930s the list of elements was not standardized, so that each statistician chose to mention the ones he considered most important. I have already mentioned Leslie Carl, the statistician from Iowa, who referred to the series of older statistics, and C. J. West, the statistician from Ohio, who conceived a social theory about the relation between the enthusiasm of reporters and their observations. These reports were relevant precisely because each statistician had the advantage of being completely independent.

The statisticians thus produced three types of documents: a coded telegram that contained only extremely condensed numbers, a summary sheet that gave an exhaustive synopsis of all the results, and detailed remarks on the various stages of production of the first two documents. Between them, the three documents recapitulated the agriculture of the state. They condensed and aggregated the masses of reports sent by the reporters, discussed and rationalized them when they contradicted each other, and presented the statistician's personal observations and some earlier statistics. These three modules took different routes (telegraph and the ordinary post), but they left for the same destination—Washington, DC—the heart of the division where the statistics of the different states would be compared.

The story of how the state figures were gathered in Washington to produce exhaustive counts for the United States as a whole is as long—if not longer—as the one that I have just told. Many more surprising steps were necessary. So I will simply refer the reader to other sources where this description is made (Didier 2005, 2009) and call on his or her confidence: after a great number of successive transformations, agricultural statisticians had indeed calculated an estimated production of this or that crop for "the US as a whole." They were able to produce an observation of the entire nation.

Conclusion: The Cunning Intelligence of Observation

We can now conclude that observation appears first and foremost as a process of aggregation. It consists in identifying diverse elements in the world and amalgamating them into a new element, which might itself be aggregated with other elements to produce another observation. In our account, the reporters gathered data about acreage and condition of growth and used them to fill out their reports. statisticians listed those reporters, collected their answers, and aggregated them to their personal observations of the field. The division gathered bits of information about agriculture in the diverse states of the American union and synthesized them into a set of national figures. At every step of the process, heterogeneous elements were put together to form a new one.

The heterogeneity of these elements is striking. Expert statisticians made alliances with lay reporters; quantitative data were combined with qualitative ones; lists were used to identify singular events; outdoor trips informed indoor clerical tasks; material tools produced abstract figures. Many opposites were reunited in the observation. All the same, the ways these elements were associated seemed infinite and imaginative—contrary to the image of the statistician as a highly boring bureaucrat. Statisticians wrote letters to the farmers who had completed the questionnaire to maintain a constructive relationship with them—but did not rely *too* much on the good graces of the farmers—and mastered agronomy as well as the manipulation of data: they established stable district boundaries; they invented machines that clipped questionnaires together; and so forth.

So the final question that we are led to ask is whether there is an actual common point between these diverse ways to observe. I propose to answer positively with the word *mètis*, which also comes from the ancient Greeks and can be described as *cunning intelligence* (Detienne and Vernant 1991), an intelligence made of detours, of tricks. Statistical observation also has its own *mètis*. It consists of finding cunning ways to associate heterogeneous elements.

Finally, this series of aggregating steps never ended. I concluded my account by referring to another paper, which tells the story of the Washington, DC, continuation of the process that I have illuminated here. Observations always come from previous observations and might always be reaggregated into some other one. And so are my own observations aggregated in this essay.

References

Akerman, James R. 1993. "Selling Maps, Selling Highways: Rand McNally's 'Blazed Trails' Program." *Imago Mundi* 45:77–89.

Becker, Joseph A. 1928. "Analysis of Assumptions Underlying the Various Indications of Change in Crop Acreage." In *Class of the Division*, March 9, Washington, D.C.

Brooks, E. M. 1977. *As We Recall: The Growth of Agricultural Estimates, 1933–1961.* Washington, D.C.: USDA.

Cassin, Barbara. 1995. *L'effet sophistique.* Paris: Gallimard.

Church, Verne H. 1943. *Personal Recollection of the Government Crop Reporting Service*. Personal printing by Huwon Productions.

Daston, Lorraine. 2010. "Observation as a Way of Life: Time, Attention, Allegory." Hans Rausing Lecture, Uppsala University.

Detienne, Marcel, and Jean-Pierre Vernant. 1991. *Cunning Intelligence in Greek Culture and Society*. Translated by Janet Lloyd. Chicago: University of Chicago Press.

Didier, Emmanuel. 2005. "Releasing Market Statistics." In *Making Things Public: Atmospheres of Democracy*, edited by Bruno Latour and Peter Weibel, 638–42. Cambridge: MIT Press.

———. 2007. "Do Statistics 'Perform' the Economy?" In *Do Economists Make Markets? On the Performativity of Economics*, edited by Donald MacKenzie, Fabian Muniesa, and Lucia Siu, 276–310. Princeton: Princeton University Press.

———. 2009. *En quoi consiste l'Amérique?* Paris: La Découverte.

Estabrook, Leon M. 1915. *Government Crop Reports: Their Value, Scope, and Preparation*. Washington, D.C.: US Government Printing Office.

Pollak, Michael. 1986. "Un texte dans son contexte: L'enquête de Max Weber sur les ouvriers agricoles." *Actes de la recherche en science sociale* 65:69–75.

Taylor, Henry C., and Ann D. Taylor. 1952. *The Story of Agricultural Economics in the US, 1840–1932*. Ames: Iowa State College Press.

US Department of Agriculture (USDA). 1863. *Annual Report*. Washington, D.C.: USDA.

———. 1933. *The Crop and Livestock Reporting Service in the United States*. Washington, D.C.: USDA.

Economic Observation and Measurement in Russia before 1917: Surveying Typicalities and Sampling Totalities

Vincent Barnett

With a few notable exceptions, economists in the West in the nineteenth century focused their attempts at gathering and analyzing observations on Western countries and institutions, and employed techniques developed within currents of Western economics. These currents varied considerably, as is fruitfully discussed in this volume. However, an instructive additional comparison can be attempted with examples of data gathering in non-Western states.

Russia is an interesting country to investigate vis-à-vis observation for various reasons: the interface between economists and governmental representatives was often fraught with conflict, the institutions of observation were distinct from those in the West, and the purposes of observation could also be different. Russia's unique position in the firmament of nation-states was recognized in the West as early as 1737, when an article titled "A Proposal for the Measurement of the Earth in Russia" declared that

> the Question concerning the Earth's Figure is not yet at an end. Nay, 'tis not impossible, that after finishing all the Observations which are actually making, new Difficulties may arise. . . . 'Tis with this View, and particularly to render such important Service to the Geography of *Russia*, that I think it necessary to undertake a Work of that Nature in *Russia*; towards executing which we have great Advantages, which

Unless otherwise indicated, all translations are mine.

History of Political Economy 44 (annual suppl.) DOI 10.1215/00182702-1631779

the other Nations have not. One of the principal of these Advantages is the great Extent of *Russia* in every way. (L'Isle 1737, 40)

The argument was that large distances between Russian cities aided the accuracy of geographic measurements. Another advantage was that Russia would benefit from existing knowledge and "may expect to succeed and execute it better than could have been done elsewhere, by applying timely Remedies against the Difficulties that occurr'd in other Places" (42). Russia's size had economic consequences. Unique forms of trade, such as the large-scale commercial fair held annually over four weeks in Nizhny Novgorod, when transport was easiest, were conditioned by the vast scale of communication, manufacturing concentration in a small range of districts, and the scarcity of commercial towns.

In selecting a non-Western state as a comparison, the differences thought to exist should be considered. For some, Russia was "first and foremost a geographical concept, and an ambiguous one at that" (Gerschenkron 1970, 1). It was ambiguous because it had one part of its geography and culture in the backyard of Europe, and the other part (beyond the Ural Mountains) in Asia. In this sense it was different from other examples of "backward" economies considered in this volume, such as Italy, where the sheer range of geography and variety of customs were less diverse.

To others, the differences between West and East were mainly institutional. Henry Sumner Maine's 1875 Cambridge lecture "The Effects of Observation of India on Modern European Thought" applied equally to Russia. For Maine (1876, 222), on observing the Indian system, Westerners found economic institutions that were "very like, yet appreciably unlike, what they had left at home": there was ownership, but joint ownership; land rent, but no market standard; profit rates, but customary ones; and competition, but only between collective bodies. What Maine called "the comparative method" of observation applied most cogently to institutions of property and contract, but his distinctive efforts were the exception in the West. Maine provided a precedent for what Mary Morgan (2010, 314) has described as "seeing with new categories," in the case of Western attempts to record the Nigerian economy in the 1950s.

My main goal here is consequently to sketch something about what economic observation meant in the Russian nineteenth-century context, as a comparison for Western history. To do this, I first consider national-level statistical organizations and then present three examples of relatively autonomous data-gathering institutions: natural resource surveys, the *zemstvo*, and the Free Economic Society. This discussion of observational issues includes individuals as diverse as the industrial economist and chemist D. I. Mendeleev and the statistical analyst S. N. Prokopovich. I conclude with a more theoretical analysis of whether there were unique Russian approaches to observational techniques, and how they might have connected to wider political and methodological debates, using the work of the agricultural economist A. V. Chayanov, the historical economist A. I. Chuprov, and his son, the statistical theorist A. A. Chuprov.

National Institutions

Sites for observation could most obviously mean central government statistical offices, which were fixed in the major urban centers (Moscow and Saint Petersburg). In 1811 the Russian Ministry of Police first organized a statistical department, which became the statistical committee of the Ministry of Internal Affairs in 1852 and then in 1857 the Central Statistical Committee, which published its own periodical presenting agricultural data. The main areas that the latter documented were population, harvest data, sown area, and livestock. In 1863 the Statistical Council was organized, composed of representatives from the statistical divisions of government departments. In different regions, *guberniya* (provincial) statistical committees also existed, but their work was often of limited value (Ezhov 1960, 52).

Government departments such as the Ministry of Trade and Industry, the Ministry of Agriculture and State Property, and the Ministry of Finance also produced statistical data in their own fields. "The Cash Accounts of the Ministry of Finance" was initially issued in 1870, and the first official data source for the Russian state budget was published in 1866 (Livshits and Belen'ky 1960, 190). However, this type of statistical yearbook was based on data that had been gathered centrally, and related only to the remits of the ministries concerned. The Ministry of Agriculture collected some data on sown area and harvests, but the quality of much of this data was questionable and was not comprehensive in terms of geographic coverage or in documenting the diversity of Russian agriculture.

Various wide-ranging quantitative surveys, such as E. F. Zyablovsky's *Statistical Description of the Russian Empire* of 1808, were published from the beginning of the nineteenth century onward, but these were primarily descriptive. One of the first analytic works on statistics in Russia was D. P. Zhuravsky's (1810–1856) *Concerning the Sources and*

Uses of Statistical Observations of 1846, which considered the budgetary expenditure of different population classes. Zhuravsky distinguished between "material" and "rational" statistics—the former being concerned with simple chronological order and classification, the latter with the scientific reworking of data to obtain conclusions. He also elaborated a system of indicators for all areas of Russian society and proposed a general program for the investigation of the Russian productive forces.

Overall census counts of the Russian population had occurred since the time of Peter the Great (1672–1725). Censuses were nothing unusual within Europe, but what was exceptional was that in Russia "communal land *must* be redistributed during the census year," that is, periodic reallocation within the peasant commune was directly linked to observations of population growth (Haxthausen [1847] 1972, 83). One of the earliest examples of more focused governmental attempts at data collection was the decision by the minister of the interior, A. I. Bibikov, to compel Russian landowners to prepare inventories of their estates listing the obligations owed to landowners by peasants, and to empower committees to gather related evidence. On reporting the results in 1846, the committees complained of inaccurate information because of a lack of skilled staff and even some landowner resistance.

There were other sources of data on aspects of the Russian economy after 1850: for example, the army horse census, usually taken every six years, which counted the number of horses fit for army service, and individual commissions created by the government to investigate certain branches of industry. The official *Proceedings of the Commission for the Study of the Handicrafts Industry in Russia* was published in a massive seventeen volumes between 1879 and 1890. However, the lack of coordination of Russian observational efforts was indicated by the fact that the mineralogist V. I. Vernadsky (1922, 31) was still calling for the creation of an official state network of scientific investigative institutes in 1916.

Natural Resource Surveys

Sites for observation could also mean more movable feasts, such as surveys of the national resources of Russia's regions and the mapping of geography, hydrography, climate, and ethnography. It was Peter the Great who, at the end of the seventeenth century, first dispatched engineers to survey the provinces of the Russian Empire and "sent persons skilled in metallurgy to the various districts in which mines were to be found"

(Society 1833, 188). This type of fact-gathering operation had a scientific component, relating to the existence of mineral deposits, and an economic component, regarding industries that could be located in specific resource-rich areas. These two aspects were sometimes blurred, as in the second quarter of the nineteenth century, when the Livonian Economic Society asked the astronomer F. G. W. Struve to cover Livonia with a trigonometric net of measurements (Witskowski 1891, 307). Accurate maps were a prerequisite of documenting raw materials deposits.

It was the Imperial Free Economic Society that joined the Imperial Geographic Society in 1867 to send expeditions to various districts to study the commercial distribution of grains and also to sponsor expeditions to examine the distribution of Russia's *chernozem* (black soil) in 1878–79 (Vucinich 1970, 85). The *Proceedings of the Expedition Equipped by the Free Economic Society for Investigating the Grain Trade* was published in four volumes in 1868–76. The Geographic Society also conducted extensive demographic surveys and organized ethnographic expeditions to document rural socioeconomic organization and customs. And it was the Russian Society of Mining Engineers that, at congresses in 1903 and 1911, studied the economics of geological prospecting activities and the legal bases of industrial exploration (Vucinich 1970, 422). A survey expedition to the Urals provided the world-renowned chemist D. I. Mendeleev (1834–1907) with evidence of iron ore deposits used to analyze mining and metals production.

However, because of Russia's size and the wider variety of its physical environments compared with West European states, surveying and prospecting were often more difficult tasks in Russia. One methodological difference between how such surveys were conducted in Russia and (say) the UK was that in the former, observation was more often seen as a comparative activity, in that Russia's "facts" were compared with those of more advanced states, as part of the process of articulating a development program. For example, in works on industry and on tariff reform, Mendeleev frequently quoted observational data on Germany, and in 1877 he published the detailed analysis *Petroleum Affairs in Pennsylvania and the Caucasus* (Barnett 2004, 2005a). In 1873–74 Yu. E. Yanson published a series of comparative statistical studies, including one on Russian and European railways and mortality, and a general two-volume *Comparative Statistics of Russia and West-European States* in 1878–80.

In 1889, in response to rumors that Baku oil supplies were being exhausted, Mendeleev compared Baku with Pennsylvania, indicating that

Baku naphtha flows had increased between 1885 and 1888. He explained why exhaustion was unlikely in the near future:

> The Devonian and Silurian sand strata of Pennsylvania are similar in this respect to the naphtha sands in the new tertiary strata of the Caucasus. The former are, however, geologically old—the latter are recent. . . . The old beds had many natural opportunities of getting opened, of letting out their naphtha supply, of getting washed away . . . but the younger naphtha deposits of the Caucasus had less chance of this. (Mendeleeff 1889, 754)

Mendeleev demonstrated that, because of the absence of storage reservoirs in Baku, the price of oil fluctuated much more in relation to changing demand compared with Pennsylvania. When demand for kerosene rose, prices in Baku increased, but this was not a sign of impending exhaustion, merely of differences in storage facilities (Mendeleeff 1889, 755). It was far less likely that US economists would write substantial works comparing their country's natural resources with those of Russia.

The vastness of Russia also obliged economists to divide the country into agricultural regions, each having its own distinct structure. The resultant agricultural geography related price variations and production intensity to distance from, and transport links to, local markets (Tchayanov 1928, 546). For example, A. I. Skvortsov (1848–1914) published *The Influence of Railway Transport on Agriculture* in 1890. Other factors influencing regional typicality were the range of soils and the diversity of climatic zones, and the distance between farms and the factories they supplied with raw materials (Chayanov [1929] 1991, 189–90).

In 1910 A. N. Chelinstev (1874–1962), a leading member of the Organisation-Production School of economists, published *Regions of European Russia as Stages of Agricultural Evolution*, arguing that different regions of Russia represented different phases of rural development and that population density was linked to production intensity. Low population regions favored extensive farming, whereas high population density favored intensive farming, with a sliding scale linking production methods with regional particularities. Outside European Russia, in Siberia, indigenous seminomadic agriculture and clan-based tent villages persisted even to 1900, with West-Russian settlement producing intermixed economic institutions. Consequently, location theory in the style of Johann von Thünen was especially relevant to Russian observational practice, more so than in substantially smaller countries.

The *Zemstvo*

Another institution with special observational duties was the *zemstvo*. The *zemstvo* was an autonomous unit of regional government first created in Russia in 1864, which had limited tax-raising abilities and some governmental functions. *Zemstvo* powers were restricted to local tasks, for example, education and roads, but they also had a special role in gathering and collating local statistics. Since the basis of *zemstvo* income was taxes levied on immovable property (land and commercial establishments), *zemstvo* statistical bureaus had a direct incentive to document local economic conditions (Matyukha, Postnikov, and Samoilov 1960, 299).

The first detailed *zemstvo* statistical investigation was begun in 1870, and by the 1880s there were twenty-one separate *zemstvo* statistical bureaus in operation. In contrast to the government's own Central Statistical Committee, which often collected data by circulating questionnaires, local *zemstvo* bureaus employed their own staff to gather firsthand information (Johnson 1982, 344). One early method of observation used by *zemstvo* statisticians was the household inventory and the house-to-house census, which was a detailed investigation of peasant farms in specific areas, often for taxation purposes, that was then published in statistical abstracts (Lenin [1899] 1960, 70, 643). In such censuses, information on total annual output, date of establishment, number of workers, and methods of cultivation were collected. According to an 1893 estimate, the *zemstvo* censuses covered 123 *uezds* (districts) in twenty-two *guberniyas* (provinces), observing 2,983,733 separate peasant households and a combined population total of 17,996,733 people (345, 142).

Another, higher estimate in 1894 put the coverage figure for the censuses made by *zemstvo* statistical bureaus at eighty thousand villages across twenty-five Russian provinces (Craigie 1897, 749). By 1917 *zemstvo* statisticians had interviewed approximately 4.5 million peasant families across thirty-four different provinces, and published approximately 3,500 separate items documenting their results (Johnson 1982, 357). As a consequence of observing "millions of separate farms," one economist explained that "it is quite beyond doubt that no other country has such an extensive collection of local statistical monographs as Russia" (Tchayanov 1928, 544). House-to-house censuses and inventories were sometimes also made for handicraft industries in certain regions. After 1900 some new *zemstvo* survey methods were developed, for example, household budget studies and peasant consumption studies.

Given the size of the Russian Empire, the ability of the central government to conduct local observations was limited, and hence the *zemstvo* was often the only institution able to collect data in more remote areas. But since conditions varied so extensively from region to region, it was found that it was not always possible to utilize a universal design for gathering data (Johnson 1982, 347). Indeed, the question of calculating the size of landholdings in various regions had been of great significance in debates over measuring the extent of rural development and setting peasant taxes. Whether average figures or more disaggregated measures should be used had provided a point of much discussion (Darrow 2000, 70). Lenin ([1899] 1960, 144–45) drew extensively on *zemstvo* data to support his argument that peasant differentiation was creating a rural bourgeoisie in Russia and hence that capitalism in agriculture was more developed after 1890 than Populist economists had acknowledged.

In the 1870s Mendeleev attempted to encourage rural *zemstvo* in using weather forecasts as an aid to agriculture, by facilitating the use of aerostats (weather balloons) to collect meteorological data at high altitudes (Brooks 2004, 45). This type of data collection provided a direct link between natural and social science observations, as climate data would be of use both to derive laws relating to changes in atmospheric layers and to assist Russian peasants in designing successful crop sowing patterns. These aerostat proposals were unsuccessful, but more important was Mendeleev's campaign for metric measurement. Appointed as director of the Chief Bureau of Weights and Measures in 1893, in 1899 he introduced a law that attempted to standardize Russian units of measurement in relation to the metric system (Gordin 2004, 164). One reason for introducing the metric system was to enable more accurate alcoholometry to improve the collection of excise duties. Another was to ensure that standardized weights and measures were used in commercial transactions across the Empire, as regional centers often used outdated and inaccurate measuring prototypes. In 1897 use of the metric system was also cited as enabling improvements in attaining accurate harvest data (Craigie 1897, 743).

Across much of the work of *zemstvo* statisticians, it is possible to identify two different observational data-gathering goals that coexisted: a narrower attempt to assess the value of landholdings and property, and a wider attempt to investigate household inventories and local socioeconomic conditions (Johnson 1982, 345, 347). The former had as its main aim to provide information to enable government and local tax collection, the latter to provide data that could be used to design policies to improve rural living conditions. The political tensions between conservatives and reformers were one overtone to these different goals, and *zemstvo* statisticians were sometimes accused of harboring radical sympathies, but in other instances *zemstvo* statisticians had freely entered government service, and hence they were not all political reformers, let alone social revolutionaries.

The Free Economic Society

The final institutional aspect of Russian observation I examine here is the work of the Imperial Free Economic Society for the Encouragement of Agriculture and Husbandry, which was created on the initiative of Catherine II in 1765 and was in existence until 1919. It was declared "free" in that it was not under the formal tutelage of the Russian government or the Academy of Sciences, although it did receive some central governmental funding. Throughout its existence it published 281 volumes under its banner and issued journals and questionnaires, as well as organizing exhibitions and competitions.

It officially requested answers to economic questions in the form of open competitions, which attracted entries from Russian and foreign authors. Examples of the question asked included "For the vigorous spread of agriculture, what should be the estate of the ploughman?" and "What is more useful for society, that the peasant have his own land or only movable property?" (Prescott 1977, 509). These prize competitions were a way to seek new ideas and to gather firsthand information. It also published individually authored pamphlets such as G. Yatsenkov's (1840) *To What Extent Is Agriculture Found in Russia*, which investigated the degree and form of crop cultivation.

The general aim of the Free Economic Society was to accelerate the development of Russian agriculture and industry. This was to be achieved by various methods such as publishing periodicals and other collections, disseminating the latest agricultural knowledge, awarding medals and prizes, organizing public lectures, giving special commissions to members, conducting field investigations, setting competitions for solutions to certain tasks and publishing the best answers, arranging exhibitions of agricultural and industrial works, organizing agricultural shows and experimental farms, collecting statistical data, and authorizing entrance to its museums and libraries (*Ustav* 1859, 13–14). The society's journal published not only conventional articles but also replies from the provinces on questions relating to soils, crops, agricultural equipment, and peasant economy more generally that had been posed in previous issues.

One noteworthy feature of the Free Economic Society was that its membership came from a wide circle of people, including aristocrats and landowners, statesmen and civil servants, writers and lawyers, those interested in political and social economy, and also natural scientists. It thus served as a point of connection for other institutions of civil society. For instance, it served as a clearinghouse for otherwise isolated *zemstvo* statistical workers, where it was "one of the very few institutions that made concerted efforts to gather valuable data related to this unique social experiment" and provide economists with usable empirical information (Vucinich 1970, 86). It also acted as a government consultant on various economic issues and organized commissions such as that of 1885 to investigate grain exports (Atkinson 1980, 97). Another example of the society's work was in researching the best varieties of crops to grow in Russian soil.

The connection between economic and scientific observation was important to the methods of key individuals associated with the society. In 1866 Mendeleev composed for the Free Economic Society a questionnaire on soil quality. As has been explained, "Similar to what he would propose for meteorological observations in the 1870s, local farmers would gather data (after being properly instructed by an expert—himself) and then he would coordinate all the results through the Free Economic Society" (Gordin 2004, 149). In the same year, 1866, Mendeleev wrote a work titled "On the Organization of Agricultural Methods under the Free Economic Society." The year before, in 1865, he had purchased his own estate of land (around 1,026 acres), on which he organized the scientific application of fertilizer to the cultivation of grain crops (Mendeleev 1991, 6–7).

Perhaps one of the most significant examples of work using economic observations published under the society's banner was that conducted by S. N. Prokopovich (1871–1955) on measuring national income. Before 1917 Prokopovich was a socialist sympathizer who witnessed the 1891–92 Siberian famine firsthand; in 1922 he was deported from Soviet Russia, and then in exile he created the renowned Prague "Economic Cabinet" for observing the Soviet economy. In a 1906 contribution to the Works of the Free Economic Society publication series titled *Experience of Calculating National Income in 1900*, Prokopovich provided the first indigenous estimate of aggregate national income for all of the Russian state (excluding Finland). He calculated that it was 8.9 billion rubles in 1900 (Prokopovich 1918, 26); what was interesting were the observations needed to reach

Table 1 Russian National Income in 1900

Branch of Production	Level in 1900 (in rubles)
Agriculture	2,985,057,000
Forestry and fishing	626,167,000
Mining and processing industries	1,402,191,000
Transport business	531,200,000
Construction business	473,100,000
Trade	561,900,000
Total	6,579,615,000

Source: Prokopovich 1918, 6, 24.

this aggregate figure. This work on national income can be seen as the culmination of data-gathering efforts that had occurred over decades.

Prokopovich declared that, in his calculation, national income was composed of the net production of six branches of material production, and for fifty *guberniyas* of European Russia, he estimated their levels as shown in table 1.

Thus total national income for fifty *guberniyas* of European Russia in 1900 was approximately 6.58 billion rubles, which increased to 11.81 billion in 1913. He recognized that figures for gross output for all branches of productive activity, and data on the consumption of material values used in production, would actually be necessary to calculate national income, but as these figures were not available, net production had been used as a substitute (Prokopovich 1918, 5–6). Prokopovich (1930, 46) later admitted that his calculation of national income in 1900 was not really an estimate of actual population income, but of the net production of the Russian national economy.

To calculate the total figures for the branches of production that were used, Prokopovich employed observational data gathered by the Central Statistical Committee (TsSK). However, the TsSK had judged some of its data, agricultural harvests, according to information gathered by *zemstvo* statisticians (Prokopovich 1918, 7). In another instance, output of cattle, Prokopovich used data from peasant budget investigations published by the Free Economic Society (10). In still other instances, Prokopovich used data from the Russian Forestry Department, the Ministry of Finance, a Special Conference on Fuel, and various monographs and statistical yearbooks on specific areas of industry.

Thus Prokopovich's national income calculation for 1900 was possible only because of the existence of a wide variety of data gathered by statistical institutions, and it can be conceived of as one of the most significant culminations of observational efforts in prerevolutionary Russia. Prokopovich's efforts did not go unnoticed. Colin Clark (1939, 5) declared that Prokopovich had adopted a "somewhat limited and materialistic definition of national income" that excluded rents and many services. Prokopovich had readily recognized this deficiency, but data limitations had tied his hand; in fact he had been a pioneer.

Observational Techniques

Having considered various institutions, it is now time to focus on the techniques employed by Russian economists. One of the most important economists to have an impact on the development of observational techniques in the prerevolutionary period was A. I. Chuprov (1842–1908), a leading Russian historical economist and president of the Statistical Section of the Moscow Juridical Society. In 1888 he defined the task of statistics as the composition of social facts describing phenomena in terms of systematic observations with the help of a special method, in order to elucidate laws that underpinned them (Chuprov [1888] 1909, 207). He outlined that the successes achieved by Russian statistics in the previous quarter century had been huge, for example, the formation of a Central Statistical Committee, which competed with government departments in providing data. Chuprov believed statistics was particularly important because an acquaintance with the facts of economic life was a necessary condition for elaborating norms for civil rights (210).

The "special statistical method" that Chuprov referred to was the "monographic method" or the "monographic description" of separate entities such as villages, which he declared was a necessary means of renewing the foundations of *zemstvo* investigations (Chuprov [1894] 1909, 225). The monographic method involved selecting a cluster of elements identified as typical of a given population in aspects that were deemed relevant, and then investigating them in substantial detail (Seneta 1985, 120). This was done either by using existing registrations or by employing local agronomical and anthropological knowledge (Chayanov [1929] 1991, 190; Morgan 2010, 312). The outcome could be detailed statistical data on production in a given area or a study of the agricultural institutions found in a specific region. In another, more-focused example that was related to household inventories: "While the data by household could be compiled in general tables, detailed descriptions should be obtained of one or more typical households in each particular district, including complete data on the budgets, and real and personal property of each household" (Craigie 1897, 751). Many of the regional studies accomplished by *zemstvo* statisticians in the 1880s could be conceived as using the monographic method, at least in part.

Chuprov outlined the reasoning for the necessity of such typicality studies and also the need for associated larger-scale investigations as follows:

> Explaining the fundamental difference between phenomena of the external [natural] world and human society consists of the fact that the former occurs under the influence of causes that are constant, identical, or uniform, whereas on the contrary, social phenomena depend on a multitude of causes that are not only constant, but also variable and random, in consequence of this they also possess individual character. The observation of various facts here cannot serve as the basis for conclusions about other cases of the same kind; the action of one individual does not resemble the actions of another. In this latter case, it is necessary to combine observations of a large number of single cases together, in order from the sum of such individual studies to obtain one total investigation—it is necessary to accomplish what is called mass observation. (Chuprov [1888] 1909, 207)

Thus Chuprov advocated focusing on the individual monographic selection of typicality and also on wider documenting of the totality of which it formed a part, as two elements of a method designed to reveal unique economic specificities and also general trends in the wider economy.

Consideration of the monographic method was quite extensive, as it was discussed at a meeting of the International Statistical Institute held in Saint Petersburg in August 1897. In addition to general statistical analysis, the need for a special committee investigating what were called "methods of typological inquiry" was asserted. Especially with regard to social questions, a large field allowing "partial investigations" was identified, either case-study monographs or statistical explorations of specific fields, although the types chosen "should be as representative as possible" and "controlled by" general statistics in many regards (Craigie 1897, 766). This latter point highlighted the selection criteria for "typicality," which should be based on a wider understanding of general trends, or so-called best representative typological methods. However, others such as S. A. Pervushin (1888–1966) argued that it was difficult to judge in isolation whether materials gathered by the monographic method were typical for peasant farms in general, and he suggested that the "expedition method" of collecting budget materials on the basis of a single-period once-only investigation were often flawed: instead, receipt and outlay accounts over a series of years should be used (quoted in Chayanov [1912] 1991, 342–43).

It was Chuprov's son, A. A. Chuprov (1874–1926), who was one of the most important theorists to challenge the relevance of the monographic method in Russia after 1900. According to J. M. Keynes (1926, 518), A. A. Chuprov was "one of the most important writers on the boundary line between statistical theory and the theory of Probability." In a 1910 work, whose title is usually translated as *Sampling*, but could more literally but less accurately be rendered as *Selective Investigation*, Chuprov provided a critique of the monographic method and its hidden sources of observational bias. Having in mind the sort of regional studies that had been commonly undertaken by *zemstvo* statisticians, Chuprov (1910, 4) explained that

> when we return from a distant journey, mapping our representations of the visit to the locality, describing aspects of the streets, the character of buildings, and type of inhabitants, then you want to recount it free from figures, but in essence it rests on the purely statistical—only subconscious—calculation of various impressions and on inference, "typical" for the total mass of your experience.
>
> In such cases of "crypto"-statistical judgment we have matters on every stage of living customs. With this underlies, in the majority of cases, a concealment of so-called "popular wisdom" finding expression in proverbs and omens. Here the same is attributed to the notorious "personal experience" of the practitioner.

Thus, according to Chuprov, when investigators produced their monographic studies of apparent typicality, they were unconsciously employing selection criteria for observations based on folk wisdom and their own selective experiences.

Clearly employing an analogy with the "correct" observational techniques used by scientists, Chuprov continued his critique of typicality as follows:

> The errors that creep into the conclusions with such unconscious use of statistical judgements have various sources. Not free from errors are, above all, those single [typical] observations that we summarize

onto one general statistical map. Such types of error, that every natu-ralist sharply knows according to their daily practice, is not necessary for us to explain. . . . But, in the large, measures serve attention in the second stage of the process—summing individual impressions into general conclusions. Here such ideas, passively providing natural cur-rents of thinking experience, meet peculiar dangers. (5)

Chuprov's solution to the problem of monographic bias was mechanically and randomly chosen samples (one out of every ten) and use of the idea of "probable error" of estimates (Seneta 1985, 120). He proposed that social science observations—"the city of Petersburg as a complicated system of mutual relationships among an aggregate of its inhabitants"—should be analyzed with the same sample count methods used in the natural sci-ences, which were based ultimately on applying the law of large numbers (Chuprov [1913] 1981, 174).

   Here was the essential methodological difference between the approaches of father and son. A. I. Chuprov, the historical economist, believed that social science observations were of a different type from those of the natural sciences, whereas A. A. Chuprov, the statistical theorist, believed they were the same. In the former case, the monographic method was deemed appropriate precisely because of this distinction, where essen-tial differences between economic phenomena had to be observed and explained in individual and historically grounded terms: whereas, in the latter case, the monographic method was seen as biased and unrepresen-tatively selective, precisely because the law of large numbers was not being consistently applied.

   It has been suggested that the monographic establishment of typical-ity involved only the use of the arithmetic average of a stratified sample, which would be a nonsensical measure if variability within the sample were large (Kotz and Seneta 1990, 77–78). E. E. Slutsky (1880–1948) made a similar point in *The Theory of Correlation* of 1912 about any sta-tistical totality of items having a common relation when not all the items had indicated relations of the same magnitude:

   There was a time when statisticians ignored these differences and only concentrated on the arithmetic mean of the indications. Nowa-days, it is not anymore necessary to struggle against this dated . . . restriction. It is almost generally understood that the mean is report-ing too little about the essence of the whole statistical group and that the aim of statistics comes to describing as completely and simply as possible the whole composition of totalities under consideration. (Slutsky [1912] 2009, 8)

However, this purely distributional characterization of the method is missing an important part of the monographic approach. Typicality could mean not simply the numerical representation of a standard commonality but the construction of complex distinctiveness.

A. I. Chuprov's concern with "the sum of individual studies" implied that typicality was assembled organically and individually from the bottom up, rather than statistically and mechanically from the top down. Beginning with detailed individual studies of specific farms, types, households, and regions, the monographic description of more general structure was then built up through later comparison and contrast. This method was similar to the idea of revealing "hidden internal structure" in the macroeconomy through cartographic description (Morgan 2010, 305). This bottom-up approach was especially relevant to a large nation such as Russia, where the diversity of agricultural economy was greater than in small Western European countries, and hence the standard deviation in relation to typicality measures would often be higher.

Another related issue that was debated in prerevolutionary Russia was the use of averages with regard to time-series observations of individual quantities. For example, in estimating the volume of oil exports, in order to detect possible errors in the data, Mendeleev recommended cross-checking independently obtained figures against each other, and if no errors were apparent, then average (arithmetic mean) figures of the various data sets should be taken (Sheynin 1996, 61). In another instance he declared that, in presenting yearly data for Russian manufactories and mills over the period 1878–90, under this averaging method "production is estimated by the approximate mean values of the articles produced" (Mendeleeff 1893, vii). Mendeleev favored the use of what he termed "harmonious" observations, that is, those in which the median value coincided with the arithmetic mean, or even better, those in which the mean of the middlemost third coincided with the mean of the means of its extreme thirds (Sheynin 1996, 63).

Problems of observing agricultural yields and use of the notion of an "average crop" were considered at the meeting of the International Statistical Institute in 1897. In some instances, only verbal statements of crop yield estimates were employed in Russia, the categories being very good, good, good-average, average, under-average, bad, and very bad. The question was then raised whether the meaning of the term *average* had any definite significance in the Russian context. Whereas in France, a 100 percent rating meant only the qualitative grading "very good" and a 20 percent rating "bad," in the United States, a 100 percent rating corresponded quantitatively to what was called a "full average crop": the basis of comparison was taken as the average of the preceding ten years. While this might be appropriate for the United States, where the yield varied comparatively little from year to year, in Russia, where production was so extensive and diverse and the climate so variable, the range of variation in the yield reached around 300 percent. In this latter instance, a "full average crop" measure would have no real observational value, partly because of the sheer size of Russia and the diversity of its agriculture (Craigie 1897, 744–45).

Perhaps the most well-known analyst of the techniques of household budget study employed by *zemstvo* statisticians was A. V. Chayanov (1888–1937), the renowned theorist of peasant farming who, in the 1920s, was director of the Moscow Institute for Agricultural Economics. In 1912 he suggested that one of the most precise techniques of budget investigation could be the self-completed bookkeeping questionnaire, which peasants themselves were trained to conduct (Chayanov [1912] 1991, 342). Tables 2 and 3 present examples given by Chayanov from 1910 of the tabular part of such questionnaires, indicating the level of factual detail that such questionnaires were intended to capture.

Table 2 was designed to collect data on the hours worked by individual farm members disaggregated by category of labor, while table 3 was designed to collect data on the costs of various types of working equipment that farms employed. Alongside such tables, for each household farmstead in a given village, numerous accompanying questions were asked, such as how much of a particular crop was grown, the associated costs of cultivation, the harvests obtained, the prices realized, the average harvest level, the prices paid for leased land, percentage outlay on specific crops, and so on.

To give an example of how Chayanov used such questionnaire data on budgetary expenditure, he presented the information shown here as table 4, comparing various peasant farms in different regions, describing it as what he called character analysis.

Analysis of this data suggested that declining consumption of tea and sugar was linked to the size of the monetary element in family budgets. In Chayanov's original yet controversial analysis of Russian agriculture, peasant behavior was based on a labor-consumption balance in which

Table 2 Calculation of Labor Expended on a Farm

Work Done	Work Time	Required Daily Work				Payment	
		Horses	Men	Women	Children	Units	Price
Ploughing I							
Harrowing I							
(number of tracks)							
Ploughing II							
Harrowing II							
(number of tracks)							
Sowing							
Closing up							
Rolling							
Weeding							
Pulling out and linking							
Bringing together with poles							
Threshing							
Spreading							
Lifting							
Trampling down							
Pulling about							
Scutching							
Connecting							

Source: Chayanov [1929] 1991, 72.

Table 3 Amortization of Tools of Production

Tool	System	Place of Purchase	Number	Cost	Yearly Maintenance	Usual Years of Service
Plough						
Holing tool						
Mangle						
Rake						
Seed divider						
Thresher						
Brake						
Winnower						
Scutcher						
Rower						
Seed grader						

Source: Chayanov [1929] 1991, 73.

Table 4 Regional Budget Data

Region	One Person's Budget (in rubles)	Monetary Percentage	Outlay on Tea and Sugar (in rubles)
Volokolamsky district	100.1	57.9%	8.0
Moscow province	79.1	52.0%	6.2
Vologodsky district	64.1	60.7%	5.4
Totemsky district	51.8	30.2%	2.5
Vel'sky district	56.7	31.2%	2.0

Source: Chayanov [1912] 1991, 346.

the monetary and nonmonetary requirements of a family unit were evaluated against the drudgery of labor performed. Part of the origins of this analysis was the data gathered through *zemstvo* budget investigations. Not everyone agreed with Chayanov's results. L. N. Litoshenko also used budget data to argue that peasant behavior was mainly acquisitive and often market-driven.

Although Chayanov was not officially a *zemstvo* statistician, in 1912 he used survey materials gathered by *zemstvo* officers in Khar'kov to verify his hypothesis that the evolving needs of the family unit were the major factor in determining peasant behavior: as previously, he compared monetary outlays in different regions with the varying character of purchasing trends (Chayanov 1915, 125–30). From the position of observational techniques, the crucial factor was that Chayanov was able to use data that were disaggregated by region and by size of peasant farm, and that observations on consumption patterns were now available. Some Russian economists also observed urban consumption budgets: in 1909 Prokopovich published an empirical study *Budgets of St-Petersburg Workers*, while in 1910 D. Shaposhnikov conducted a regional account of factory worker budgets in Bogorodsk *uezd*. And although Slutsky's 1915 article "On the Theory of the Budget of the Consumer" became famous as a contribution to microeconomic theory, it was also intended to stimulate the study of measurable budgetary data (Barnett 2011, 42).

Political Ramifications

One way to determine the observational "typicality" identified by historical economists was to group peasant farms by some category of socioeconomic stratification, by size of allotment, number of draught horses owned, or the size of the monetary element in the household budget. Methods of grouping indicators into more complex systems were also proposed. Chayanov ([1929] 1991, 189) defined rural typicality in relation to family landholdings within a region: each social stratum had its typical farm. Another example of typicality was in organizational forms of economy: the *obshchina* (rural commune), *artel* (industrial collective), *kustar* (small-scale handicrafts), and various types of cooperative association were all subject to statistical-monographic study.

Although the publications produced from *zemstvo* survey data were most often framed in terms of regional divisions, and hence the typicality that might emerge from the observational data was geographic, it is not true to suggest that *zemsvto* statisticians (or others gathering data) were always blind to socioeconomic divisions. For example, in his prerevolutionary analysis of twenty village communities within Ryzan *guberniya*, the geographer and statistician P. P. Semenov (1870–1942) plotted six types of peasant household: very wealthy, prosperous, well-to-do, middling, poor, and very poor (Matyukha, Postnikov, and Samoilov 1960, 298). In 1915 he even published a book titled *Types of Locality in European Russia and the Caucuses*.

In a study of peasant budgets of four *uezds*, the director of the Voronezh *zemstvo* statistical section, F. A. Shcherbina (1849–1936), presented statistics on sixty-seven budgets of what were called typical farms. Shcherbina also published budget studies under the auspices of the Free Economic Society. According to Lenin, however, Shcherbina's use of all-around averages produced misleading results, as it concealed the socioeconomic differentiation that had developed (Lenin [1899] 1960, 149). Shcherbina divided land income by the total number of farms to obtain an overall average figure for the *uezds* in question. For Lenin, it was not peasant farming in totality that constituted a special "type of development" but the rural proletariat and the peasant bourgeoisie, as these groups should be separately classified by size of allotment and number of animals owned (171). Even so, as Lenin recognized elsewhere, other *zemstvo* statisticians did group peasant households according to area under crops, in the Taurida region finding that 20 percent of the households owned over 50 percent of the total area under cultivation (71).

Observations of industrial data did not escape consideration in political debates. Mendeleev provided analysis of the distribution of factory workers, noting in 1893 that there were forty-three workmen per manufactory (Mendeleeff 1893, lii). Although such data might seem uncontroversial, in

Russia they were subject to significant political debate. The conflict between Social Democrats like Lenin, Populists like V. P. Vorontsov, and Legal Marxists like M. I. Tugan-Baranovsky about estimating the growth of factory and worker numbers has been documented, as the question of the extent of capitalist development in Russia during the 1890s was crucial to resolving questions of political strategy (Barnett 2005b, 93–96).

In such debates, the unit of industrial observation was an essentially contested quantity, as definitions of "factory," "manufactory," "handicraft unit," and so on were subject to elementary dispute. One part of this dispute related to the size of enterprises categorized as "factories": should they include smaller artisan units? Another was whether a linear scheme of industrial transformation applied across the nineteenth century: did handicrafts precede, coexist with, or follow on from the factory system? In both cases, dispute over what should be observed was fundamental. The issue of averages also reappeared: Tugan-Baranovsky warned that "average numbers of workers" or "value of output" did not provide a reliable measure of industrial concentration in cases of heterogeneous enterprises (Tugan-Baranovsky [1907] 1934, 290–91).

Part of the problem was that three separate government institutions had responsibility for collecting data on Russian industry in the second half of the nineteenth century. The Ministry of Agriculture and State Property gathered information on mining and metallurgy, the Ministry of Finance gathered information on industries in which production was assessed for excise duties, and the Ministry of Trade and Industry gathered information on industries in which production was not assessed for excise duties: different methodologies and programs of collection proliferated, making it more difficult to calculate aggregate industrial growth. Factory inspectors also produced firsthand reports on working conditions by visiting individual factories, but their scope was severely limited by personnel shortages and travel limitations (Tugan-Baranovsky [1907] 1934, 311).

Finally, the nature of the factories being documented had consequences for the observations that were (or were not) being made. After 1750 two basic types of Russian factory existed: the manorial (*votchinnye*) factory, which was owned privately by the gentry and often used serf labor, sometimes without payment, and the possessional (*posessionnye*) factory, which either received state subsidies in the form of land or buildings, or was constructed with state aid and used workers bound to it by law. If the owners of possessional factories did not fulfill their obligations for production, then the factory (along with its workers) could be sequestered by the state (Tugan-Baranovsky [1907] 1934, 84). Unsurprisingly, in the early nineteenth century the Russian government collected extensive statistical data on this latter type of factory, whereas data on the former type were relatively neglected.

Conclusions

One issue that arises from the above discussion was the consequences of scale for economic measurement, as was highlighted in the 1737 article on measuring the earth. In opposition to the notion that the extent of Russia assisted accurate scientific observations, Russia's vast scale often hindered the making of accurate economic observations, at least outside the major urban conurbations like Moscow and Saint Petersburg, and made a single methodology much harder to implement. Alfred Marshall's (1919, 162) description of Russia as "large, continuous and self-contained" was consequently correct only in its first and last characterizations. Institutions such as the *zemstvo* evolved to fill the regional gap to some degree, but the information thus gathered was not always easily available to government departments and was sometimes subject to fierce political debate. The size of Russia also had consequences for the specific economics that developed, as seen in the examples of location theory and typicality studies.

Another point that arises was whether specifically Russian institutions and techniques of observation could be detected. There were certainly unique Russian institutions, which conducted observations and were the subject of them, but perhaps less so were there unique techniques. *Zemstvo* surveys of peasant households were pioneering, as were Prokopovich's efforts at least in the Russian context. Certainly, the sheer volume of localized economic studies published in late nineteenth-century Russia was unprecedented, although as noted elsewhere, masses of raw facts can languish unutilized or be put to widely different purposes. But the debate over the "monographic" methodology of the historical school versus the aggregate sampling favored by statisticians was part of a wider continental trend, as the historical school came under attack for its "unscientific" approach. In Russia the question of whether averaging lost more typicality information than it gained in overall representativeness still remained open in 1917. As the scale of the averaging sample increased, the representative nature of the average sometimes declined: who decided at what level an average was taken was therefore crucial.

Finally, the political components of the Russian debates over observation grew in intensity as the nineteenth century gave way to the twentieth. Today, it is understood how these debates were resolved after 1917: Lenin's sociological classification of peasant farms by size of allotment and number of animals owned was transformed in the late 1920s into the ideological attempt to measure the political "sin" of class differentiation, which after 1929 became the chilling governmental attempt to "annihilate the kulaks as a class." Of course it is not inevitable that, if an attempt is made to observe class as a category, then this will be followed by a Marxian attempt to "abolish" such categories and the individuals who constitute them.

Other Russian Marxists, such as Tugan-Baranovsky, moved in the opposite political direction to Lenin, and even cautiously welcomed some aspects of the development of capitalism in Russia after 1900, based in Tugan-Baranovsky's case on his extensive observations of the Russian factory past and present. But the Russian/Soviet example provides an instructive tale of how the term *observation* has various nuances of meaning: *study* and *inspection* can give way to *surveillance* and *judgment* in certain acute circumstances.

References

Atkinson, Dorothy. 1980. "The Library of the Free Economic Society." *Slavic Review* 39 (1): 97–103.

Barnett, Vincent. 2004. "Catalysing Growth? Mendeleev and the 1891 Tariff." *Research in the History of Economic Thought and Methodology*, ser. A, 22:123–44.

———. 2005a. "D. I. Mendeleev, Russian Protectionism, and German Political Economy." In *Deutsche und russische Okonomen im Dialog*, edited by H. Rieter, L. D. Shirokorad, and J. Zweynert, 169–84. Marburg: Metropolis.

———. 2005b. "Tugan-Baranovsky and *The Russian Factory*." In *Late Imperial Russia: Problems and Prospects*, edited by I. D. Thatcher, 84–100. Manchester: Manchester University Press.

———. 2011. *E. E. Slutsky as Economist and Mathematician: Crossing the Limits of Knowledge*. London: Routledge.

Brooks, Nathan. 2004. "Dmitrii Mendeleev and Russian Meteorology." *Proceedings of the International Commission on History of Meteorology* 1 (1): 41–47.

Chayanov, A. V. (1912) 1991. "Iz oblasti metodologii byudzhetnykh issledovanii." In *Izbrannye Trudy*, 342–50. Moscow: Fin-Stat.

———. 1915. *Byudzhety krest'yan: Starobel'skago uezda*. Khar'kov: Khar-Zem.

———. (1929) 1991. "Byudzhetnye isslevodaniya." In *Izbrannye Trudy*, 25–341. Moscow: Fin-Stat.

Chuprov, A. A. 1910. *Vyborochnoe izsledovanie*. Moscow: Lissner.

———. (1913) 1981. "The Law of Large Numbers in Contemporary Science." In *The Correspondence between A. A. Markov and A. A. Chuprov on the Theory of Probability and Mathematical Statistics*, edited by Kh. O. Ondar, 164–81. New York: Springer.

Chuprov, A. I. (1888) 1909. "O snachenii statistiki dlya pravovedeniya i eya uspekhakh v Rossii za poslednee vremya." In *Rechi i stati*, 1:204–24. Moscow: Sabashnikov.

———. (1894) 1909. "O monograficheskom opisanii otdel'nykh selenii, kak sposob dopolneniya i podnovleniya osnovnykh zemsko-statisticheskikh izsledovanii." In *Rechi i stati*, 1:225–33. Moscow: Sabashnikov.

Clark, Colin. 1939. *A Critique of Russian Statistics.* London: Macmillan.

Craigie, P. G. 1897. "Notes on the Subjects Discussed at the St Petersburg Meeting of the International Statistical Institute." *Journal of the Royal Statistical Society* 60 (4): 735–88.

Darrow, David. 2000. "The Politics of Numbers: Zemstvo Land Assessment and the Conceptualization of Russia's Rural Economy." *Russian Review* 59:52–75.

Ezhov, A. I. 1960. "Gosudarstvennaya statistika." In *Istoriya Sovetskoi gosudarstvennoi statistiki*, 51–75. Moscow: GosIzdat.

Gerschenkron, Alexander. 1970. *Europe in the Russian Mirror.* Cambridge: Cambridge University Press.

Gordin, Michael. 2004. *A Well-Ordered Thing: Dmitrii Mendeleev and the Shadow of the Periodic Table.* New York: Basic.

Haxthausen, August. (1847) 1972. *Studies on the Interior of Russia.* Chicago: University of Chicago Press.

Johnson, R. E. 1982. "Liberal Professionals and Professional Liberals." In *The Zemstvo in Russia*, 343–64. Cambridge: Cambridge University Press.

Keynes, J. M. 1926. "Professor A. A. Tschuprow." *Economic Journal* 36:517–18.

Kotz, S., and E. Seneta. 1990. "Lenin as a Statistician." *Journal of the Royal Statistical Society*, ser. A, 153 (1): 73–94.

Lenin, V. I. (1899) 1960. "The Development of Capitalism in Russia." In vol. 3 of *Collected Works*, 25–607. Moscow: L&W.

L'Isle, J. N. de. 1737. "A Proposal for the Measurement of the Earth in Russia." *Philosophical Transactions* 40:27–49.

Livshits, F. D., and Y. S. Belen'ky. 1960. "Statistika finansov." In *Istoriya Sovetskoi gosudarstvennoi statistiki*, 189–212. Moscow: GosIzdat.

Maine, H. S. 1876. *Village-Communities in the East and West.* London: Murray.

Marshall, Alfred. 1919. *Industry and Trade.* London: Macmillan.

Matyukha, I. Y., S. V. Postnikov, and V. A. Samoilov. 1960. "Statistika byudzhetov naseleniya." In *Istoriya Sovetskoi gosudarstvennoi statistiki*, 297–316. Moscow: GosIzdat.

Mendeleeff, D. 1889. "The Present Position and Prospects of the Caucasian Petroleum Industry." *Journal of the Society of Chemical Industry* 8 (10): 753–57.

Mendeleeff, D. I. 1893. "Introduction." In *The Industries of Russia, Manufactures, and Trade*, edited by J. M. Crawford, i–liv. Saint Petersburg: Min-Fin.

Mendeleev, D. I. 1991. *C dumoyu o blage rossiiskom.* Novosibirsk: Nauka.

Morgan, Mary. 2010. "Seeing Parts, Looking for Wholes." In *Histories of Scientific Observation*, edited by L. Daston and E. Lunbeck, 303–25. Chicago: University of Chicago Press.

Prescott, J. A. 1977. "The Russian Free Economic Society." *Agricultural History* 51 (3): 503–12.

Prokopovich, S. N. 1918. *Opyt" ischisleniya narodnago dokhoda 50–gub: Evropeiskoi Rossii.* Moscow: Koop.

———. 1930. *Narodnyi dokhod Zapadno-Evropeiskikh stran.* Moscow: GosIzdat.

Seneta, E. 1985. "A Sketch of the History of Survey Sampling in Russia." *Journal of the Royal Statistical Society* 148 (2): 118–25.

Sheynin, Oscar. 1996. "Mendeleev and the Mathematical Treatment of Observations in Natural Science." *Historia Mathematica* 23:54–67.

Slutsky, E. E. (1912) 2009. *Theory of Correlation and Elements of the Doctrine of the Curves of Distribution.* Berlin: Verlag.

Society for the Diffusion of Useful Knowledge. 1833. "Peter the Great." In vol. 2 of *Gallery of Portraits*, 182–92. London: Knight.

Tchayanov, A. 1928. "Agricultural Economics in Russia." *Journal of Farm Economics* 10:543–49.

Tugan-Baranovsky, M. I. (1907) 1934. *Russkaya fabrika.* Moscow: Gos-Izdat.

Ustav Imperatorskago Vol'nago Ekonomicheskago Obshchestva. 1859. Saint Petersburg: Akad-Nauk.

Vernadsky, V. I. 1922. *Ocherki i rechi.* Vol. 1. Petrograd: NKhTI.

Vucinich, Alexander. 1970. *Science in Russian Culture, 1861–1917.* Stanford, Calif.: Stanford University Press.

Witskowski, B. 1891. "History of Geodetic Operations in Russia." In *Annual Report of the Smithsonian Institution for 1890*, 305–14. Washington, D.C.: Government Printing Office.

Yatsenkov, G. 1840. *Na kakoi stepeni nazhoditsya zemledelie v Rossii.* Saint Petersburg: Iversen.

The Economist as Surveyor: Physiocracy in the Fields

Loïc Charles and Christine Théré

François Quesnay strove his entire life to better his social condition, leaving early on the modest rural neighborhood where his parents lived to try his luck in Paris, then Mantes, Paris again, and finally Versailles. After turning sixty, he landed in the middle of what the French monarchy could best afford in terms of luxury, privileges, and frivolity, in charge of Louis XV's favorite mistress, the powerful Madame de Pompadour. Yet it was in this context that Quesnay began to investigate what he had quite consciously turned his back on in his youth: the countryside, the peasantry, and its rural and unpolished simplicity.

Wealth was from the start the prime interest of Quesnay's social investigations. More precisely, Quesnay and the physiocrats believed that their theory of wealth was the only one that was able to go beyond appearances to uncover the true nature and source of wealth. While most people, including the most learned French intellectuals, believed that the splendor of the king's palace and court was a convincing sign of the economic power of the French kingdom, Quesnay believed that the spectacular display of luxuries, far from signaling an enduring wealth, presaged a rapid and violent downfall.[1] Indeed, the kind of economic theory Quesnay was building in the midst of a busy social life was conveying a straightforward

---

1. "Never had Rome been richer and more luxurious than when it devastated the provinces it subjugated to its rule, but its splendor was the flame of the fire that was consuming the forces of the Empire, and that in the end submitted it to the power of its enemies" (Quesnay 1757b, 315). Unless otherwise indicated, all translations are ours.

History of Political Economy 44 (annual suppl.) DOI 10.1215/00182702-1631788

critique of the world of the court. Likewise, most contemporary economic writers believed that French enrichment came from the recent rise of colonial trade, industry, and manufactures. Quesnay had a different view and believed that all wealth originated in agricultural activities. To prove his point, he had to create a whole new way of looking at the economy.

To meet this challenge, Quesnay, a physician-surgeon and amateur economist, devoted himself to a major analytical effort and created what was at the time, like today, assessed as an original and far-reaching social theory. It is less commonly assumed, however, that he was also very much concerned with developing a systematic inquiry into the French economy and society. In this article, following the lead of Jean-Claude Perrot ([1978] 1992), our claim is that this program of observation was for Quesnay and the physiocrats no less important than their theoretical investigations. The results of the surveys and agricultural accounts that the physiocrats produced were integrated into their main works such as the *Philosophie rurale*, in more or less stylized form.[2] As Quesnay passed on his passion for counting and accounting to some of his assistants and pupils, they were able to conduct large—at least for the time—land survey experiments that applied physiocratic knowledge to measuring concrete economic activities. In the heyday of physiocracy, the integration of empirical and theoretical inquiries was sufficiently developed for one of Quesnay's closest disciples, Charles Richard de Butré (1725–1805), a bodyguard of the king and a gifted agronomist and calculator, to conceive of a plan for some sort of national accounting.

1. From Secondhand Observations to Systematic Investigation

The first economic texts, "Fermiers" and "Grains," that Quesnay (1756, 1757a) wrote used and presented—to an unusual degree for the time—quantitative and qualitative data. In the first of these texts, he distinguished between two categories of cultivation: *petite culture* and *grande culture*. Typically, this distinction was both theoretical and empirical, and these two dimensions were in Quesnay's discourse integrated to the point of becoming somewhat indistinct. On the one hand, they were characterized as different techniques of production—*petite culture* was less capital

---

2. This has been completely neglected by historians of economic thought. To our knowledge, Jean-Claude Perrot is the only one who has discussed this aspect of physiocratic thought in any detail. See Perrot [1978] 1992 and 1988, and Perrot and Woolf 1984.

intensive (and more labor intensive) and provided lower capital returns, while *grande culture* was more capital intensive and yielded higher capital returns. They were also based on different socioeconomic systems: in the *petite culture*, the sharecropper paid a share (half) of the profits of his farm to the landowner, while in the *grande culture*, the farmer paid a fixed rent and kept all the profit. On the other hand, Quesnay integrated the distinction he made with a set of empirical observations. When he first introduced this distinction, he presented it as an observation: "The land is commonly cultivated either with horses by farmers, or with oxen by sharecroppers" (Quesnay 1756, 129). Then he compared in detail the relative costs and performance of each animal for plowing based on minute computations and observations (129–39). The multiple dimensions of the opposition between *petite culture* and *grande culture* are underlined by the fact that Quesnay used several expressions to designate them; for the former, he used, interchangeably, "cultivation by sharecroppers," "poor cultivation," and "cultivation by oxen"; for the latter, "cultivation by farmers," "wealthy culture," and "cultivation by horses."[3]

In "Grains" he integrated the distinction into a macroeconomic setting by providing a detailed account of French agricultural output. To demonstrate the relevance of his economic categories, Quesnay furnished his reader with a great number of detailed observations, most of them quantitative, including accounts of agricultural microeconomic units and other economic, geographic, and social data such as prices of agricultural goods, population, crop returns, and the size of various types of land areas. Tied to the service of the Pompadour, Quesnay had gathered his information from printed sources. These sources raised two sets of issues: first, several of them did not originate from acknowledged and reliable primary sources, and second, most of the data did not fit into Quesnay's economic categories. Consequently, Quesnay's first articles were plagued with methodological problems. For example, the agricultural account Quesnay used in "Fermiers" was left incomplete: it concerned only the *grande culture* and therefore it was only loosely integrated into his more general reasoning. In "Fermiers" and "Grains," as Quesnay tried to reconcile data from several sources, his computations were full of errors, misprints, and inaccuracies, which cast doubt on his whole theoretical project, as his critics were to point out. François Véron de Forbonnais (1767, vol. 2), in particular, attacked the empirical bases and the calculations of these

---

3. The blurring was later criticized by Turgot ([1765] 1983).

two texts.[4] In a staggering phrase, he opposed to physiocracy "the true philosophy" that "will never put aside factual observations . . . on the contrary she will always draw carefully the real limits of the application of abstract truths in positive and empirical matters" (95–96).

Quesnay himself was aware of the limitations of his printed sources, and he looked for ways to improve and widen his set of observations on French agriculture. It was for that purpose that he conceived of the *Questions intéressantes sur la population, l'agriculture et le commerce*, which was integrated into the sequel of *L'ami des hommes* released in June 1758. In the foreword, the marquis de Mirabeau explained that the *Questions* emerged out of a suggestion made to him, that he should publish "a kind of abridged and simple agricultural manual for the countrymen." Mirabeau consulted Quesnay on the issue, and the latter replied that this kind of manual would be of no avail because "there should be a different manual for every district, for every village, for every hamlet" (Quesnay and Marivetz 1758, 335). Hence the *Questions* in its form and its topics can be best described as a kind of questionnaire for a general survey of the French kingdom. Made of a long list of queries, it was intended to prompt the "zealous citizens who have the good of the state in mind" to provide their observations on the French territory and economy, preferably by addressing them to the *Journal oeconomique*, the main economic and agronomic publication of the day.

Produced by two different authors, the well-known Quesnay and the obscure petty courtier Etienne-Claude Marivetz, the *Questions* is an unusually complex and odd text.[5] Part of its mystery lies in its uneven style: short and factual questions probably written by the amateur natural philosopher Marivetz are mixed with long and sophisticated ones, which sometimes more resemble instructions than questions, written by Quesnay. For example, item 5 in the theme devoted to the trade of local foodstuffs reads: "The advantages of the external trade of local foodstuffs or gifts of the earth over that of manufactured goods" (Quesnay and Marivetz 1758,

---

4. Forbonnais (1722–1800) was one of the most successful French political economists of the 1750s and 1760s. Author of several entries in the *Encyclopédie* and economic essays, he corresponded with Quesnay on economic subjects in 1758 (INED 2005, 1173–80). On Forbonnais, see Fleury 1915 and Charles, Lefebvre, and Théré 2011. On Forbonnais's conceptions and the physiocrats' response to his critiques, see Van den Berg 2002.

5. Marivetz (1729–1794) had been living in Versailles since 1752, where he had a small office of Écuyer de Mesdames de France. Enjoying the life of a petty courtier, he, like his mentor Quesnay, took an interest in agricultural matters in the 1750s. His best-known work is *La physique du monde*, published in seven volumes (1780–87), which he wrote with the natural philosopher Louis-Jacques Goussier.

370).[6] Indeed, the fourteen themes decomposed into 228 items that structured the several hundred queries are of very different lengths. The first theme, "Climates of the [French] provinces," is made up of 15 items ranging from one single query—"Whether hail is frequent [in this location or not]?"—to two items on winds and heats that comprise several queries. Some themes are longer than others: those that can be related to Quesnay's research program such as "Territory," "Cultivation of land," "Population," "Grains," "Livestock," "Vines," "Cities," "Trade of local foodstuffs," and "Wealth" are double or more the size of those that are not, such as "Climate of the provinces," "Linen, hemp, and oils," "Fruit trees," "Rivers," and "Customs" (the shortest of all).

Even in the themes themselves, one finds a surprising heterogeneity between the items, sometimes even within each item. In this perspective, it is worthwhile investigating the different sources that could have informed the two authors. From the references given in the *Questions* and other writings to which Quesnay contributed in this period, we can safely assume Quesnay and Marivetz drew inspiration from three different types of general surveys.

By the 1750s the French state had launched several surveys of the kingdom, each one addressed by the controller general of finances to the provincial intendants.[7] The first ones dated from the seventeenth century. The most well known of these administrative surveys was the one conducted in 1697 for the instruction of the Duke of Burgundy, then heir to the French throne. It was compiled and extracted by Henri de Boulainvilliers, a member of the duke's circle, in the beginning of the eighteenth century and finally published posthumously in 1727 to great success among the French public.[8] The seventeenth-century surveys were very broad—they

6. This is not a query per se, since there is no question mark; moreover, the way it is phrased prevents the reader from even considering the reverse case (that it would be more advantageous to trade manufactured goods for agricultural ones from other countries). Another significant example is item 14 of the theme "Cultivation of land": "The destructive effects of the implementation of duties detrimental to trade, to vent, to price, to consumption, to the production of foodstuffs, to the yield of landed properties and to the source of the king's income" (Quesnay and Marivetz 1758, 345).

7. Our presentation is based on Gille [1964] 1980, 23–80; Perrot and Woolf 1984, 5–10; Bourguet 1988, 22–34; and Brian 1994, 160–68.

8. See Ellis 1988. Boulainvilliers worked on the results of the survey at the end of the seventeenth century up to at least the 1710s. Several manuscript copies of his work or part of it existed in French libraries. The *État de la France*, as it was called, was reprinted throughout the eighteenth century. However, it did not present the entire survey but an abridged version with comments and remarks from Boulainvilliers. The marquis de Mirabeau had it in his personal library and cited it in *L'ami des hommes*; it is beyond doubt that Quesnay knew it as well.

included all kinds of geographic facts, human and physical, as well as natural resources and the mores of the people inhabiting the area—and were not particularly directed to the gathering of quantitative facts. Three other, more-focused surveys were made during the eighteenth century, in 1724, 1730, and 1745. All these surveys were conceived as unique synchronic syntheses that should be conducted again from scratch each time.[9] Indeed, no continuity existed in their general structure, the labeling of their questions, and the topics addressed by the inquiries.[10]

The second category of works that may have inspired Quesnay was that of semipublic surveying projects, two of which were quoted by Quesnay in his economic writings. The first one was the map of Cassini, which Quesnay knew firsthand as a member of the Paris Academy of Sciences and a financial contributor to the map. It was a state project, although it was financed mostly by private funds and conducted by members of the French Academy of Sciences, the Cassinis, a renowned family of geographers and astronomers. The project conducted by Cassini de Thury produced the first complete and nearly exact map of the kingdom. Although the last part was published only in 1815, the main results were already known at the time of Quesnay's first economic writings and may have emulated him.[11] Another semipublic survey that Quesnay used in one of his early economic articles is Pierre Doisy's *Le royaume de France*, originally published in 1745 and reedited in 1753 (the one edition Quesnay had in his possession).[12] To these two projects that were completed, one can also add the *Enquête du régent*, launched after Louis XIV's death. This survey, which aimed to inventory the natural resources, with a special emphasis on minerals and manufacturing techniques, was never completed, but it was at the outset of the multivolume *Description des arts et*

9. In other words, the surveys were syntheses of several local surveys conducted in the French provinces at about the same time, and they used categories that were specific to each one and not intended to be reused or replicated in subsequent surveys.

10. The 1724 survey was focused on fiscal matters. The 1730 survey was conducted in the aftermath of a major food shortage (1725) and was first and foremost concerned with food distribution throughout the kingdom and the construction of a rational policy in this matter at the national level (Zeller 2007, 145). Finally, the 1745 survey and its possible revision from 1755 were intended as part of France's preparation for war against England and its allies, first in the War of Austrian Succession and then in the Seven Years' War. For that purpose, the survey looked for information such as the quantity of precious silver and gold that individuals possessed in wares and jewelry or the evaluation of the level of wealth of the king's subjects and what part could be subjected to new taxes if needed.

11. Quesnay (1756, 139) cited Cassini's measurement of France's land area in "Fermiers."

12. On Doisy and his survey, see Brian 1994, 165–67.

métiers published by the French Academy of Sciences throughout the eighteenth century (Demeulenaere-Douyère and Sturdy 2008).[13]

The third kind of literature that might have helped Quesnay to conceive of the *Questions* was the writings of the political arithmeticians.[14] Quesnay was aware of this literature through different sources. Several texts of the English political arithmeticians, including William Petty, had been translated in the *Journal oeconomique* in the 1750s, at a time when Quesnay was reading it thoroughly.[15] Quesnay also had access to translations of texts providing the methodological background of political arithmetic such as Charles Davenant and Petty. Quesnay also knew very well the *Essai sur les monnoies* by Nicolas-François Dupré de Saint-Maur, which resembles the English treatises and contains series of grain prices as well as several other kinds of economic data. Indeed, this book was by far the most quoted source in Quesnay's early economic writings. Finally, Quesnay also knew Sébastien Le Preste Vauban's *La dîme royale*, a book of detailed estimates of the French population and agricultural yields.[16] "Grains," with its numerous tables of data and tedious computations to provide an estimate of the French kingdom's wealth, had a lot in common with political arithmetic treatises.

Like the state and semistate surveys, the *Questions* was intended to produce a full description of the French kingdom. Quite possibly Quesnay and Marivetz's text was inspired by the project of a *Notice générale de la France* advertised in the May 1756 issue of the *Journal oeconomique*.[17]

13. Because it focused on the natural resources of the territorial state, the *Enquête du régent* shared some similarities with the cameralist literature, which, however, belonged to a different tradition foreign to France. On cameralism, see Tribe 1988, especially chapters 2 and 3.

14. For an overview of the French literature on political arithmetic, see Martin 2003. Quesnay did not read English and therefore knew only that part of political arithmetic literature translated into or written in French.

15. Indeed, he made a direct reference to these translations in one of his early articles (Quesnay 1757b, 265).

16. On Vauban, see Meusnier 2003, 95–97, and Virol 2007. Vauban (1686) published a theoretical essay on how to make surveys before he used the data he collected all those years to write one installment of the *Projet d'une dixme royale*, one of the most famous and debated French fiscal projects of the eighteenth century. Dupré de Saint-Maur (1695–1774) was the author of *Essai sur les monnoies ou réflexions sur le rapport entre l'argent et les denrées* (1746), which was widely used at the time by political economists, most notably Quesnay and Adam Smith.

17. This survey would have included a detailed map of every diocese and an alphabetical dictionary of each parish. Each entry was supposed to include such information as the individual businesses in the area, the quality of land, the state of cultivation, wealth, the number of inhabitants, the number of horses and carts, and the number of rich landowners. It would have also included a normative part on the causes of poverty in the country, the means to overcome

However, much more than the *Notice*, the *Questions* was conceived of not as a geographic or a topographical description but as an economic survey. For example, in the category "Territory" (Quesnay and Marivetz 1758, 338–42) the inquiries about the physical nature of the soil and the role of climate are an introduction to economic themes such as the price of the land, the cost of the rent, the quantity of land cultivated, and so on. Moreover, the agricultural and cultivation techniques that were investigated in several of the articles were absent from the state surveys. The *Questions* was even more focused on the economic dimension than the political arithmetic literature. References from recent economic literature including Quesnay's entries in the *Encyclopédie*, "Fermiers" and "Grains," made in the *Questions* signal that the text was framed by Quesnay's theoretical agenda. For example, the distinction between *petite culture* with oxen and *grande culture* with horses was taken up, and readers were asked to verify that theoretical proposition. In the "Population" theme, Quesnay's main theoretical findings were presented as truths, sometimes in an interrogative form.[18] This is particularly true of themes that Quesnay had discussed in-depth in his economic articles, such as the trade in corn and other agricultural commodities. In the items that belonged to these themes, one finds an exposition of Quesnay's doctrine rather than an invitation to provide facts. However, taken as a whole, the *Questions* was genuinely concerned with gathering information, qualitative as well as quantitative. The authors were particularly interested in getting concrete figures on agricultural work : How many animals are "ordinarily" put on each cart, how much land can a cart plow per day, how many plows did the cultivation of wheat need, at what depth or at what time of the year should one plow? (Quesnay and Marivetz 1758, 343).

To whom was the text directed? First and foremost, as its title indicates, it was intended for provincial academies and scientific societies and their members. One important point is that these institutions, which had been

---

it, and suggestions of the kinds of manufactures that might be well suited to the area and of relief the government could provide ("Notice générale de la France" 1756, 88). The project was never realized, but it may account for Quesnay and Marivetz's suggestion to send the answers to the *Questions* to the *Journal oeconomique*.

18. For example: "It is not population that can repair wealth, but wealth that can repair population." In the third article, the authors asked: "Is, or is not, a man profitable for the state in proportion to his production and in proportion to his gains and income? Is it not through consumption and reproduction that men perpetuate and augment riches?" (Quesnay and Marivetz 1758, 347, 352).

little concerned with economics issues, were experiencing some change in this regard. A few of them such as the academy of Amiens were showing a new interest in economic issues and offered prizes for economic dissertations. In 1757 the estates of Brittany backed by the intendant of commerce Vincent de Gournay and some local merchants and manufacturers created a society devoted exclusively to the study and discussion of economic issues.[19] Indeed, the fact that the creation of that society was mentioned in the *Questions* leaves no doubt that Quesnay had been struck by this fact and saw in it a possible outlet for his theories (Quesnay and Marivetz 1758, 346). Another public that Quesnay and Marivetz were aiming at was the elites, including the provincial and central government administrators. The first edition of *L'ami des hommes* had been a staggering success inside and outside the administration, and the inclusion of the *Questions* in its sequel was a promise that it would be read by many people.

However, none of these possibilities ever materialized. The *Questions* went unnoticed in the periodicals of the time, which devoted their reviews of the sequel of *L'ami des hommes* to the other texts it contained. Even the *Journal oeconomique*, which was supposed to publish whatever responses the *Questions* might provoke in the public, did not mention it once. And there is no indication that Mirabeau or Quesnay and Marivetz ever got any response through other channels. This complete failure may be explained on several grounds. First, Quesnay and Marivetz's questionnaire was simply too huge and complex. Moreover, it was based on ideas and concepts that were for the most part groundbreaking and unknown to their readers.[20] Second, the status of the authors of the text was unclear to the reader: they wanted to be answered in the *Journal oeconomique*, but they were not journalists; they aimed their text at the provincial academies, but they did not present it to any academy in particular; they wanted to emulate the state surveys, but they were not part of the administration. Finally, the timing was simply wrong. The second part of 1758 resonated with the battles of the Seven Years' War, and the news of one defeat after another

19. In the years after the publication of the *Questions* from 1760 to 1765, several agricultural societies were founded with the help of the French government, which acted through its local representatives, the provincial intendants. All but one, in Limoges, were founded from 1762 on, after the government had given clear instructions to the provincial intendants to take over the process. On the royal agricultural societies, the main reference is Justin 1935. On their link with political economists and physiocrats in particular, see Charles 1999.

20. Quesnay's economic articles for the *Encyclopédie* went largely unnoticed at the time, and it was only in the beginning of the 1760s that Quesnay's economic theories began to spread.

created an improper setting for the kind of work Quesnay and Marivetz had assigned to their readers.

2. Seeing the World like a Physiocrat

As the *Questions* did not elicit any response from the wide-ranging readership of *L'ami des hommes*, Quesnay rethought his approach. He turned instead to his existing social network and, in parallel, tried to establish connections with individuals already interested in economic matters and who could collect salient observations for him. One was a young man named Pierre-Samuel Du Pont (later Du Pont de Nemours) who wrote two of the several fiscal pamphlets that circulated in 1763 and signed them "D. P." Reading them, Quesnay saw a potential recruit in the anonymous author and tried to locate him. When he finally succeeded, Quesnay immediately set his newest pupil to work and assigned him fact-gathering tasks (Théré and Charles 2008, 14–16). More generally, from the beginning of the 1760s and throughout the decade, Quesnay himself or his closest fellow physiocrats such as Du Pont and Butré developed prolonged interactions either inside the French economic administration or at its borders, with the newly founded royal agricultural societies. This move was facilitated by the atmosphere that reigned in the royal administration at that time, which was prone to reform and ready to engage, at least to some degree, with administrative experimentations suggested by economists.[21]

Thanks to his reputation as a political writer and the incredible success of *L'ami des hommes*, Mirabeau was receiving memorandums, solicitations, and projects from every corner of France, which he forwarded to Quesnay. Among these, some documents contained useful information for their work in political economy. One example is an important memorandum on *corvée* written by the intendant of Caen, François-Jean Orceau de Fontette (1718–1794), that Quesnay got through Mirabeau during the summer of 1760 (Théré and Charles 2008, 17).[22] Quesnay's position at court gave him access to some of the highest-ranking administrators such as

21. Because of the Seven Years' War, the French state was in dire need of resources to finance its huge deficits and debts.

22. The *corvée* was a tax that took the form of free labor to build or repair roads. Besides Fontette, Quesnay also benefited from contacts with several authors through Mirabeau such as one abbé Thomas-Jean Pichon, coauthor of *La France agricole et marchande*, a reasonably successful book published in 1762, or with Georges-Marie Butel du Mont, author of several books on colonies and commerce (see INED 2005, 699, 1190, 1208, 1318, 1322).

Henri-Léonard-Jean-Baptiste Bertin, controller general of finances from 1760 to 1763 and a protégé of the Pompadour (INED 2005, 717–26). Quesnay was kept aware of the various policies Bertin developed to favor French agriculture. For example, in August 1760 Bertin wrote to the intendant of the generality of Soissons, Charles-Blaise Méliand (1703–1768), that "the king wanted to be informed of the means necessary to extend and improve agriculture in the province." Méliand forwarded the order to his representatives as well as to locals knowledgeable in matters of agriculture in the form of "a sufficiently instructive letter." Several persons sent him "memorandums from which he made extracts" that he "added to those he made from conversations he had with locals during his tour in the province." From all these, Méliand wrote a synthetic report where he "limited himself to expose the general and principal subject-matters that merited your attention," which he sent back to Bertin in November of the same year.[23] Bertin gave a copy of Méliand's report to Quesnay, who, probably with the blessing of Bertin, wrote a long letter to Méliand suggesting further inquiries along the lines set by the *Questions*.[24]

Méliand drafted his report in the manner of the late seventeenth-century administrative surveys: it was mostly descriptive and did not contain systematic quantitative data. Méliand's memorandum was also akin to the extracts made by members of the French Royal Society of Medicine in the mid-1770s when they tried to answer Turgot's "loosely formulated six queries" (discussed in Mendelsohn 2011). From a myriad of individual and local observations, Méliand extracted a few general descriptions that did not constitute a general observation, that is, one commensurable with others made in different provinces or by different individuals. To some extent, Méliand's report answered part of the program underlined by Quesnay and Marivetz in the *Questions*. When describing the localities of his generality, Méliand provided a detailed topography that put in context the dominant type of agricultural production. Méliand also shared with Quesnay several of his conceptions such as the idea that free trade in grain will benefit agriculture, that farmers were the key economic agents, and that the French tax system was putting a heavy burden on agriculture. However, as Quesnay remarked, the details furnished by Méliand's report

23. Citations are from the French National Archives, K 906 no. 36, f. 1r–v. A significant part of the original reports and letters from Méliand's correspondents has been preserved and may be found in the departmental archives of Aisne, box D1.

24. Copies from the hand of Mirabeau's secretary of this report and another letter from Méliand to Bertin are in the French National Archives (see INED 2005, 1209–17, 1318, 1320).

were not satisfactory. For, he wrote, "it is not enough to represent the general aspect of the different cultures of a country, neither is it enough to speak vaguely of the quality of the different lands. One should go through the net product yields of farmers' investments and agricultural spendings, and mark the actual money value of landed properties set in different classes and their number in each class. It is also necessary to declare the price of the rent calculated by *arpent* of land, to go into the details of the tax burden, the operating costs, the variation in crops and the variation of the prices of these crops" (INED 2005, 1216). Hence Quesnay's comment on the report and, in particular, his emphasis on computable facts were perfectly consonant with the project outlined in the *Questions*.

In his letter to Méliand, Quesnay was, however, more specific about the core economic observations that were needed. He told the intendant that "the benefits of alternate cultivations and land uses must be calculated by the net product, that is by the rent." And he added that "to speak like a tax official, rent ought to serve as a yardstick for a land tax and neither men, nor their cattle, nor their personal properties, nor their salaries, nor their advances" (INED 2005, 1215). Quesnay was perfectly aware that his suggestions went against the normal practice of French administration: in the regular tours the intendant made, Méliand evaluated or reevaluated the amount of personal and land taxes according to the gross product of farms and personal properties. In the context of the acute fiscal debates of the early 1760s that took place inside as well as outside the administration, Méliand was willing to experiment, and he invited, with Quesnay's blessing, Du Pont to conduct an experimental physiocratic survey in one of the districts of his province.[25] Du Pont's work provides an interesting application of Quesnay's program of observation, although it was limited to the fiscal domain. Indeed, he followed thoroughly the program outlined by Quesnay in his letter to Méliand. Du Pont constructed four classes of farmers according to the amount of capital invested on their land and the net product their farms yielded on average.[26] The survey was based on

25. In his autobiography, Du Pont made clear that Méliand believed that a detailed survey made on the basis of Quesnay's economic principles might advance his career—he was indeed made councillor of state in 1765. He also testified that Quesnay had "charged me with a multitude of questions" (Du Pont de Nemours [1906] 1984, 252, 273–74). For a historical overview of the tax debates in 1760s France, see Alimento [1995] 2008 and Decroix 2006, especially part 1.

26. According to Quesnay's theory, these two variables were linked: the amount of net product was proportional to advances. Our account is based on the fragments of Du Pont's survey we have identified and examined, one in Mirabeau's papers, another in Du Pont's papers, and the last one in Butré's papers.

individual statements that Du Pont collected on each farm. He added the individual amounts to compute a general result for each of the four categories.[27] He then calculated their operating costs and returns, and compared the actual amount of their tax with the one they would pay if the French tax system were built on physiocratic principles. Du Pont also collected a few agricultural accounts of individual farms—one in particular he would pass over to Butré, who would include it in his 1767 publication.

Although Du Pont conducted this survey in late 1763 and early 1764, he never finished it. On his return to Paris, he was given the general editorship of the *Journal d'agriculture, du commerce et des finances*, which took most of his time. After his ousting from the *Journal* in November 1766, he considered resuming his survey, but by this time Méliand had resigned as head of the province. Turgot, then intendant of Limoges, solicited Du Pont for a fiscal survey he was conducting in his province. Like Méliand, Turgot wanted to contribute to the ongoing French and European fiscal debate by showing how physiocratic theories could be applied in this matter.[28] It seems that Du Pont conducted a preliminary work for Turgot in 1768, but it never went beyond that point, likely because of a shortage of funds.

At the time Quesnay wrote to Méliand, he was also soliciting the collaboration of a wide range of often obscure individuals. For example, when working on the *Théorie de l'impôt*, a bulky work he wrote with Mirabeau in a hurry because of their political agenda, he received help from two men, one "Legrand"—who produced several large tables of data on French incomes and taxes—and one "Morin," who did some calculations for him.[29] He was in parallel working with Butré,[30] who furnished him with detailed agricultural accounts and also played an important part in the calculations Quesnay had to do for his *Tableau économique*.

Butré was the individual most engaged in Quesnay's program of a physiocratic survey. His observations were included in the most important

27. The husbandmen are classified in three categories, of the first, second, and third order, and one special category for the "nineteen privileged" (lords).

28. For details on Turgot's plan, see Alimento [1995] 2008, 49–56.

29. See INED 2005, 1185, 1251, 1288, 1295–97. The *Théorie de l'impôt* was written in 1760 and finally published at the end of that year.

30. Butré is an interesting and unusual character who has been unduly neglected by commentators. Born in Pressac, in the midwest of France, Butré was incorporated in the third company of the king's bodyguard on December 26, 1743, at the age of eighteen. He stayed in the service of Louis XV for eighteen years, retiring in February 1761. He later bought a small estate in Touraine, in the center of France, in June 1762. According to the sales contract, the land was composed of ten arpents, half of vines, three to be plowed and two in pasture and heath.

theoretical physiocratic work, the *Philosophie rurale*, published in 1763.[31] Compared with the observations made by other physiocrats, Butré's work is distinctive in that his observations were more integrated into the building of physiocratic economic theory. In the *Philosophie rurale*, the agricultural accounts he provided were used as theoretical cases by Quesnay and Mirabeau. For example, the *grande culture* was discussed through exposing the account of the farm of Lisoir (Mirabeau and Quesnay 1763, 238–40). Comparing the published version with the several drafts of this account shows that this practice involved a degree of transformation of the original empirical material gathered by Butré. Some of the categories of the original survey, such as the *avances primitives* (more or less equivalent to fixed capital), were reconstructed—from two subcategories to four in the final version—and some items such as animal farms were removed from the *avance primitives* to a stand-alone category (*bestiaux de profits*). Moreover, the figures were slightly altered. Hence the total of the return of *avances primitives* is less in the final version compared with the one originally registered in the account (from 84 to 70 percent). Finally, the description of the *grande culture* was concluded by a *tableau économique* that presented the proportion between the variables—that is, the advances, on the one hand, and gross and net product, on the other—in an abstracted form. The result of these operations was to translate the empirical microeconomic data into a device that could be used at the macroeconomic level, either for theorizing the distinction between *petite culture* and *grande culture* or for measuring the macroeconomic consequences of the choice between those two types of cultivation.

Throughout the 1760s Butré continued to work in a similar vein to combine detailed empirical observations with the development of a more theoretical inquiry both in a publication that covered several issues of the *Ephémérides du citoyen* in late 1767 as well as in texts that were never published. The first two parts of his 1767 publication were based on a dozen detailed agricultural accounts that Butré (1767a, 9:9) had gathered over the last few years during his journeys in "a large part of the provinces of Touraine, Poitou, du Limo[u]sin, de la Marche, du Berry, de la Xaintonge [*sic*], de l'Angoumois." It gave him the materials for a detailed survey of French agriculture whose aim was to provide an answer to Forbonnais's (1767) critique of Quesnay's distinction between *grande* and *petite culture*. Forbonnais had stated that this theoretical distinction was too

31. Butré provided the three agricultural accounts that are included in the *Philosophie rurale* (Mirabeau and Quesnay 1763, 238–43, 254–56). On the attribution of these accounts to Butré, see INED 2005, 1238, 1319). We later found copies of these accounts in Butré's papers.

crude to be empirically relevant; Butré countered his argument by disaggregating each of Quesnay's two categories into three subcategories, or "types," of agricultural units of production.

In the last part of the text, Butré went beyond individual observations to calculate a general evaluation of the actual and potential output of French agriculture.[32] To do so, he multiplied the amounts from each of his six categories of cultivation by the quantity of land that was occupied by each of them according to his evaluation. This way, Butré (1767a, 12:73) claimed, one can oppose successfully Forbonnais's critique on empirical grounds while showing that the theoretical distinction introduced by Quesnay was meaningful to provide a satisfactory measurement of French output.

In a text written at about the same time but never published that Butré titled *Élémens d'oeconomie politique*, he was contemplating an even grander survey project integrating more fully the empirical observations into a macroeconomic model. Butré stated that each government ought to make an *État constitutif* of his territory—that is, a detailed description of the country's agricultural sector and its output. Aside from this survey that was close to his 1767 published text, it was also necessary to draw a "political map of a nation," which described the general distribution and circulation of wealth inside and outside the economy, including the industrial and trade sectors as well as the balance of external trade (Butré 1767b, "1er cayer," 8).[33] This later document, a crude input-output table, Butré believed could be applied to study real-world economies by replacing the theoretical figures he used with those that governments may have gathered from their *État constitutif*, that is, general surveys conducted according to physiocratic principles. However, Butré worked in relative isolation, and it seems that his program for linking micro-observations in the form of agricultural accounts to what can be described as a primitive national account system went unnoticed in administrative circles and even in the physiocratic school.[34]

32. Butré's calculation was both a continuation of, and an improvement on, previous evaluations of French agricultural output provided by Quesnay in "Grains" and in the seventh chapter of the *Philosophie rurale*. Indeed, Butré had been deeply involved in the last one (see INED 2005, 641, 689–715).

33. Butré (1767b) articulated the two types of inventories as follows: "We can see without going into further detail that the political map is the representative picture of the economic interplay of the annual expenditures of a nation and of its relations with foreign countries, or the plan of the government management; this plan cannot be developed without having the *État constitutif*, which is as we have seen above the general inventory of the products of a territory."

34. Indeed, when he was hired by the margrave of Baden in the 1770s, Butré was assigned a task similar to what he had done in his 1767 publication and the work Du Pont made for Méliand and Turgot.

3. Concluding Remarks

Two general concluding remarks can be made from our study. The contributions of Du Pont and Butré illustrate two possible applications of Quesnay's program of observation of the creation of wealth. That of Du Pont was based on individual statements that were collected, classified, and then averaged. The contribution of Butré was different, since what he did was to begin by observing an area and select individual farms that he assessed as representative of a whole category of individual observations that he could not or would not make. After Butré had defined types based on detailed individual statements he had recorded, he derived the total output of each category by multiplying the quantities/values that accounted for each type of cultivation according to the area it occupied.[35] This way he was able to provide a reasonable assessment of French wealth with limited means.

The method of observation followed by Du Pont was more comprehensive than that of Butré, but it was also much more demanding in terms of resources. Hence it could be implemented only with the help of the administration and its resources. For example, after several months of work and with the aid of a secretary lent by Méliand, Du Pont could do only one of the seven *élections* (administrative subdivisions) of one generality, of which there were no less than thirty-two in the whole kingdom. Moreover, he was unable to complete it. On the other hand, with the multiplier method one could provide estimates of French total product or even be able to disaggregate this product into agricultural items such as corn, vines, and so forth, much faster. The only problem was that these evaluations were often questionable—as those of "Grains" made by Quesnay on the narrow basis of secondhand sources had shown—and depended heavily on the choice of the values of the type(s) that were multiplied and the multiplier itself. To improve the quality of these observations, Quesnay put Butré in charge of providing case studies to feed his theoretical observation of the existence of two categories of cultivation. These were included in the *Philosophie rurale*. But Butré did not stop there, and his 1767 publication provided further refinements by breaking each category into three typical cases. The method of observation devised by Quesnay in "Grains" and refined by Butré was disseminated at the end of the old regime throughout Europe. Butré himself was hired by the margrave of Baden in 1775 and was

---

35. Hence Butré's method is akin to the one followed by the Italian agricultural economists in the early twentieth century described by Federico D'Onofrio in this volume.

charged with surveying the territory to prepare for a reform of the tax system according to physiocratic principles. In France the physiocratic way of observing the French economy was well represented in the revolutionary debates over the economic management of the nation and its taxation system: several important works such as Du Pont's *Aperçu de la valeur des récoltes du royaume* (1786) and Antoine-Laurent Lavoisier's *De la richesse territoriale de la France* (Perrot 1988) borrowed from Quesnay and Butré both the definition of wealth as the net product of agriculture and the method of the multiplier to assess the nation's wealth.[36]

References

Alimento, Antonella. (1995) 2008. *Réformes fiscales et crises politiques dans la France de Louis XV*. Brussels: Peter Lang.

Bourguet, Marie-Noëlle. 1988. *Déchiffrer la France: La statistique départementale à l'époque napoléonienne*. Paris: Editions des Archives contemporaines.

Brian, Eric. 1994. *La mesure de l'État: Administrateurs et géomètres au XVIIIe siècle*. Paris: Albin Michel.

Butré, Charles Richard de. 1767a. "De la grande et de la petite culture." *Ephémérides du citoyen* 9:5–81; 10:73–134; 11:71–114; 12:73–136.

———. 1767b. *Eléments d'oeconomie politique*. Archives Départemental d'Indre-et-Loire, C 101.

Charles, Loïc. 1999. "La liberté du commerce des grains et l'économie politique française (1750–1770)." PhD diss., Université de Paris I.

Charles, Loïc, Frédéric Lefebvre, and Christine Théré, eds. 2011. *Le cercle de Vincent de Gournay: Savoirs économiques et pratiques administratives en France au milieu du XVIIIe siècle*. Paris: INED.

Decroix, Arnaud. 2006. *Question fiscale et réforme financière en France (1749–1789): Logique de la transparence et recherche de la confiance publique*. Aix-en-Provence: Presses universitaires d'Aix-Marseille.

Demeulenaere-Douyère, Christiane, and David Sturdy, eds. 2008. *L'enquête du régent, 1716–1718 [Texte imprimé]: Sciences, techniques et politique dans la France pré-industrielle*. Turnhout, Belgium: Brepols.

Du Pont de Nemours, Pierre-Samuel. 1786. *Aperçu de la valeur des récoltes du royaume*. Papers of Pierre-Samuel Du Pont de Nemours and his two wives, Eleutherian Mills Historical Library, Greenville, Del.

———. (1906) 1984. *The Autobiography of Du Pont de Nemours*. Translated by Elizabeth Fox-Genovese. Wilmington, Del.: Scholarly Resources.

Ellis, Harold A. 1988. *Boulainvilliers and the French Monarchy*. Ithaca: Cornell University Press.

36. On these debates and the influence of the physiocratic writings of the 1758–67 period on them, see Perrot 1988.

Fleury, Gabriel. 1915. *François Véron de Fortbonnais [sic]: Sa famille, sa vie, ses actes, ses oeuvres 1721–1800*. Le Mans: A. de Saint-Denis.

Gille, Bertrand. (1964) 1980. *Les sources statistiques de l'histoire de France: Des enquêtes du XVIIe siècle à 1870*. Geneva: Droz.

INED (Institut national d'études démographiques). 2005. *Oeuvres économiques complètes de François Quesnay et autres textes*, edited by Christine Théré, Loïc Charles, and Jean-Claude Perrot. 2 vols. Paris: INED.

Justin, Emile. 1935. *Les sociétés royales d'agriculture au XVIIIe siècle (1757–1793)*. Saint-Lo: Impr. Barbaroux.

Martin, Thierry, ed. 2003. *Arithmétique politique dans la France du XVIIIe siècle*. Paris: INED.

Mendelsohn, J. Andrew. 2011. "The World on a Page: Making a General Observation in the Eighteenth Century." In *Histories of Scientific Observation*, edited by Lorraine Daston and Elizabeth Lunbeck. Chicago: University of Chicago Press.

Meusnier, Norbert. 2003. "Vauban: L'arithmétique politique, ragot et autre cochonnerie." In Martin 2003.

Mirabeau, Victor Riqueti, and François Quesnay. 1762. "Philosophie rurale." Manuscript. National Archives, M 779 no. 3–2, Paris.

———. 1763. *Philosophie rurale, ou économie générale et politique de l'agriculture réduite à l'ordre immuable des loix physiques et rurales, qui assurent la prospérité des empires*. Amsterdam: Libraires associés.

"Notice générale de la France." 1756. *Journal oeconomique*, May.

Perrot, Jean-Claude. (1978) 1992. La comptabilité des entreprises agricoles dans l'économie physiocratique. In *Une histoire intellectuelle de l'économie politique (XVIIe–XVIIIe siècle)*. Paris: EHESS.

———, ed. 1988. *De la richesse du royaume territorial de France*, by Antoine-Laurent Lavoisier. Paris: Éditions du CHTS.

Perrot, Jean-Claude, and Stuart J. Woolf. 1984. *State and Statistics in France, 1789–1815*. London: Harwood Academic.

Quesnay, François. 1756. "Fermiers." In INED 2005.

———. 1757a. "Grains." In INED 2005.

———. 1757b. "Hommes." In INED 2005.

Quesnay, François, and Etienne-Claude Marivetz. 1758. *Questions intéressantes sur la population, l'agriculture et le commerce, proposées aux Académies et autres Sociétés savantes des Provinces*. In INED 2005.

Théré, Christine, and Loïc Charles. 2007. "François Quesnay: A 'Rural Socrates' in Versailles?" In *Economists' Lives: Biography and Autobiography in the History of Economics*, edited by E. Roy Weintraub and Evelyn L. Forget. *HOPE* 39 (supplement): 195–214.

———. 2008. "The Writing Workshop of François Quesnay and the Making of Physiocracy (1757–1764)." *HOPE* 40 (1): 1–42.

Tribe, Keith. 1988. *Governing Economy: The Reformation of German Economic Discourse, 1750–1840*. Cambridge: Cambridge University Press.

Turgot, Anne-Robert-Jacques. (1765) 1983. *Sur la grande et la petite culture*. Edited and translated by P. D. Groenewegen. Sydney: University of Sydney.

Van den Berg, Richard. 2002. "Contemporary Responses to the Tableau Econo-
mique." In *Is There Progress in Economics? Knowledge, Truth, and the History
of Economic Thought*, edited by S. Boehm, C. Gehrke, H. D. Kurz, and R. Sturn.
Cheltenham: Edward Elgar.

Vauban, Sébastien Le Preste. 1686. *Méthode généralle et facile de faire le dénom-
brement des peuples*. Paris: Chrestien.

Véron de Forbonnais, François. 1767. *Principes et observations oeconomiques*.
Amsterdam: M.-M. Rey.

Virol, Michelle, ed. 2007. *Les oisivetés de Monsieur Vauban*. Seyssel, France: Champ
Vallon.

Zeller, Olivier. 2007. "Changement agraire et récession démographique: La première
enquête Orry (1730); L'exemple d'Issoudun." *Annales de démographie historique*
2:143–61.

**Part 2
The Fragile Dynamics of Trust**

Making Variety Simple: Agricultural Economists in Southern Italy, 1906–9

Federico D'Onofrio

It is a well-established maxim of politics that *prius consultatu quam factu opus est.*[1] The process of deliberation in turn is ideally nourished by facts gathered to support the competing arguments. Hence *fact gathering* becomes preliminary to *action*. In the nineteenth and twentieth centuries, inquiries (from the celebrated British parliamentary inquiries to the German inquiries of the Verein für Sozialpolitik) played an essential role in steering and influencing deliberation by influencing public opinion, parliaments, and cabinets. Inquiries were specific forms of investigation of social issues based on a combination of different sources. Not all of them proved successful in influencing deliberation, as political plots or technical reasons could undermine their effectiveness, but inquiries seemed to be a necessary source of information in nineteenth- and twentieth-century Europe. In this article I examine the case of the Italian parliamentary inquiry into the conditions of peasants in the southern provinces and Sicily, the so-called Faina inquiry (1906–9). The collection of facts for the Faina inquiry, as for most inquiries of this kind, was subjected to three intermingling classes of problems: the problem of indisputability, the problem of remoteness, and the problem of packaging.

First, let us consider *indisputability.* Ideally, facts had to be so indisputable that they could determine the outcome of deliberations. How to put facts above the disputes of politicians and parties? The Italian parliament

Unless otherwise indicated, all translations are mine.
1. "It is necessary to deliberate before taking action."—Sallust

History of Political Economy 44 (annual suppl.) DOI 10.1215/00182702-1631797
Copyright 2012 by Duke University Press

turned to specialists in data-gathering in order to found its work on solid bases: statisticians and experts in agricultural economy thus collected information. Because of their disciplinary training not only were they more skillful in collecting information than, say, state officials but they were expected to be more "independent" from political interests. Hence they could summarize the opinions of various social actors, making the facts they collected less disputable in the arena of public opinion. Agricultural economists acted as experts in different ways: First, as *experts* in opposition to *politicians* in the parliament; second, as members of a national and international scientific community distinct from the hyperlocal perspective of peasants and landlords in the South; third, as experts of agriculture and experts in techniques for collecting and handling information. I do not want to stress here the intrusion of a foreign and hostile expert rationality into the life of laypeople, as Judith Pallot (2000) does with the case of "rationalization" of landholding in Russia under Pietr Stolypin's reform. My desire instead is to stress how agricultural economists were asked to act as a communication channel between different elements of Italian society, which meant their work depended on the *trust* they earned. Beyond the "postmodern" critiques of modernist attempts at creating legible spaces for domination (Scott 1999), I intend to show how information was exchanged in the actual fieldwork of an inquiry, with local agents contributing to shape the representation of their own lives through the investigators' expertise.

Second, let us consider *remoteness*. For facts on southern peasants to reach the study rooms of the educated public, they had to travel a long distance through language, class, and geographic barriers.[2] This implied that inquirers had to travel far, into the southern provinces. In 1875, when three students from Pisa, Enea Cavalieri, Leopoldo Franchetti, and Sidney Sonnino, decided to make an inquiry into the conditions of the peasants in Sicily, they brought with them a panoply of revolvers and rifles (Franchetti and Sonnino 1925).[3] Agricultural economists who took part in the Faina inquiry traveled safely through the Italian countryside of the early 1900s, but their writings reveal how remote Mezzogiorno's peasants appeared to the educated elite. Most reports transmit the same feeling that Carlo Levi ([1947] 2006) described in *Christ Stopped at Eboli*: investigators were overwhelmed by local specificities, by different and competing visions of society, or on the contrary they were met with the hostility of groups and regions that, for different reasons, refused to cooperate with them.

2. On traveling facts, see Howlett and Morgan 2011.
3. On Italy's Mezzogiorno as exotic Orient, see Schneider 1998.

This is what I call the problem of remoteness. The task of agricultural economists who engaged in the Faina inquiry was to *translate* locally embedded knowledge into a framework that could be understood elsewhere, to sever its ties with a specific configuration of politics, geography, and routines in order to mobilize it for nationwide political and scientific debates.[4] At the same time, for this process to succeed, they had to engage local interests in the inquiry; they had to mediate between the distant ruling classes represented in the parliament and provincial needs, hopes, and aspirations.

Third, let us consider *packaging*. The issues of mobilization and representation raise the problem of "packaging" facts.[5] Only those facts could be politically relevant that were easily produced and easily read, for neither parliament nor public opinion generally had time to examine an endless list of particular observations. The Italian parliamentary inquiry on agriculture of 1874, for instance, was forgotten on bookshelves because it lacked a synthesis (Valenti 1907, 6). Statistics—in this case a large, comprehensive collection of observations—by means of averaging and graphs, seemed to offer early twentieth-century positivists a good synthetic representation of facts.[6] But statistics took time to produce, and facts that were known too late would have no effect. Moreover, they required permanent institutions and rarely reached the adequate level of detail.

The facts inquirers collected concerned the way of life of peasants: their income, their labor participation, their patterns of consumption, their health, their propensity to crime, and their political associations. All factors varied greatly across southern Italy and were heavily affected by local contexts. To detach such local and varied facts from their context and make it possible for them to reach the public, they had to be packaged in such a way as to preserve variety and specificity but also to allow handling far away from the places and the people described. *Types* were the available format to crystallize varieties (Desrosières 1988).

In the tradition of agricultural economics, farm types were classes of farms similar for some geographic, dimensional, technological, and juridical features, like the extensive farm of Basilicata or the Tuscan *podere*. Types presupposed structural differences imposed by natural (climate, altitude, soil) or social (contracts, labor conditions, technologies) constraints, instead of a continuum of variation. The concept had a multiplicity of intellectual roots and a plurality of empirical applications in farm

4. On mobilization, see Latour 1987.
5. I take this definition from Howlett and Morgan 2011.
6. On the importance of Adolphe Quételet's average, see Porter 1986.

appraisal, tax surveys, farm management, and so forth.[7] To study types, observers selected *typical* farms, real farms that were *representative* instances of the type. In this way it was possible for agricultural economists, by studying a single carefully selected farm, the typical one, to study a whole class of farms for which no statistics were available. As a result, types made differences easy to handle.

The following paragraphs describe the political context that led the parliament to summon Faina's commission, how the work of investigation was structured and divided between a *technical* and a *political* part, the role of agricultural economists, and the methods applied for the *technical* inquiry to deal with the three problems listed above.

The Faina Inquiry

On July 13, 1906, after long discussions in the two houses of the Italian parliament, the senate finally passed a new law whose substance is indicated by its title: "Provisions for the Southern Provinces, Sicily and Sardinia" (Legge 15 luglio 1906, n. 383). The law contained a series of tax reductions to stimulate the (fundamentally agricultural) economy of the dilapidated Mezzogiorno, together with a list of public works to be funded. The most controversial measure the law introduced, though, was a complete revolution in land tenancy contracts. The law aimed to extend to the South the Tuscan sharecropping system (thirty years after Sonnino's journey through Sicily) and replace the huge variety of tenancy and lease contracts in use in southern Italy. A vast coalition of interests opposed this idea, and although the law was approved, the application of the part that concerned land-lease contracts was suspended, pending on the results of a parliamentary inquiry that was summoned, immediately afterward, by a second law passed by the Senate on July 19.[8]

The inquiring commission was "to inquire into the conditions of peasants, their relationships with landlords, and especially into the nature of the land tenancy contracts [*patti agrari*] in the southern provinces and in Sicily" (quoted in Rogari 2002, 27).[9] In fact, some commissioners wanted to turn the inquiry into a narrow discussion of contracts, while others

7. It suffices to look at Nou 1967, especially chapters 5, 6, and 8 on Albrecht Thaer, Johann Heinrich von Thünen, and the Swiss school of agricultural economics, to see how deeply rooted the idea of structural differences among types of farms was in agricultural economics.

8. On the political maneuvers that led to the laws of 1906, see Prampolini 1981 and Rogari 2002.

9. The commission had eighteen commissioners, nine members of the lower house of the Italian parliament, the Chamber of Deputies, and nine senators.

expected an all-encompassing investigation into the conditions of peasants, the state of agriculture, the reasons for peasants' discontent, emigration, and so forth. The convergence of right-wing opponents to the law (who wanted to gain time through a long inquiry) and left wingers (who hoped to direct the attention of the public to the poverty of southern peasants) finally extended the commission's mandate and the inquiry's object.

This was not the first time the Italian parliament formed an inquiring commission on economic matters. A much-talked-about parliamentary inquiry on agriculture had been carried out in the late 1870s; it was known as the Jacini inquiry, after the name of the inquiry's president. A previous inquiry had targeted industrial potential. The model for nineteenth-century inquiries, as for the inquiry that began in 1906, was British parliamentary inquiries: alongside a large mass of statistical data collected in various ways, a preeminent place was reserved for the declarations of various social characters, who testified in front of the parliamentary commission on their views and opinions of the problems at hand.[10] Through inquiries, the parliament listened to the country.

Testimonies in general show two dimensions: on the one hand, they allowed inquiring commissions to listen to the *voti* (what the population desired, hoped, and expected from the government) and specific needs of certain areas, remote from the country's political centers; on the other, commissions listened to a vast range of classes and people, thus letting the country express its social diversity. Geographic and social diversity had, of course, different levels of importance according to the different topics of inquiry, but they both contributed to the political and informational meaning of it.

When the commissioners first gathered in the winter of 1906–7, after electing their president, Senator Count Eugenio Faina, they decided to split the workload in two: "The preliminary collection of material, i.e. documentable data, should be carried out by special technical delegates; the parliamentary commission, instead, should reserve for themselves, besides the task of control, etc., only the political work, that is, the survey of the mood of the population, and the vows, insofar as they address the State, of the different agricultural classes in the territories touched by the inquiry" (Archivio centrale dello stato [ACS], Giunta parlamentare d'inchiesta sulle condizioni dei contadini nelle provincie meridionali e nella Sicilia, b. 5, f. 6, *Verbali della Giunta plenaria*, Verbale 2, February 2, 1907). The commission's activities were thus divided into "political" and

10. On the Jacini inquiry, see Caracciolo 1959; on the industrial inquiry, see Baglioni 1974; for the British influence on the 1906 inquiry, see Coletti 1906b, 36–52.

"technical." For each of the six regions of Sicily and the Mezzogiorno,[11] a subcommission of three commissioners fulfilled the "political" task, while a technical delegate collected the "documentable data" (for a total of seven technical delegates). Politicians should synthesize the demands of the population and eventually translate them into proposals; "technicians" should provide neutral and objective information that could offer the politicians grounds for their synthesis. This was considered all the more important because the data already available in official publications were regarded as old and unreliable, and statistics did not provide enough ground for arguments.[12]

The Technical Delegates

Francesco Coletti was chosen as the commission's secretary-general with the task of writing the program and questionnaires for the inquiry (ACS, Giunta parlamentare d'inchiesta sulle condizioni dei contadini nelle provincie meridionali e nella Sicilia, b. 5, f. 5, *Verbali della Giunta plenaria*, Verbale 2, January 24, 1907). Since Coletti was professor of statistics and demography at the University of Sassari, his nomination shows that statistics was awarded pride of place among "techniques" that could provide objective and incontestable data. But Coletti was hardly an arid technician, without political connections. First of all, he was known to most of the commissioners as the former secretary-general of the Società degli agricoltori italiani (SAI), a nationwide association of Italian landowners. For SAI, he had coordinated a number of inquiries into strikes in agriculture. Since many of the commissioners were also SAI members, they probably expected Coletti to understand the viewpoint of landowners (who strongly opposed the law on tenancy contracts) and also to be sensitive to the problems of agriculture in general. Moreover, Coletti was close to the leader of the radical (left-wing) opposition Francesco Saverio Nitti, also a commission member: Coletti had collaborated on agricultural problems with Nitti's celebrated journal, *La riforma sociale*.[13] Coletti's objectivity thus resulted from three elements: a methodology of investigation, a good

11. The current administrative Italian regions did not yet exist as such, but *compartimenti* existed as statistical units. On the statistical treatment of regional differentiation, see Patriarca 1996.

12. This point was raised by Francesco Saverio Nitti in the committee's meetings; on the inadequacy of official data on agriculture, see Federico 1982 and its bibliography.

13. See the entry on Coletti in the *Dizionario biografico degli italiani*.

knowledge of agriculture, and a political stance in between the different groups that formed the commission.

Coletti and Faina, then, hired the technical delegates. Unfortunately, it is not clear how the six delegates were selected, but they shared some characteristics. They were almost all scholars of economics and agricultural economics (with the exception of the rural sociologist Giovanni Lorenzoni and the lawyer Enrico Presutti). The Neapolitan Oreste Bordiga was already an established professor at the Scuola superiore di agricoltura (SSA) of Portici and taught agricultural economics, accounting, and land valuation. Ernesto Marenghi, a graduate of the SSA of Milan, held the chair of agricultural economics, accounting, and land valuation in Perugia (see Gabba 1995). Eugenio Azimonti, after graduating from the SSA of Milan, had moved to Basilicata (in the far south) as the director of the Cattedra ambulante di agricoltura in Potenza, a local institution of technical assistance to the peasants (Musella 1995). Cesare Jarach was a graduate in economics whose main achievement had been an empirical research on the financial sheets of Italian joint-stock companies; after the inquiry he became Faina's personal secretary at the International Institute for Agriculture (Forte 2009). Lorenzoni was educated in Austria and Germany (he dedicated his main book to the cooperative movement in Germany); as head of the Labor Office at the Società umanitaria di Milano (SUM) he had directed the SUM's social inquiries.[14] Coletti and Faina entrusted these men with the technical inquiries: a short preliminary examination of the sources already available in Rome; the collection of information on the ground, on the basis of the program that Coletti had elaborated; and the writing of a synthetic report (ACS, Giunta parlamentare, b.5, f.5, Adunanze dell'ufficio di presidenza, Verbale 2, January 24, 1907). This division (i.e., elaboration of data vs. collection of information) is mirrored by the competences required for both technical delegates and secretary-general: familiarity with the methodologies of inquiries and knowledge of agriculture (method and content).

The inquiry's program was "to investigate in particular the relationships between land laborers and landowners." Hence "it was necessary to examine both terms of this relationship, and reveal, together with the condition of workers, that of proprietors, or, more precisely that of property, i.e. that of agriculture which is the concrete expression of property" (Coletti 1906b, 56). The conditions of peasants were deemed inseparable from that of

14. Gioia and Spalletti 2005; on SUM, see Granata 2003. Lorenzoni gave an account of his inquiries for SUM in Lorenzoni 1903.

landownership and agriculture, as a whole economic sector. The first two parts of the inquiry's program focused, therefore, on "land and agriculture" and "patterns of landownership," and the remaining five on peasants. Part 3 investigated the different classes of smallholders and peasants according to tenancy and labor contracts. It inquired into the budget of peasant families, their income, salaries, the distribution of revenues according to the different patterns of land tenancy, and employment. Part 4 concerned the standard of living, including health and moral conditions of peasant life, as well as their demographic consequences. If part 3 discussed income, part 4 investigated expenditures and consumption. Parts 5 and 6 examined the peasant within a wider range of relationships: part 5 investigated credit and charity; part 6 the political grouping of peasants. Part 7 was dedicated to emigration, probably the most powerful factor of change in southern societies. Part 8 summarized the previous parts and made explicit the relationships connecting them (Coletti 1906b, 56–60).

This being the inquiry program, the technical delegates should proceed to fulfill it, with their own direct field surveys (*rilievi*), and through questionnaires sent to individuals and institutions. Such alternatives were named *direct* and *indirect* inquiry. Documents (i.e., contracts) formed a third source of information. Matters of landownership (part 2), for instance, were to be discussed in terms of total product, net income, and rent of agricultural estates. These data could be obtained either through direct surveys and estimates of the fundamental parameters of individual estates (this was called "farm monograph" and was a type of direct inquiry) or by requiring information from somebody knowledgeable and willing to answer, for instance, an official of the Inland Revenue (indirect inquiry). Also, part 3 was to be based on a variety of sources: technical delegates should collect contracts and describe the most common for each area; they should also note family budgets and farm accounts for which direct survey of some families was integrated by the answers provided by local informants to the questionnaires. The combination of multiple sources was a characteristic of inquiries.

Already available statistics would have been of great help. For Coletti, had statistics like that of Belgium been available, the inquiry would have been altogether unnecessary. But Coletti lamented that Italian statistics on agriculture "lack(ed) almost entirely reliable and homogeneous data."[15] For practical as well as theoretical reasons, technical delegates should

15. He was not alone in complaining: the Ministry of Agriculture, Industry, and Trade engaged in a complete renovation of agricultural statistics in 1907. See Federico 1982.

hence limit themselves, in their direct inquiry, "to the survey of typical instances of the various phenomena": since it was impossible and superfluous to examine all individual instances of a phenomenon, "it (was) necessary to concentrate on the various categories or degrees that are typical for a given phenomenon, and within these categories or degrees, it (was) necessary to single out and survey an average case" (Coletti 1906b, 60). The observation of typical (*tipico*) instances was regarded by Italian social investigators as the only legitimate alternative to a complete survey of the population, which alone deserved the name of "statistics."[16]

The Typical Farm

Coletti placed the typical at the crossing of two ways of investigating social phenomena. In the first place, the typical was the final result of surveys and elaborations: Adolphe Quételet's average man was constructed by combining the average dimensions of human organs in a single individual and could be treated as the "type" of a nation (Porter 1986, 52–53). Thus, in Coletti's (1906b, 61) view, "statistics survey statistical units. On their basis, they construct the datum. Out of a mass or series of data, statistics extract what is typical." According to the method of monographs popularized by Frederic Le Play, instead, identification of typical cases preceded the collection of information. It was based on "prudent and careful inspection, together with the information provided by experienced and knowledgeable men, of those whom Frederic Le Play, called 'social authorities'" (Coletti 1906b, 61). The latter's reliability derived from their lifelong exchange with the people observed and their *goodwill* to serve the cause of social peace.

Coletti believed these two methods were not incompatible and derived his faith in the conciliation of Le Playan monographs and Quételetian statistics (based on complete census) from Émile Cheysson. For Cheysson, while "the role of the monograph was to describe a subject (individual, family, workshop, commune, or nation); the role of statistics was to insure scientifically the subject's typicality" (Rabinow 1989, 174). As Alain Desrosières pointed out, Quételet's stress on the stable and essential nature of averages enabled Cheysson to assume that an individual, *close* to the average for *some significant* features, could totally substitute its group for *all* features. In this way, monographic study fleshed with details the

16. For the conception of "inductive method" that prevailed in Italy, see Baffigi 2007.

generality of the inquiry, expanding in-depth what the inquiry depicted in extension (Desrosières 1988, 96).

Typical objects allowed generalization and represented satisfactorily a complex phenomenon. As Desrosières put it, "They depicted the characters of the story to be told"; they built collective actors of the social drama (96). But they had to display such characters in their completeness, in their purest (even when socially pathological) form. So, for instance, Coletti (1906a, 124) recommended studying "complete" families with kids of different ages, rather than families without kids.

In empirical practice, this meant a two-step procedure, faithfully mirrored in Coletti's instruction. Statistical information was required for a preliminary of types. In an area where a majority of farms grew wheat extensively and a minority had orange and lemon orchards, for instance, at least two types could be identified beforehand on the basis of even rough figures of production. The technical delegates were compelled to begin their investigation in Rome by diving into all the published sources available, to familiarize themselves with such general data. The next step was the choice of the individual cases to summarize such types. This, instead, was considered to depend on a network of "experienced and knowledgeable individuals" who lived in the area. Coletti (1906a; 1906b, 61) suggested the delegates "mobilize" such forces so that they could select the right family whose budget to make, the right farm whose crop rotation to study, whose revenues to analyze, the right peasant house to take a picture of, and so forth. This second step could not be strictly planned for. Only when they were on the spot, in the presence of variable and unforeseeable local conditions, could the delegates select their typical cases. It was experience and skillfulness that would suggest to them what to take and what to leave out.

Unfortunately, the field notebooks that inquirers usually took with them on their journeys have not survived.[17] We can get an idea of the social authorities delegates might have turned to for selecting "typical" instances from the interviews carried out by some of the subcommissions during their journeys.[18] As I pointed out before, though, subcommissions had a "political" task and acted differently from delegates. Subcommissions interviewed the authorities in charge of the different aspects of the life of the countryside, a sort of Foucauldian biopower of notables. Medical doctors reported on health and hygienic conditions; judges, police officers, and king's prose-

17. For notebooks, see Lorenzoni 1929.
18. Those collected for Abruzzo and Molise, Sicilia, Campania, and Puglia are preserved in the ACS.

cutors on crime statistics and crime determinants; notaries on trends in the land market;[19] inland revenue officers (especially the engineers working for the Land Register) were asked for information on land rent and prices. Mayors presented schematic reports on their municipalities, touching on demographics, the municipality's balance sheets, schooling conditions, patterns of ownership, land and labor prices, peasant housing, health and hygiene, and emigration. While village notables dominated the interviews with the subcommissions, they were not the only interviewees. A crowd of different economic characters, sometimes invited by the commissioners, sometimes testifying spontaneously, also had their opinions recorded in the subcommissions' proceedings: peasants, landowners, administrators of large estates, industrialists, craftsmen, and so forth (even some women!).

Something more specific on the work of the technical delegates can be deduced from their own reports. Let us examine Azimonti's report on Basilicata. Of the three sources of information that Coletti distinguished (questionnaires, documents, field trips), the questionnaires were addressed to more or less the same type of individuals as those interviewed by the subcommission. Only about one-third of the questionnaires sent were returned completed. As for the documents, Azimonti found no material on the managing of agricultural businesses, "since it was everywhere lacking a systematic and orderly record of the facts of the administration of farms and estates," and if that existed it was nowhere disclosed. In the case of farm accounting, as for other topics, direct survey remained the only available source for these kinds of data, and Azimonti engaged in extensive surveys (Giunta parlamentare d'inchiesta 1909b, 14).

Unlike other technical delegates, Marenghi in Calabria, Jarach in Abruzzi, or Lorenzoni in Sicily, who were unfamiliar with and foreign to the region they studied, Azimonti knew part of Basilicata very well, since he had already been for a few years the director of the Cattedra ambulante in Potenza (one of the region's main towns). Scattered through the kingdom in provincial capitals and minor centers, *cattedre* (traveling chairs of agriculture) stimulated the introduction of the best suited and innovative technologies: better crop rotations, chemical fertilizers, new machines, and so forth. They propagandized novelties by giving public lectures to farmers and assisting them (Failla and Fumi 2006).[20] Azimonti thus personally

19. Italy is a Roman law country, and notaries are state officials.
20. *Cattedre* were financed in general by local governments (province) and associations of agriculturalists. They were thus *private* institutions with partly public funding. In the south and in Basilicata in particular, instead, *cattedre* had been established by the central government alone as part of a program of regional development launched in 1904 (Legge 31 marzo 1904

knew a relevant number of farmers, peasants, and landowners. He also knew his district very well from an agricultural point of view.

Apart from Azimonti, who declared he could not separate the work he did for the inquiry from what he did for the *cattedra*, so closely related they were, the directors and staff of the *cattedre* were in a good position to cooperate with the inquiry. They graduated from schools of agriculture, just like the majority of technical delegates of the Faina inquiry. Their job appeared to them as the dissemination of advanced techniques (that circulated in the world of science, experiments, and academia) into often neglected corners of the country: "The professor of the Cattedra ambulante accomplishes a pioneering task, wherever the word of science, for a number of recent or remote reasons, has not yet penetrated, there he is the pioneer of agriculture. He prepares the environment, he looks—as a friend and a counselor—after the farmer and he suggests to him things that he otherwise would never know" (Patrizi 1910). But the word of science would have been meaningless without the work done to adapt it to local contingencies and local practices. Adaptation involved experiments with crops or fertilizers, that is, *experiences* as they were called, but also selection of the best local practices. The anonymous director of a *cattedra* gave, for instance, a decidedly bottom-up interpretation of his teaching: "What else should we teach within our *cattedre*, if not the best of what we have learned (from the farmers)?" (quoted in Marenghi 1922). The *cattedre* acquired over time an essential knowledge of the territory they operated in, of its farmers and their habits, while preserving the ability to interact with the nationwide community of agricultural experts.

In general, technical delegates began the research of the "typical" from the suggestions of directors of *cattedre*. In Basilicata (there were four *cattedre* in the small region), Azimonti often traveled with his colleagues, and—in their districts he relied on his colleagues' recommendations when choosing the farms to study; they introduced him to peculiar traditions, put him in touch with relevant private individuals, and vouched for him in front of generally diffident farmers. Without the mix of general notions of agricultural management (agricultural economics) and local, contextual knowledge that the *cattedre* represented, it would have been impossible for technical delegates, who were often completely foreign to the territory and equipped with scanty statistics, to identify within a reasonable time span typical families, typical farms, typical villages for their surveys.

n. 140). Each *cattedra* was staffed by a director (*il professore*) and a few helpers. One helper was usually a young graduate in agricultural sciences.

Observation: A Farm Monograph

To illustrate this point, let us now examine what kind of observation technical delegates could perform thanks to the *cattedre* and the form they gave them. In his report, to illustrate the conditions of agricultural business in Basilicata, Azimonti presented to his readers a series of monographs on one farm for each prevailing farm type. The typology considered geographic factors, farm size, and usual combinations of enterprises. It thus relied on data that could be extracted from published and widely available sources (maps, reports, harvest statistics for the prevailing crops) or that were macroscopically evident in the landscape as well as in the everyday life of markets and people. The choice of the actual farms to be observed and the carrying out of the survey, instead, depended on personal contacts that only insiders could have.

One of the farms described represented the type of the extensive cereal farm joined with husbandry in the eastern zone of Basilicata. Clearly, this typology combines geographic elements with broad characteristics relating to production and production patterns. I discuss this monograph in detail because it shows the sensitivity of the information that the investigation required (such as could never be attained without active collaboration from the farmer) and the way the monograph was structured. In a farm monograph, the technical delegate's ability to obtain information from the farmer was preliminary to the framing of the farmer's information into basic categories of agricultural economics: the farm budget made the fundamental economic and technical features of the farm explicit.

The farm, owned by D. R., was composed of various plots for a total of approximately 889 hectares; Azimonti records its climatic conditions, soil, distance from market, and roads available. For each crop, Azimonti gives the acreage and rotation; for livestock, the number of each species and the surface dedicated to grazing. Livestock's most common illnesses are reported. D. R.'s farm also included tools and machines that constituted the so-called dead stocks. Fertilizers (actually, their scarcity) completed the picture. All this was the farm's *inventory*. It must be noted that machines, livestock illnesses, species of herd, different rotations were all familiar entities to the readers of the inquiry, much more than they are to us now. What readers wanted to learn from the inquiry was the peculiar combination of such elements that constituted a typical farm of Basilicata.

The farm consisted of its inventory, but also of workers. Azimonti discusses the budget (income and expenditures) of each category of workers, including the farm manager, that is, D. R. himself. Considerations on management led to the core of the farm monograph: the farm's cash flows, which Azimonti had to compute himself with the help of the owner and of an assistant to the local *cattedra*, since "there exist(ed) no bookkeeping whatsoever, Mr. D. R. being almost illiterate" (Giunta parlamentare d'inchiesta 1909b, 311).

Azimonti starts with gross production of crops and husbandry, the only data available for the years 1905–6, when Azimonti himself recorded the returns. For crops, after subtracting the products consumed within the farm, Azimonti computes 644 hundred kilograms of hard wheat, 132 hundred kilograms of soft wheat, and approximately 200 hundred kilograms of lesser crops (beans, etc.). The yield of husbandry is computed more easily, by the number of lambs for sale (180 at 1.10 lire per kg), and wool (785 kg, at 265 lire per hundred kg), dairy product (cheese and ricotta, around 700 kg), kids (around sixty kids for sale at 1.20 lire per kg), old sheep sold (100 at 25 lire the pair), and so forth.

Once the gross product is known (notice that the computation of the gross product value requires that prices are known for wheat and other commodities), Azimonti lists all the detractions that have to be subtracted from the gross product value to obtain rent, rent being the remuneration of the services of land. Among such detractions are expenses for labor, including the manager wage (notice that this is computed anyway, although the manager coincides with the owner); returns on capital, that is, the remuneration of the services provided by live stocks, dead stocks (machines, seeds, fodders, manure), and circulating capital, as if they had been borrowed by the entrepreneur; amortization; taxes on rent (*imposta fondiaria*). In particular, the calculation of returns on capital (*beneficio industriale*) involved first an appraisal of all forms of stocks (live and dead, for a value of 57,175 lire). On this value an interest was imposed of 5 percent, resulting in a subtraction of 2,858.75 lire from the rent. On the circulating capital, instead, represented mainly by cash payments for labor and amounting to 10,000 lire, Azimonti estimated an interest of 6 percent. The total detraction for remuneration of capital and stocks is thus 2,858.75 lire plus 600.

In a good year like 1905–6, D. R.'s revenues amount to 34,459 lire, while his expenses (including the remuneration of capital) reach 29,826 lire. What remains to D. R. amounts to 4,633 lire. By simply applying the equations of land valuation, imposing a standard interest rate of 4.50 percent, the returns on the value of land capital (approximately 90,000 lire) would be 4,050 lire, that is, the rent, what D. R. earns for owning the land. There are hence 583 lire that D. R. earns as his profit as an entrepreneur.

It is evident that this way of describing a farm originated in the principles of accounting and in the practices of land valuation (these two disciplines formed such a great part of the technical delegates' education). In the prevailing tradition of agricultural economic studies in Italy, in analogy with German *landwirtschaftliche Betriebslehre*, agriculture consisted of farms, and farms were fully described by their inventory and by "the proportions of the single constitutive parts and their reciprocal interrelations" (Cuppari 1869). These proportions were expressed in terms of distribution of the farm gross product among the economic factors of production.[21] Vittorio Niccoli (1898), who taught agricultural economics to both Marenghi and Azimonti in Milan, published influential sketches of regional farm types.[22] Farm types thus acquired a substantial stability as entities that could be studied and observed.

Thanks to the concept of typical farm, then, Azimonti's account of an individual farm acquired a larger significance and was taken to summarize local patterns of production, for instance, the interdependence of shepherding and extensive cultivation of cereals. Such monographs served, for instance, as the basis for Nitti's and Azimonti's own claims that *latifundia* functioned as complex productive units and could not easily be broken into smaller parts, a conclusion with strong political significance (Azimonti 1921).

Observations of such significance rested on fragile dynamics of trust: inquirers had to *trust* the local and contextual knowledge of their local guides (in the case of Azimonti's farm monograph, other agrarian economists working for the *cattedre*); the farmer had to *trust* the inquirer (and previously the inquirers' local guides) in order to disclose information that was so sensitive and could be so easily concealed. The same held for farm and family monographs: who would have let a foreigner enter the house to compute the value of furniture without *trust*? In fact, trust was only one aspect of the interaction between inquirers and "inquirees." Peasants and farmers who decided to collaborate with inquirers were actually those who desired to be interviewed: they were eager to communicate. As Coletti

---

21. Factors of production were called *cooperatori* in the language of the manuals of agricultural economics: land, labor, capital, entrepreneurship, and so forth.

22. The innumerable editions of Niccoli 1897, Niccoli's handbook for agricultural engineers, also containing directions for farm description, witness how the study of individual cases of farms as types was clearly part of the standard training of agricultural engineers, agronomists, and agricultural economists. Nou 1967, chapter 4, traces the origins of this way of investigation to Arthur Young and after him to Albrecht Thaer. The categories used in the calculations derive entirely from the Italian tradition of land valuation.

(1906b) put it, "The inquirer needs to select a family *willing* to be observed" (quoted in Serpieri 1929, 125; my emphasis). The motives, obviously, could vary greatly: pleasure of showing one's own achievements or requests for help. Arrigo Serpieri (1910), for instance, reports that during his inquiry on the conditions of peasants in the area of Milan (carried out for SUM almost in the same years as the Faina inquiry in the south), as soon as they heard that somebody was investigating their conditions, some peasant women encouraged him to visit their dwellings, to show him their appalling conditions, with the hope that their landowner would build new houses. Many requested an audience from subcommissions to complain about their problems and ask for help of some kind. It was so much so, that the commission even discussed the possibility that mayors might hide the arrival of the commissioners from the population to prevent complaints.

While Theodore Porter (2009) stressed the political conservatism that influenced Le Play's method of monographic inquiries, his dependence on "social authorities," I would like to highlight here the necessary interactions between local and foreign, between observed and observer built into this type of observation. Both social and geographic remoteness required guides and translators in order for technical delegates to overcome them, and the literate, Italian-speaking, university-educated locals—when willing to cooperate—constituted the most obvious starting point of observation, just like Neapolitan aristocrats had guided their European guests into the exotic kingdom, during the Grand Tour (Placanica 1987). As Azimonti wrote: "Out of necessity, due to the illiteracy that dominates among peasants, we were forced to ask the *galantuomini* for intelligence of the life of the peasants" (Giunta parlamentare d'inchiesta 1909b, 15), thus stressing the divide caused by literacy. But were the *galantuomini* faithful interpreters for the peasants? The technical delegates found, instead, their best supporters in the assistant and directors of the Cattedre ambulanti and in the teachers of the schools of agriculture disseminated in the south.

The *cattedre* were able to translate the "word of science" into propaganda for the peasants,[23] but they were also able—at least in principle—to transform the tacit world of local agricultural practices into a language that could be understood by the general community of experts: accounting sheets, respective proportions of fertilizers, yearly rotations, and so forth.[24] Not to mention the translation—*sensu stricto*—from local dialects into Italian.

---

23. "Peasants need to see, or they won't trust" is a common statement in the answers of *cattedre* directors to the inquiring commission.

Observations such as those combined in a farm monograph contained a great deal of communication and translations, as I showed; a mechanism similar to Bruno Latour's (1987) *mobilization*, but bidirectional, as the observed actively pursued their own representation.[25] In the case of southern Italy, in fact, for the mobilization to take place, the distant periphery should have an interest in providing information to the "centre of calculation"; otherwise, data could be misreported or simply hidden.[26] Consequently, the effectiveness of both direct and indirect inquiry varied greatly depending on the interest shown by observed populations. Marenghi, for instance, lamented that in Calabria "the inquiry would have been more complete had public and private offices showed . . . more collaboration": "private individuals did not welcome the inquiry" (Giunta parlamentare d'inchiesta 1909a, xxvii). Azimonti complained that in Basilicata the collaboration of private individuals "was, altogether, very deficient and—so to say—offered unwillingly," "the civilized strata [*ceto civile*] seemed not to acknowledge the practical utility of the inquiry and of collaborating with it" (Giunta parlamentare d'inchiesta 1909b, xvi). In contrast, Lorenzoni praised the welcome received in the Sicilian villages he visited, and in particular the collaboration of peasants "full of trust and—so to say—of gratitude for the interest shown in them." And he could not "recall without emotion the long evening meetings . . . when they orderly and without impatience or exaggeration . . . , explained their conditions." It was together with such peasants or with equally participative landowners that Lorenzoni visited cooperatives and estates (Giunta parlamentare d'inchiesta 1911, introduction).

Conclusions: Communication, the Typical, and Statistics

It might seem that the two aspects of observation that emerged from the discussion of the Faina inquiry, that is, the role of a seemingly subjective

24. A similar notion can be found in Collins and Evans 2002.

25. Investigation of agriculture has often been seen in terms of "quantification" and "mapping," with statistics making the countryside "appropriable" for the state (unidirectional): for instance, James C. Scott (1999) stresses the top-down character of cadastres in continental Europe and Southeast Asia. In fact, a closer look at the way cadastres were actually made shows that local communities participated in the making of maps and the attribution of values; the landowners interviewed by the Faina inquiry, for instance, almost invariably invoked the completion of the *catasto terreni* that they expected would lower the land tax to more reasonable levels.

26. Emmanuel Didier (2009) stresses the importance that reliable information had for American farmers against speculators. On deception, see also Boumans, this volume.

element as the "typical" and the importance of communication, are limited to that form of social investigation that went under the name of inquiry and that positivist scholars such as Giovanni Battista Salvioni (1892) regarded as not quite statistics because of its qualitative character. It was not so: the most seemingly objective numerical statistics relied on the same elements.[27] I mention only a few facts about Italian statistics on harvest, as they were prepared after Ghino Valenti's reform of 1910. The system for computing harvest was based, for each district, on the production coefficients and rotations of typical farms. Such typical farms were identified by the directors of the Cattedre ambulanti, and the coefficients were estimated by them as in Azimonti's monograph discussed above (Valenti 1907). The whole organization of agricultural statistics, moreover, depended on the collaboration of local associations of landowners: without their help and supervision, data on acreage and per hectare productivity could not have been updated.[28] Hence, also in the case of statistics, the statistician's ability to build a network and alliances within the population he studied was a necessary condition of observation, as well as his own ability to identify what was typical.

There was no opposition between the subjectivity of inquiring methods and the indisputability of the resulting facts. The description of types *was* a reasonable way to summarize variety for politics and science. It was the expertise of technical delegates to combine consistently answers to questionnaires (indirect inquiry) and their own investigations and travel impressions (direct inquiry) that made the conditions of the poorest part of its population observable for the Italian state.

Questionnaires were answered by a variety of individuals, with different degrees of precision, dominated by diverging concerns, and referring to different experiences and places. They had to be merged into a unique text: "Once the questionnaires were collected—wrote Lorenzoni—we had to think how to summarize them: by municipalities first, by district afterward. Neither of the two was an easy job. The questionnaires coming from the same municipality but from different individuals frequently diverged from one another. And the difference was not only merely formal or quantitative but sometimes, although rarely, substantial. How to select?" (Giunta parlamentare d'inchiesta 1911, xxv). It was a direct knowledge of places, direct observation of circumstances and a survey of typical

27. I define here "objective," and conversely "subjective," following Porter 1995, as "knowledge based completely on explicit rules."

28. For a list of the agricultural associations that took part in the making of the statistics, see Ministero agricoltura industria e commercio 1907.

instances of social phenomena (direct inquiry), that guided the selection of questionnaires and the judgment on their reliability.

In principle, the observation of a whole region—of all the farms, families, villages—could be accomplished only through a continuous and comprehensive census, through statistics, but, since statistics were not at hand, the technical delegates of the Faina inquiry traveled almost through a terra incognita of social phenomena. Only the observation of a few "typical" points (and not random samples) made generalization possible, on the basis of "typicality," at a reasonably economic cost. The choice of the typical instances preceded, out of necessity, the observation of them and was thus confided to the expert's coup d'oeil. Although it depended on a complex interaction between different kinds of expertise, local and academic, tacit and explicit, methodological and agricultural, and different interests, the farmers' and the inquirers', the final decision rested entirely on the shoulders of the technical delegates.

The characteristics that in principle made the delegates suited for making the right observations and giving to such observations their best synthesis were two: their university training (i.e., decontextualized knowledge), and their ability to translate such university training into local context. These characteristics they shared with their fellow graduates from agricultural schools who worked in the Cattedre ambulanti. In fact, they belonged to the same group—that of agricultural experts—whose task was *translating* the expertise of local agriculturalists and farmers about contracts, techniques, technologies, and human factors into the language of economic theory and vice versa. By doing so, the community of agricultural experts gave stability and substance to agricultural types (types of farm, types of peasant families) that the government and the parliament could make laws about and that agricultural experts themselves could study in further investigations (as in the case of statistics of harvest). If the political impact of the Faina inquiry was in the end rather limited, its volumes nevertheless offered for a very long time a reference point for every researcher interested in southern Italian agriculture.

References

Azimonti, Eugenio. 1921. *Il Mezzogiorno agrario qual è*. Bari: Laterza.

Baffigi, Alberto. 2007. "Cultura statistica e cultura politica: L'Italia nei primi decenni unitari." Quaderni dell'ufficio ricerche storiche della Banca d'Italia 15. Rome: Banca d'Italia.

Baglioni, G. 1974. *L'ideologia borghesia industriale nell'Italia liberale*. Turin: Einaudi.

Caracciolo, Alberto. 1959. *L'inchiesta agraria Jacini*. Turin: Einaudi.

Coletti, Francesco. 1906a. *Come si compilano le monografie di famiglia: Estratto dallo Cheysson e Focillon*. Rome: Bertero.

———. 1906b. *Programma questionario dell'inchiesta per i delegati tecnici*. Rome: Bertero.

Collins, Harry M., and Robert Evans. 2002. "The Third Wave of Science Studies: Studies of Expertise and Experience." *Social Studies of Science* 32:235.

Cuppari, Pietro. 1869. *Manuale dell'agricoltore*. Florence: Barbera.

Desrosières, Alain. 1988. "La partie pour le tout: Comment généraliser? La préhistoire de la contrainte de représentativité." *Statistique et analyse des données* 13 (2): 93–112.

Didier, Emmanuel. 2009. *En quoi consiste L'Amérique? Les statistiques, le New Deal et la démocratie*. Paris: La Découverte.

Failla, Osvaldo, and Giampiero Fumi, eds. 2006. *Gli agronomi in Lombardia: Dalle cattedre ambulanti ad oggi*. Milan: Franco Angeli.

Federico, Giovanni. 1982. "Per una valutazione critica delle statistiche della produzione agricola italiana dopo l'Unità (1860–1913)." *Società e storia* 15 (2): 87–130.

Forte, F. 2009. "Cesare Jarach e Achille Necco." In *La scuola di economia di Torino*, edited by Roberto Marchionatti, 149–63. Florence: Olschki.

Franchetti, Lepoldo, and Sidney Sonnino. 1925. *La Sicilia nel 1876*. 2nd ed. Florence: Vallecchi.

Gabba, A. 1995. "L'opera Ernesto Marenghi." *Pubblicazioni Ce.S.E.T., seminari* 15, 5–14. Aspetti evolutivi della scienza estimativa: Seminario in onore di Ernesto Marenghi.

Gioia, Vitantonio, and Stefano Spalletti, ed. 2005. *Etica ed economia: La vita, le opere e il pensiero di Giovanni Lorenzoni*. Soveria Mannelli: Rubbettino.

Giunta parlamentare d'inchiesta. 1909a. *Relazione del delegato tecnico Prof. Ernesto Marenghi*. Vol. 5, *tome* 2. Rome: Bertero.

———. 1909b. *Relazione del delegato tecnico Prof. Eugenio Azimonti*. Rome: Bertero.

———. 1911. *Relazione del delegato tecnico Prof. Giovanni Lorenzoni*. Vol. 6. Rome: Bertero.

Granata, Ivano. 2003 *In difesa della terra: L'ufficio agrario della Società umanitaria, 1905–1923*. Milan: Franco Angeli.

Howlett, Peter, and Mary Morgan, eds. 2011. *How Well Do Facts Travel? The Dissemination of Reliable Knowledge*. Cambridge: Cambridge University Press.

Latour, Bruno. 1987. *Science in Action: How to Follow Scientists and Engineers through Society*. Cambridge: Harvard University Press.

Levi, Carlo. (1947) 2006. *Christ Stopped at Eboli*. New York: Farrar, Straus and Giroux.

Lorenzoni, Giovanni. 1903. *Le inchieste statistiche dell'ufficio del lavoro*. Milan: Ufficio Del Lavoro Editore.

———. 1929. *Introduzione e guida ad un'inchiesta sulla piccola proprietà coltivatrice postbellica in Italia*. Rome: Treves Dell' Ali.

Marenghi, Ernesto. 1922. *Lezioni di contabilità agraria*. Milan: Politecnica.

Ministero agricoltura industria e commercio. 1907. *Esperimenti di statistica agraria in alcune province del Regno*. Rome: Bertero.

Musella, Luigi. 1995. "Il Mezzogiorno agrario di Eugenio Azimonti." In *La federconsorzi tra stato liberale e fascismo*, edited by Severina Fontana, 108–27. Bari: Laterza.

Niccoli, Vittorio. 1897. *Prontuario dell'agricoltore: Manuale di agricoltura economia, estimo e costruzioni rurali*. Turin: UTET.

———. 1898. *Economia rurale, estimo e computisteria agraria*. Turin: UTET.

Nou, Joosep. 1967. *The Development of Agricultural Economics in Europe*. Uppsala: Almqvist and Wiksells.

Pallot, Judith. 2000. "Imagining the Rational Landscape in Late Imperial Russia." *Journal of Historical Geography* 26 (2): 273–91.

Patriarca, Silvana. 1996. *Numbers and Nationhood: Writing Statistics in Nineteenth-Century Italy*. Cambridge: Cambridge University Press.

Patrizi, Ugo. 1910. "La discussione sul bilancio dell'agricoltura." *Bollettino dell'Associazione delle cattedre ambulanti di agricoltura*, vol. 2, no. 6, p. 1.

Placanica, Augusto. 1987. "La capitale, il passato, il paesaggio: I viaggiatori come 'fonte' della storia meridionale." *Meridiana* 1:165–79.

Porter, Theodore. 1986. *The Rise of Statistical Thinking, 1820–1900*. Princeton: Princeton University Press.

———. 1995. *Trust in Numbers: The Pursuit of Objectivity in Science and Public Life*. Princeton: Princeton University Press.

———. 2009. "The Engineer and the Sage: Le Play's Quest for Social Renewal and the Reconstruction of Observation." History of Observation in Economics Working Paper Series, no. 2.

Prampolini, Antonio. 1981. *Agricoltura e società rurale nel Mezzogiorno agli inizi del '900*. Milan: Franco Angeli.

Rabinow, Paul. 1989. *French Modern: Norms and Forms of the Social Environment*. Chicago: University of Chicago Press.

Rogari, Sandro. 2002. *Mezzogiorno ed emigrazione*. Florence: CET.

Salvioni, Giovanni B. 1892. "Ai confini della statistica." *Rassegna di scienze sociali e politiche* 1:25–42, 95–107.

Schneider, Jane, ed. 1998. *Italy's "Southern Question": Orientalism in One Country*. Oxford, UK: Berg.

Scott, James C. 1999. *Seeing like a State: How Certain Schemes to Improve the Human Condition Have Failed*. New Haven: Yale University Press.

Serpieri, Arrigo. 1910. *Il contratto agrario e le condizioni dei contadini nell'alto milanese*. Milan: L'Ufficio Agrario della Società Umanitaria.

———. 1929. *Guida a ricerche di economia agraria*. Rome: INEA.

Valenti, Ghino. 1907. *Per l'ordinamento della statistica agraria in Italia: Relazione a S. E. il comm. Cocco-Ortu*. Rome: Bertero.

Observations in a Hostile Environment: Morgenstern on the Accuracy of Economic Observations

Marcel Boumans

> The world would, indeed, be even more of a miracle than it is if
> the influence of one set of errors offsets that of another set of errors so
> conveniently that we need not to bother much with the whole matter.
> —Oskar Morgenstern, *On the Accuracy*
> *of Economic Observations* (1963)

I am not aware of any other book in economics that discusses observations so extensively as Oskar Morgenstern's (1963a) *On the Accuracy of Economic Observations*, but even this book focuses much more on "accuracy" than on "observations" (as the title indicates). Morgenstern uses the term *accuracy* as synonymous with *reliability*, expressing how much (less) "error" is involved in the observations. The book is a 340-page detailed discussion of various sources of errors, how to deal with, to reduce, or—if at all possible—to avoid them.[1]

The sources of errors are legion. In an abstract of the first edition, Morgenstern (1951a) emphasized that the sources of errors are more numerous and the problem of treating them is far more serious in the social sciences than in the natural sciences.[2] "We have made detailed studies in

---

1. This 1963 edition is a "completely revised" version of the first 110-page edition published in 1950.

2. This abstract (Morgenstern 1951a) was presented at the "Conference on Linear Programming" in June 1949, whose proceedings were published as *Activity Analysis of Production and*

History of Political Economy 44 (annual suppl.) DOI 10.1215/00182702-1631806

Princeton of the kind of information currently used in economics and, as a rule, found the results absolutely shocking" (Morgenstern 1949, 239). For example, one has to deal with deliberate lies, hiding and suppression of information, and conflicts with the interests of private business. Moreover, observations are "most frequently made of *unique* phenomena. Sometimes the same event is observed simultaneously by different observers who are, however, seldom scientific observers" (Morgenstern 1951a, 284).

What the book shows is that a treatment of observations is a treatment of sources of observational errors, which can only be but a detailed discussion of idiosyncratic circumstances leading to these errors. The book does not present a "theory of observations" or a "theory of errors." If Morgenstern aimed at arriving at such a theory, he would have done something very opposite to the book's intentions, namely, to abstract from these idiosyncratic circumstances. A theory of error could arise only when observational errors were divorced from cause and effect, from the individual observer, from actual measurements, from time, and so forth (Klein 1997). Abstraction from these circumstances led to the mathematical theory of errors based on the works of Carl Friedrich Gauss, Adrien-Marie Legendre, and Pierre-Simon Laplace.[3] With key elements as the least squares method and the normal distribution, this theory is based on the assumption that by averaging the observations, the observational errors will cancel each other out. This is a history of creating objectivity: the elimination of personal judgment by mechanical rules of calculation. It was meant to "filter out local knowledge such as individual skill and experience, and local conditions such as this brand of instrument or that degree of humidity" (Daston 1995, 9).

Morgenstern's book, however, is not part of this history. To account for this book, another historical line should be drawn, a line going through field disciplines where a statistical mean of observations is meaningless, or lacks relevance. Although the method of least squares became the standard tool to deal with errors across many different disciplines, its legitimacy depends on the availability of a large number of independent observations, equally trustworthy so far as skill and care are concerned, and obtained

---

Allocation (Koopmans 1951). Linear programming and Wassily Leontief's input-output tables use "great masses of economic data" and require "enormously large numbers of operations" (Morgenstern 1951a, 283, 282). To make any progress, "a thorough exploration of the nature of the observations" (284) was needed. Morgenstern 1949 contained the very same message.

3. This history of a mathematical theory of errors is well exposed by Judy Klein (1997), L. E. Maistrov (1974), and Stephen Stigler (1986).

with precise instruments. In astronomy and geodesy, these requirements were no problem, but there are a lot of field disciplines where these requirements can never be met (see Boumans 2008).

Morgenstern (1963b) "condensed" the main concerns of the 1963 edition of *On the Accuracy* in an article "Qui Numerare Incipit Errare Incipit" ("He Who Begins to Count Begins to Err") in *Fortune*. The title of this article was the epigraph of this second edition. His concerns were broadly shared among people involved with social statistics.

In his presidential address to the American Statistical Association in 1963,[4] Raymond T. Bowman (1964a, 2) addressed, besides such issues as the improvement of federal statistics for use in economics and social analysis and the relationship of the American Statistical Association (ASA) to such improvements, the general development of statistical science: "I shall also argue, however, that the newer areas of statistical methodology and their development, and the application of such methodology to a variety of fields other than those of social aggregates, must be given attention." After giving a brief history of the ASA, he made more precise in what direction such statistical methodology should be advanced:

> It is appropriate at this point to note that some of the advances in statistical methods may not have the same relevance and significance to social science problems that they do for other more experimental sciences. The stress now being placed on sampling errors in official statistics is entirely appropriate. I am not sure, however, that the people who use and interpret data understand the sense in which sampling errors are useful as contrasted with other types of errors in the data. I believe, therefore, that we should give more attention to errors other than those of sampling. Errors arising from biases induced by falsehood or ignorance, or by the enumeration process, are important and real and warrant the research efforts of statisticians concerned with methodology to find ways to eliminate them. (15)

So Bowman agreed with Morgenstern's concern that economic statistics should be used with a fuller understanding of their errors and their relevance. But Morgenstern's message was, according to Bowman, too negative. In a comment on Morgenstern's article in *Fortune*, Bowman (1964b, 10) noted that recognizing and emphasizing the need for attention to error will not lead to "an uncritical discrediting" of economic and social statistics. According to Bowman, Morgenstern set up the natural sciences

---

4. Bowman was president of the American Statistical Association in 1963.

"as the ultimate standard by which the achievements of the social sciences should be judged" (10).

To evidence this view on Morgenstern's position, Bowman referred to a comment that Simon Kuznets made in a review of the 1950 edition of *On the Accuracy*. Kuznets, who had presented, on behalf of Morgenstern, the abstract of *On the Accuracy of Economic Observations* (1951a) at the twenty-sixth session of the International Statistical Institute (ISI), which took place in September 1949 in Bern, Switzerland (Morgenstern 1963a, v–vi), had also written a review of the book (Kuznets 1950b). Because of his involvement with the US national income accounts, his discussion on inaccuracies of economic observations suggested a different direction for dealing with errors than Morgenstern had proposed in his book.

Kuznets argued as follows: Economic statistics are products of changing social institutions and relate to changing historical reality. Errors in such data are, therefore, complex and largely unique historical phenomena, "which is but another way of saying that we are not dealing here with the results of designed, controlled experiments" (577). Lack of attention paid to errors in economic statistics compared "to those data in the natural sciences" may have been because of "a feeling of helplessness and a realization of the difficulties involved in dealing with them effectively" (577). Economic statistics have to be seen as records of institutional conventions rather than experimental conventions, "as defined under imaginatively controlled conditions" (577). Therefore Kuznets suggested dealing with accuracy by the rules of accounting. Moreover, in research or in policy-making, one does not rely on a single series but on a variety of data. So error evaluations are based on consensus of these various data. According to Kuznets, Morgenstern tends in his discussion "to set up the natural sciences as a feasible ideal" (579), so to understate that economic statistics are records of constantly changing institutional settings. But Kuznets also noted that Morgenstern is quite aware of the principal difference between natural and social data: "The reader might too easily conclude from Professor Morgenstern's discussion that the trouble lies largely in the lack of attention paid by economists and statisticians to the problem; and that increased attention would go far towards solving the problem, as it has been solved in the natural sciences. To such a conclusion the reviewer, and most likely also the author, would enter a strong objection" (579).

In his presidential address to the ASA,[5] Kuznets (1950a), like Morgenstern, made a similar distinction between observations in natural science

5. Kuznets was president of the American Statistical Association in 1949.

and in social science and its consequence for the reliability of the statistics: in natural science, "where controlled experiment is possible, the experimenter produces his own data—in accordance with his analytical goals," whereas social statistics are produced by various agencies, and "the production of the data is a *social*, not an individual, act" (2).[6] "The views of these agencies necessarily differ from those that would be entertained by a scientifically minded analyst, even one who happened to live at the same time and in the same place. Consequently, the supply of data is capricious as judged by any consistent and reasoned standard for scientific analysis" (Kuznets 1950b, 3). So the social origin, which is acquired in an experimentally uncontrolled way, of social statistics affects, according to Kuznets, their reliability.

Errors may arise from three different sources: lack of control by the respondent, lack of control from the collecting agency, and lack of control by the "analytically minded final user."[7] Errors from the respondents "may easily arise either because they deliberately falsify or because their knowledge is not full or accurate" (4). All three problems can be minimized in controlled experiments where the observations are made by the experimenter self.

So although both Bowman and Kuznets shared Morgenstern's concerns with respect to the reliability of social statistics, they did not share his pessimism about improving its reliability, because they did not share his natural science ideal. This ideal kept Morgenstern from developing a methodology for achieving more accuracy. "Professor Morgenstern is an eminent mathematical economist who has done service in calling the attention of less alert users to error in economic statistics. But I am disappointed that his book and article have contributed little to proposing the framework or the practical procedures which might advance the work now going forward on the reduction of statistical errors" (Bowman 1964b, 19).

This article provides a history of the treatment of observational errors where conditions cannot be controlled to reduce inaccuracies, in other words, the history of the treatment of errors in social statistics. The main focus is on Morgenstern's atypical position. It is atypical because he took the natural science approach as the ideal standard for dealing with errors, in contrast with contemporary social statisticians. His position is, how-

6. This remoteness of data from observations is also discussed by Emmanuel Didier (this volume) and Thomas Stapleford (this volume).

7. Federico D'Onofrio (this volume) discusses similar problems in agricultural statistics of early twentieth-century Italy.

ever, not atypical when one compares it with contemporary natural science perspectives. It appears that Morgenstern's view was attuned with the view of logical empiricism of the 1950s on the difference between natural science and social science.

1. A Life in Economic Statistics

Morgenstern had a lifelong interest in statistics. In a letter to Eve Burns (March 2, 1928) Morgenstern stated, "I deal extensively with the question of quantitative and qualitative methods and with the statistification [sic] of economic theory etc. . . . You say that you study science. This is very laudable, but again I want to warn you not to forget, that the method and aims of our social sciences are very much different from the natural sciences" (quoted in Mirowski 1992, 130). In 1931 he succeeded Friedrich Hayek as director of the Vienna Institute for Business Cycle Research, a position that he held until his move to America in 1938. He became an elected member of ISI in 1937 and maintained membership until 1973.

Morgenstern's early experiences with statistics were reported in his *Wirtschaftsprognose* (1928). In a review of this book, Arthur Marget (1929, 313) summarizes Morgenstern's methodology of economic forecasting as three propositions:

1. Forecast in economics by the methods of economic theory and statistics is "in principle" impossible.
2. Even if it were possible to develop a technique of economic forecasting, such a technique would be incomplete, by virtue of its necessary limitation to methods based on a knowledge of economics alone; it would therefore be incapable of application in actual situations.
3. Moreover, such forecasts can serve no useful purpose. All attempts to develop a formal technique for forecast are therefore to be discouraged.

Marget then distinguishes three "subpropositions" that support the first proposition:

1. The data with which the economic forecaster must deal are of such a nature as to make it certain that the prerequisites for adequate induction, that is, the application of the technique of probability analysis, must always be lacking.

2. Economic processes, and therefore the data in which their action is registered, are not characterized by a degree of regularity sufficient to make their future course amenable to forecast, such "laws" as are discoverable being by nature "inexact" and loose, and therefore unreliable.

3. Forecasting in economics differs from forecasting in all other sciences in the characteristic that, in economics, the very fact of forecast leads to "anticipations" which are bound to make the original forecast false. (313–14)

Marget's review summarizes not only a very early work by Morgenstern but also, as I show, the two themes he continued to work on in his later works on economic statistics:

1. The inadequacy of the statistical approach.
2. Economic laws are inexact and loose.

The problem of inaccuracies, however, was a topic Morgenstern had to deal with even more prominently when he was, from 1936 to 1946, a member of the Committee of Statistical Experts of the League of Nations.[8] As a member of this committee, he had to deal with the main problem of international statistics, namely, comparability. "Summarizing, we can state that statistics giving international comparisons of national incomes are among the most uncertain and unreliable statistics with which the public is being confronted. The area is full of complicated and unsolved problems, and in spite of the great efforts to overcome them, the progress is slow. This is a field where politics reigns supreme and where lack of critical appraisal is particularly detrimental" (Morgenstern 1963a, 282; see also 1963b, 173).

8. The Committee of Statistical Experts was established in 1928 to coordinate the unification and standardization of international statistics. This committee met once a year between 1931 and 1939. The committee members were not official delegates of their countries, but acted in their personal capacity. In addition to these members chosen from individual countries, the committee included one member from the International Labour Office and one from the International Institute of Agriculture. The convention contained no limitation as to the number of committee members, but during most of the committee's existence the number was ten. There were no official representatives from the ISI, although most committee members were also members of the ISI. Of the methodological studies made by the committee, six were published in the League of Nations series "Studies and Reports on Statistical Methods." For more details, see Nichols 1942.

For example, in the case of international foreign trade statistics, there are many reasons for divergence in the data relating to the same trade flow in statistics of partner countries. These reasons can be grouped under three headings (see Federico and Tena 1991, 261–63). The first is "unavoidable" differences arising between nonbordering countries because of the time and cost of transportation. The second is "structural" differences in compilation criteria, which could be eliminated by standardization. The third is actual errors, that is, cases where recorded data differed from the real flow; they can be classified as follows: (1) failure to record because of smuggling; (2) inaccurate recording following wrong declarations because of negligence or fraud; and (3) errors by statistical offices.

2. On the Accuracy of Economic Observations

A discussion of the accuracy of economic observations is a discussion of the specific nature of economic data, a subject that had "always occupied a central role" (Morgenstern 1963a, vii) in Morgenstern's work, but was discussed most extensively in *On the Accuracy of Economic Observations* (1963a).

The book's main message was that in comparison with data used in the natural sciences, economic and social statistics have additional peculiarities: "at least all sources of error that occur in the natural sciences also occur in the social sciences" (7). Therefore the treatment of errors in economic data has necessarily to be a commonsense approach.

The accuracy of economic observations cannot "be formulated according to a strict statistical theory for the simple reason that no such exhaustive theory is available for many social phenomena" (7). The reason for not being able to apply statistical theory is that the nature of economic data prevents "normal distribution of the observations, creating circumstances which cannot be readily treated according to classical notions of probable error" (13): see the epigraph that begins this essay. "The notion that errors do cancel out is widespread and when not explicitly stated, it appears as the almost inevitable argument of investigators when they are pressed to say why their statistics should be acceptable. Yet any statement that errors 'cancel,' neutralize each other's influence, has to be proved. Such proofs are difficult and whether a 'proof' is acceptable or not is not easy to decide" (Morgenstern 1963a, 53).

Morgenstern (1963a) listed ten sources for errors in economic statistics:

1. Lack of designed experiments
2. Hiding of information, lies
3. The training of observers
4. Errors from questionnaires
5. Mass observations
6. Lack of definition or classification
7. Errors of instruments
8. The factor of time
9. Observations of unique phenomena
10. Interdependence and stability of errors

These sources of errors were discussed by Morgenstern in comparison with natural science observations. Economic statistics are not the result of designed experiments, and besides they are often dependent on legal rather than economic definitions of processes. Moreover, even when planned, economic statistics are generally not gathered by "scientific observers." "A scientific observer is the astronomer at his telescope, the physicist recording the scatter of mesons, the biologist determining the hereditary behavior of some cells, etc.; all are themselves scientists; they do not operate through agents many times removed" (Morgenstern 1963a, 27).

Because of the enormous amount of data needed in economics, "scientific observations" would be physically impossible: "We cannot place technically trained economists or statisticians at the gates of factories in order to determine what has been produced and how much is being shipped to whom at what prices. We will have to rely on business records, kept by men and, increasingly, by machines, none of them are part of the ideally needed scientific set-up as such" (27).

What Morgenstern saw as a main source of errors in economics, namely, that most observations were nonscientific, was emphasized once more in his 1959 book *International Financial Transactions and Business Cycles*: "Economic statistics are—in the overwhelming majority of cases—*not scientific observations*. This is a point of primary significance. They are at best historical accounts; mostly they are byproducts of business operations or of administrative acts. They are, as a rule, badly collected by scientifically untrained minor officials at the customhouses, warehouses, on street markets, etc. In other words they are not the results of carefully set experiments, or of strictly controlled measurements as are astronomical observations" (9).

Many economic observations concern events that are unique and not reproducible. One is usually confronted with historical processes. In the case that a unique event is observed more or less simultaneously by several independent but differently placed observers, one has to consider the following problem:[9]

> It is then necessary to decide which one is to be trusted (with his own observational errors still remaining), or whether averages are to be taken, what kind of averages, etc. . . . The same problem occurs occasionally also in physics and astronomy, e.g., in the field of extraordinary sound propagation, the measurement of explosions, the accounts of eruption of volcanoes, spring tides, and the observation of novae. Statistical theory adequate for full consideration of all issues raised under these conditions apparently does not exist and will be difficult to develop. (Morgenstern 1963a, 48)

The most "profound" difference between natural science data and social science data, however, is that the latter are "frequently based on evasive answers and *deliberate lies* of various types. These lies arise, principally, from misunderstandings, from fear of tax authorities, from uncertainty about or dislike of government interference and plans, or from the desire to mislead competitors" (17).

Nature may hold back information, may be difficult to understand, but "she does not lie deliberately" (17). To clarify what he meant by this, Morgenstern refers to Albert Einstein's famous pronouncement: "Raffiniert is der Herr Gott, aber boshaft ist er nicht," inscribed on the mantle of a fireplace in Fine Hall in Princeton University, and which Morgenstern translated as follows: "The Lord God is sophisticated, but not malicious."[10]

---

9. It is the same problem as Galileo's discussion of the problem of determining the position of the new star of 1572. Twelve observations were made, all of which gave conflicting positions. The problem was expressed by the character Simplico: "I should judge that all were fallacious either through some fault of the computer or some defect on the part of the observations. At best I might say that a single one, and no more, might be correct, but I should not know which one to choose" (Galilei 1967, 281).

10. There exist various translations, of which Abraham Pais's is my favorite: "Subtle is the Lord, but malicious He is not." Pais (1982, 114) provides the following story that goes with it: Oswald Veblen, a professor of mathematics at Princeton and a nephew of Thorstein Veblen, wrote in 1930 to Albert Einstein, asking his permission to have this statement chiseled in the stone frame of the fireplace in the common room of Fine Hall. In his reply to Veblen, Einstein consented and gave the following interpretation of his statement: "Die Natur verbirgt ihr Geheimnis durch die Erhabenheit ihres Wesens, aber nicht durch List," translated as "Nature hides its secret because of its essential loftiness, but not by means of ruse."

"We observe here a significant variation in the structure of the physical and social sciences, provided it is true that nature is merely indifferent and not hostile to man's efforts to finding out truth—it certainly not being friendly" (18).

This was not a loose remark: in at least two research papers, one written in 1951 and the other in 1966, Morgenstern also referred explicitly to Nature's benevolence. In the 1951 paper "Prolegomena to a Theory of Organization" (Morgenstern 1951b), he introduces Nature's benevolence when discussing the signaling system of an organization. For a signaling system of an organization there is no distinction between event and signal: an event becomes known only through a signal, so for an organization they are inseparable. Morgenstern classified the events relevant to an organization into "events of the organization" and "other events" that are either "physical, i.e., produced by Nature" or "other organizations' choices" (55). "Events of Nature" are determinable if their probability distributions are known. But even if their probabilities cannot be estimated, Morgenstern emphasizes that "Nature is never malevolent, i.e., bent on impeding the organization in the pursuit of its aim" (55).

In a 1966 paper, Morgenstern elaborated in more detail "Nature's attitude" to discuss its epistemological consequences: while man's behavior is "mostly hostility," "Nature, however, may be benevolent, or at least indifferent, to us. Nature is generally not considered malevolent to man" (8).

> If nature is indifferent to man or even benevolent, we may proceed with our methods as we have done; but if there is a suspicion of hostility, our approach would become most difficult indeed. Instead of using pure, direct strategies in questioning nature we would have to develop different ideas, perhaps similar to those needed in social science, where often an indirect approach is needed in order to elicit the truth from the subjects studied and to avoid the contamination of the observer due to his immersion in the society he studies. (18)

While deliberate untrue statistics, according to Morgenstern, offer a most serious problem with broad ramifications in the realm of statistical theory, and the nature and consequences of such statistics are not explored sufficiently, he nevertheless mentioned that "a theory of 'sampling in a hostile environment' is now under development" (Morgenstern 1963a, 21). The development of such a theory was seen by Morgenstern in the context of game theory, the setup of a nonstrictly determined two-person game where both sides have to resort to mixed or "statistical strategies": "It is an ironic circumstance that in order to get good statistics, 'statistical strategies' may have to be used!" (22).

Morgenstern emphasized that to get good statistics, it is important "to understand that there is a fundamental difference (in the field of economics) between mere *data* and *observations*" (88). Observations are planned, designed, and guided by theory, such as, for example (and not necessarily), obtained in a controlled experiment. Data are merely obtained, gathered, and collected statistics even though this involves administrative planning.[11] To explain how he saw the difference between statistics, data, and observations and their relation to theory, Morgenstern provided the following figure:

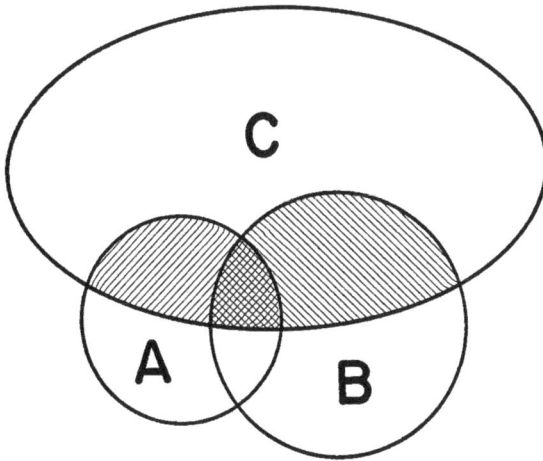

Figure 1 Morgenstern's (1963a) diagram showing the difference between data, information, description, and observation

A is the body of data in the above sense, **B** represents "other data, such as historical events or non-measurable data," and **C** is the theory "partly based on **A** and **B**." Morgenstern defines "scientific information" as the intersection of **A** and **C** ("quantitative information"), the intersection **B** and **C** ("description"), and the intersection of **A, B,** and **C** ("observation"). Scientific information is thus always related to theory. Most economic

11. For a closely related distinction between data and facts of phenomena, see Duarte and Hoover, this volume.

data, according to Morgenstern, are of the class **A** minus **C**: "These data as such tell no story" (89).

3. Data and Observations

While his 1950 book on observations did not further explore this distinction between data and observation, two years later Morgenstern provided a fuller account of this distinction in a paper on experiment and computation in economics. The paper was presented at an eight-week seminar, "The Design of Experiments in Decision Processes," which was held in Santa Monica to accommodate the game theorists and the experimenters associated with the RAND Corporation. This event has been viewed as the birthplace of experimental gaming (Innocenti and Zappia 2005, 80). Thirty-six papers were presented. A smaller number of the papers (nineteen) were published in *Decision Processes* (Thrall, Coombs, and Davis 1954), of which only six were reporting results of experiments (Roth 1993, 194). Both authors of *The Theory of Games* (1944) presented a paper, which did not appear in *Decision Processes*, and interestingly were about computers: John von Neumann's "Remarks on Chess-playing Automata" and Morgenstern's "Experiment and Computation in Economics." The latter paper was published in 1954 in a collection of papers edited by Morgenstern on economic activity analysis and linear programming (Roth 1993, 194), now with a slightly extended title: "Experiment and Large Scale Computation in Economics." Morgenstern discussed the relation of experiment to computation, that is, computational experiments, which did not involve, or at least not explicitly, decision processes or game theory.

Morgenstern's (1954) starting point is that experiment and computation are closely related. To clarify this relation, he distinguishes between two ways of using computations: first, as substitutes for experiments, and second, to generate new data. Elaborating on this, he subsequently distinguishes two types of experiments:

> (1) Experiments of the *first kind* are those where new general properties of a system are to be discovered by its manipulation on the basis of a theory of the system;

> (2) experiments of the *second kind* do not primarily rely on a theory but aim at the discovery of new, individual facts. (499)

Using these definitions, Morgenstern's main "thesis" was the following: "Every computation is equivalent to an experiment of the first kind and vice versa" (499). This equivalence was, according to Morgenstern, already emphasized by Ernst Mach through his notion of thought-experiment. "Its methods involve imagining conditions that differ from the known conditions and then attempting to identify the proper factor to which the imagined variations could be ascribed. This procedure consists in the drawing of implications and like other experiments may lead to the discovery of new facts" (Morgenstern 1954, 486). Thought-experiments were "vitally affected" by the new possibilities created by computers.

Subsequently, he also equated "planned and controlled observation or measurement" with experimentation: measurement is "at least an experiment of the second kind, but may be one of the first kind. This implies that there is no sharp dividing line between experiment and measurement" (506).

According to Morgenstern, there was no principal distinction between the physical experiment, "one in which physical reality is being subjected to desired conditions" (486), and planned observation. "The definition of an experiment as a process in which primarily a change in the direction of forces or the like is considered would definitely be too narrow if sensible at all. The largest part of scientific activity which is unmistakably experiment would be left out of account" (508). Experiment, observation, and measurement are so intricately interrelated that a distinction between observational sciences, such as astronomy, and experimental sciences, such as physics, is doubtful.

> It is true that the astronomer cannot change the course of stars and in that crude sense cannot make an experiment (i.e., make those observations and measurements which such interferences would make possible). But he does approach the multiple phenomena of the stars experimentally, for example by the use of telescopes, photography, spectroscopy, etc. That is, the experiment consists in approaching the basic phenomenon by means of numerous devices thereby improving its description. . . . The devices used in astronomy are in no way different from those applied to conditions in a laboratory. (507–8)

Likewise, in economics, planned observation is principally not different from experimentation:[12]

---

12. Cf. Warwick 1995, where mathematical calculation and precision measurement are seen as similar activities—because of the same involvement of instruments—in particular in acquiring reliable results.

It is enough to have to count anything at all (let alone the population of a whole nation) or to make a simple enumeration of the units of some good produced, in order to be confronted with the entire array of questions that have to be considered when setting up an experiment in the conventional sense. There must be "strict control" of as many parts of the process of counting as it is possible to achieve. When the counting requires more than a piece of paper and a pencil of one man, the social scientist, precisely as the physical scientist, is immediately involved with the interaction of men and machines of all kinds from the simplest abacus to electronic IBM equipment. All these involve as much "experiment" as anyone may wish to have to deal with, even though the name is not customarily attached to the procedure. (506–7)

For planned observations to be scientific, however, Morgenstern emphasized the essential role of theory: "If there were no theory behind the experiment but still the intent to discover general properties of a system, there would be no experiment at all, only a meaningless muddling" (502). In the first place, theory reduces the amount of required measurements: "The better the underlying theory the fewer will the direct experimental trials (measurements) have to be and the more weight can be thrown on the computations (at a given technology of computing)" (509). This specific role of theory was also mentioned in his 1959 book on international financial statistics: "*The amount of statistical data* needed depends on the state of the theory that can be used in the exploration of a field. The better the theory, i.e., the fewer the principles it uses, the fewer additional statistics are needed to test or advance it" (11).

In the second place, theory is needed to attach any meaning to data. Without theory, one would be "just looking" or "merely looking." In an early stage of science this may lead to data of a new kind. When the telescope and the microscope were invented, "all that mattered was to take these wonderful new instruments and to look, to look practically anywhere. Some phenomena would turn up, totally unsuspected, be they the moons of Jupiter or some tiny amoebae in a drop of water" (540). But "one would not get very far today either in astronomy or biology if one were merely to look around as one did then: now theory is guiding the direction of the search for facts and phenomena, sometimes for exceedingly esoteric and elusive ones" (540).

This situation where new instruments lead to data of a new kind by merely looking is, according to Morgenstern, the current situation of economics. Comparable to the telescope and the microscope, we have the "high-speed electronic computer." But this new possibility of process-ing enormous amounts of data is, according to Morgenstern, still "mere looking." Though "the field for 'mere looking' in biology having practi-cally vanished," in the "comparatively undeveloped state of economics the 'mere looking' by means of computers occupies still a very large field for the future" (542).

So to Morgenstern "scientific observation" meant experimentation of the first kind, that is, not merely looking around but theory-guided planned observation. But unfortunately—according to Morgenstern (1963a, 88)—in economics, however, theory is not exact, is never based solely on data; it is "constructed and invented" and to "a very high extent in addition related to non-constructively obtained material, such as personal experi-ence." This lack of exact theory in economics was the main reason for Morgenstern to be pessimistic about improving the accuracy of social sta-tistics. Morgenstern's view on scientific observation in relation to experi-mentation and theory reflected a more general view held at that time on experimentation and theories and their roles in science. So to better under-stand what Morgenstern meant by "scientific" in this sense and his reasons for pessimism, I move the focus to two persons who have written on this issue more explicitly than Morgenstern has done in his work: the two log-ical empiricists Olaf Helmer and Carl G. Hempel.

4. Economics as an Inexact Science

Olaf Helmer studied mathematics and logic at the University of Berlin, and he earned in 1934 his doctorate in mathematics at the University of Berlin with a dissertation begun under Hans Reichenbach.[13] Later that year he emigrated from Nazi Germany to Britain where he earned a sec-ond doctorate in philosophy at the University of London. In 1937 Helmer moved to the United States. In 1944–45 Helmer was drawn into mathe-matics-based work for the National Defense Research Council under the direction of John Williams, and in 1946, when Williams became one of the founding fathers of RAND Corporation, Helmer joined him there. Helmer stayed at RAND till 1968. The interaction between Helmer and Morgenstern started in 1948, when Helmer sent papers on game theory to Morgenstern.[14]

---

13. For more biographical details, see Rescher 2006.

14. For more details on this interaction, see Leonard 2010. I would like to thank Robert Leonard for pointing me to Helmer.

Helmer, together with Nicholas Rescher, wrote a paper "On the Epistemology of the Inexact Sciences," which appeared as a RAND working paper (1958) and was published the next year in *Management Science*. The RAND paper opens with a long quotation of Alfred Marshall's ([1890] 1930, 32) famous remarks on the tendencies of human action, of which the first two sentences are as follows: "The laws of economics are to be compared with the laws of the tides, rather than with the simple and exact law of gravitation. For the actions of men are so various and uncertain, that the best statement of tendencies, which we can make in a science of human conduct, must needs be inexact and faulty" (quoted in Helmer and Rescher 1958, iii). In Helmer's view, these inexact laws, which he calls "quasi-laws," require a different epistemology and methodology, namely, the systematic employment of expert judgment.

According to Robert Leonard (2010, 340), Helmer saw the need for this new epistemology because of his dissatisfaction with formal, mathematical game theory as a guide to strategy: "Some of these wargames were, in Helmer's terms, quite rigid: the strategies were chosen at the outset and, given the rules and the parameters, the consequences were calculated by computer. There was little room for interpretation and judgment after the button had been pushed, so to speak." Helmer was much more interested in games that "depended crucially on the exercise of both player judgement and umpire discretion—for example, in filtering intelligence or ruling out certain moves as unrealistic" (340).

These quasi-laws are generalizations, less-than-universal principles, that are neither fully nor even explicitly articulated or even articulable. The example Helmer and Rescher (1958, 32) gave is revealing: "One is unable to set down in sentential form everything that would have to be included in a full characterization of one's knowledge about a familiar room." I assume that the example of a "familiar room" is chosen intentionally. Ernst Mach (1959) uses this example to discuss sensations, which led to the famous drawing of his room, as he was lying on his sofa, presented to his left eye, indeed not in a sentential form.

The key argument in Helmer and Rescher's (1958, 30) paper is that in the inexact sciences, for example, economics and engineering, statistics is "not the sole and sometimes not even the main form of evidence":

> In fact the evidential use of such *prima facie* evidence must be tempered by reference to background information, which frequently may be intuitive in character and have the form of a vague recognition of underlying regularities, such as analogies, correlations, or other conformities.

For quasi-laws,

> statistical information matters less than knowledge of regularities in
> the behavior of people or in the character of institutions, such as tradi-
> tions and customary practices, fashions and mores, national attitudes
> and climate of opinion, institutional rules and regulations, group aspi-
> rations, and so on. (30)

For this kind of knowledge we need experts and expertise. The expert has

> at his ready disposal a large store of (mostly inarticulated) background
> knowledge and a refined sensitivity to its relevance, through the intui-
> tive application of which he is often able to produce trustworthy per-
> sonal probabilities regarding hypotheses in his area of expertness. (31)

Helmer's epistemology for the inexact sciences in which experts with intuitive and not-articulable knowledge have an essential role fit to a broader
discussion about whether social science needs a different epistemology
than that of natural science.

Hempel, also a student of Reichenbach, developed a closely related
account.[15] In a paper on the differences between methods in the natural
and social sciences, Hempel (1952) distinguishes between two kinds of
"imaginary experiment": the "intuitive" and the "theoretical." An imaginary experiment is aimed at anticipating the outcome of an experimental procedure that is just imagined. Anticipation is guided by past experience with particular phenomena and their regularities, and occasionally
by belief in certain general principles that are accepted as if they were
a priori truths. An imaginary experiment is called intuitive when

> the assumptions and data underlying the prediction are not made
> explicit and indeed may not even enter into the conscious process of
> anticipation at all: past experience and the—possibly unconscious—
> belief in certain general principles function here as suggestive guides
> for imaginative anticipation rather than as a theoretical basis for sys-
> tematic prediction. (76)

In contrast to the intuitive experiment, a "theoretical kind of imaginary
experiment"

---

15. According to Rescher (2006), Hempel and Helmer constitute the "middle generation"
of the Berlin School of Logical Empiricism because they both were students of Reichenbach.
For more biographical details and the interrelationships between Hempel and Helmer, see
Rescher 2006.

> presupposes a set of explicitly stated general principles—such as laws
> of nature—and it anticipates the outcome of the experiment by strict
> deduction from those principles in combination with suitable bound-
> ary conditions representing the relevant aspects of the experimental
> situation. (76)

This distinction between theoretical and intuitive is subsequently used
to distinguish between idealizations in economics, which are intuitive,
and those in the natural sciences:

> The corresponding "postulates" are not deduced, as special cases, from
> a broader theory which covers also the nonrational and noneconomic
> factors affecting human conduct. No suitable more general theory is
> available at present, and thus there is no theoretical basis for an appraisal
> of the idealization involved in applying the economic constructs to
> concrete situations. (82)

It should, however, be noted that Hempel did not explicitly account for
who should run the intuitive imaginary experiment, who should have the
appropriate economic intuitions.[16]

Because of the state of economics, that is, incomplete and inexact
theory, and the nature of economic phenomena, that is, quasi-lawful and
often unique, Morgenstern's (pessimistic) view was that scientific observation in the sense of theoretical experiment is hard to achieve in economics.
The alternative of "just looking," however, is too vulnerable for deceit;
therefore Morgenstern suggested "intuitive experiments" run by scientific
observers, having inexact but appropriate knowledge. So in a field that
does not have explicit and exact theories, a scientific observation is an
observation made by an expert having intuitive knowledge of the relevant
phenomena.

When drafting the outlines for a theory of "sampling in a hostile
environment," Morgenstern had a specific role for "scientific observers"
in mind.[17] As a member of the Committee of Statistical Experts of the
League of Nations, he had to deal with hostile governments, like that of
Nazi Germany in the 1930s and later, being affiliated with RAND in the
1940s and 1950s, with those of the Soviet Union and China.

---

16. An example of an approach where experts explicitly are being used to run imaginary
experiments, that is, a combination of the approaches of Helmer and Hempel, is the approach
developed in the 1990s by Roger Cooke (see Boumans 2009).

17. For a nice example of observations in a hostile environment, where the observer therefore has to go undercover, see Rutherford, this volume.

A special problem is offered by the Soviet Union. The statistics of that country are exceedingly difficult to assess, but it is generally known that they are seldom what they purport to be. There has been a great deal of deliberate doctoring of statistics at many levels, in order, for example, to make production results appear better than they are or to receive assignments of raw materials that would not otherwise be allocated. Even Khrushchev has repeatedly referred to falsified accounts of various activities, especially in farming, and there is no reason to assume that statistical practices were better in Stalin's time. (Morgenstern 1963b, 173; see also 1963a, 280)

It is therefore not surprising to see that in this sphere of distrust more people saw the importance of having scientific observers to assess data coming from these hostile environments. The most telling example is Reginald Victor Jones, "father of scientific intelligence." The main task of an intelligence agency is to understand how to assess information, particularly when fraud or deception may be expected to be involved. Jones advocated the role of scientific experts in intelligence. To underline the necessity of scientists being involved, Jones referred to Francis Bacon's (1869, 80) analogy between spies and scientists: "And therefore as secretaries and spials of princes and states bring in bills for intelligence, so you must allow the spials and intelligences of nature to bring in their bills; or else you shall be ill advertised."[18] The function of an expert is that of a spy on the laws of nature and the limits that they impose on a particular line of development. "Because, however, of the fallibility of individual observations—either on account of inexperience or stress in the agent making the observations, or of deliberately false information planted by the opponent—the scientific method has to take also into account those parts of legal and historical method which apply to the consideration of evidence" (Jones 1956, 348).

5. Conclusions

According to Morgenstern, for an observation to be scientific, it should be planned, designed, and guided by theory. He compared scientific observation with experimentation, but in contrast to physics, in economics the theoretical guidelines are inexact and more intuitive. Because economic theory is not as developed as physics, we need experts to assess the supplied economic statistics.

---

18. A spial stood for a spy (Bacon 1869, 357).

These experts are necessary for another reason, beyond the inexactness of economic laws. Morgenstern, when discussing the accuracy of economic information, is well aware of the distinction between observations of nature and observations of business, institutions, and governments. Observations of natural phenomena can be inaccurate, but the only one to blame for this is the observer: nature does not lie. In contrast, a human agency providing information can also be the cause of inaccuracies, sometimes deliberately. A scientific observer, however, because of his or her knowledge of the "laws" of economics, may be able to see whether a picture based on economic data is diverging from a "natural" picture.

The history of the theory of errors is a history in which the errors were attributed elegant bell-shaped characteristics that enabled mathematization and the creation of objectivity. Observations can be made by laypeople, because personal biases can easily be neutralized mathematically. The underlying assumption is that nature is benevolent. The world of the 1940s and 1950s, however, was hostile and more secretive. Attributing simple and nice characteristics would not do. It required the development of a theory of sampling in an unfriendly environment. Getting information about such a world asks for scientists who are experts of hidden and tacit regularities and are able to distinguish between counterfeit and fact. A history of observation covering Morgenstern's work is a history on subjectivity, scientific intuitions, and idiosyncrasy.

References

Bacon, Francis. 1869. *Of the Advancement of Learning*. Edited by W. A. Wright. Oxford: Clarendon.

Boumans, Marcel. 2008. "Measurement and Error Problems (1800–1900): Buys Ballot and Landré's Critique on the Method of Least Squares." In *The Statistical Mind in Modern Society: The Netherlands, 1850–1940*. Vol. 2 of *Statistics and Scientific Work*, edited by I. H. Stamhuis, P. M. M. Klep, and J. G. S. J. van Maarseveen, 179–97. Amsterdam: Aksant.

———. 2009. "Observations of an Expert." History of Observation in Economics Working Paper 4, University of Amsterdam.

Bowman, Raymond, T. 1964a. "The American Statistical Association and Federal Statistics Presidential Address." *Journal of the American Statistical Association* 59 (305): 1–17.

———. 1964b. Comments on "Qui Numerare Incipit Errare Incipit" by Oskar Morgenstern. *American Statistician* 18 (3): 10–20.

Daston, Lorraine. 1995. "The Moral Economy of Science." *Osiris* 10:2–24.

Federico, Giovanni, and Antonio Tena. 1991. "On the Accuracy of Foreign Trade Statistics (1909–1935): Morgenstern Revisited." *Explorations in Economic History* 28:259–73.

Galilei, Galileo. 1967. *Dialogue concerning the Two Chief World Systems—Ptolemaic and Copernican*. Translated by Stillman Drake. 2nd ed. Berkeley: University of California Press.

Helmer, Olaf, and Nicholas Rescher. 1958. "On the Epistemology of the Inexact Sciences." P-1513, October 13, RAND.

———. 1959. "On the Epistemology of the Inexact Sciences." *Management Science* 6 (1): 25–52.

Hempel, Carl G. 1952. "Symposium: Problems of Concept and Theory Formation in the Social Sciences." In *Science, Language, and Human Rights*, 65–86. Philadelphia: University of Pennsylvania Press.

Innocenti, Alessandro, and Carlo Zappia. 2005. "Thought- and Performed Experiments in Hayek and Morgenstern." In *The Experiment in the History of Economics*, edited by Philippe Fontaine and Robert Leonard, 71–97. Oxon: Routledge.

Jones, Reginald Victor. 1956. "Scientific Intelligence." *Research—a Journal of Science and Its Applications* 9:347–52.

Klein, Judy L. 1997. *Statistical Visions in Time: A History of Time Series Analysis, 1662–1938*. Cambridge: Cambridge University Press.

Koopmans, Tjalling. 1951. *Activity Analysis of Production and Allocation: Proceedings of a Conference*. New York: Wiley.

Kuznets, Simon. 1950a. "Conditions of Statistical Research." *Journal of the American Statistical Association* 45 (249): 1–14.

———. 1950b. Review of *On the Accuracy of Economic Observations*. *Journal of the American Statistical Association* 45:576–79.

Leonard, Robert. 2010. *Von Neumann, Morgenstern, and the Creation of Game Theory: From Chess to Social Science, 1900–1960*. Cambridge: Cambridge University Press.

Mach, Ernst. 1959. *The Analysis of Sensations*. New York: Dover.

Maistrov, L. E. 1974. *Probability Theory: A Historical Sketch*. Translated and edited by S. Kotz. New York: Academic.

Marget, Arthur W. 1929. "Morgenstern on the Methodology of Economic Forecasting." *Journal of Political Economy* 37 (3): 312–39.

Marshall, Alfred. (1890) 1930. *Principles of Economics*. 8th ed. London: Macmillan.

Mirowski, Philip. 1992. "What Were von Neumann and Morgenstern Trying to Accomplish?" In *Towards a History of Game Theory*, edited by E. Roy Weintraub. *HOPE* 24 (supplement): 113–47.

Morgenstern, Oskar. 1928. *Wirtschaftsprognose: Eine Untersuchung ihrer Voraussetzungen und Möglichkeiten*. Vienna: Springer.

———. 1949. "Input-Output Analysis and Its Use in Peace and War Economies." *American Economic Review* 39 (3): 238–40.

———. 1950. *On the Accuracy of Economic Observations*. Princeton: Princeton University Press.

———. 1951a. "The Accuracy of Economic Observations." In Koopmans 1951, 282–84.

———. 1951b. "Prolegomena to a Theory of Organization." RM-734, December 10, RAND.

———. 1954. "Experiment and Large Scale Computation in Economics." In *Economic Activity Analysis*, edited by O. Morgenstern, 484–549. New York: Wiley.

———. 1959. *International Financial Transactions and Business Cycles*. National Bureau of Economic Research Book Series in Business Cycles. Princeton: Princeton University Press.

———. 1963a. *On the Accuracy of Economic Observations*. 2nd ed. Princeton: Princeton University Press.

———. 1963b. "Qui Numerare Incipit Errare Incipit." *Fortune* 68:142–44, 173–74, 178, 180.

———. 1966. "Nature's Attitude and Rational Behavior." Econometric Research Program Research Paper 13, Princeton University.

Nichols, Charles K. 1942. "The Statistical Work of the League of Nations in Economic, Financial, and Related Fields." *Journal of the American Statistical Association* 37 (219): 336–42.

Pais, Abraham. 1982. *"Subtle Is the Lord . . ." The Science and the Life of Albert Einstein*. Oxford: Oxford University Press.

Rescher, Nicolas. 2006. "The Berlin School of Logical Empiricism and Its Legacy." *Erkenntnis* 64:281–304.

Roth, Alvin E. 1993. "The Early History of Experimental Economics." *Journal of the History of Economic Thought* 15:184–209.

Stigler, Stephen M. 1986. *The History of Statistics: The Measurement of Uncertainty before 1900*. Cambridge: Harvard University Press.

Thrall, Robert M., Clyde H. Coombs, and Robert L. Davis, eds. 1954. *Decision Processes*. New York: Wiley.

Von Neumann, John, and Oskar Morgenstern. 1944. *Theory of Games and Economic Behavior*. Princeton: Princeton University Press.

Warwick, A. 1995. "The Laboratory of Theory or What's Exact about the Exact Sciences?" In *The Values of Precision*, edited by M. N. Wise, 311–51. Princeton: Princeton University Press.

Observing Attitudes, Intentions, and Expectations (1945–73)

José M. Edwards

The economic use of data on attitudes, intentions, and expectations is an interesting vehicle for analyzing some of the multiple purposes of observation in economics. However, and although the history of the collection and analysis of these kinds of facts has been greatly influenced by the economic effects of the Great Depression and World War II, it has been studied mainly by historians of psychology (Herman 1995), statistics (Converse 1987; Desrosières 1998), market research (Arvidsson 2004), and social studies (Bulmer, Bales, and Sklar 1991; Igo 2007).[1] According to that literature, the analysis of public opinions and attitudes began during the nineteenth century, and its history is characterized, first, by a turning point during the 1930s with the "scientific measurement" of subjective outcomes (Converse 1987, 125), and second, by an upsurge during World War II, usually "treated as 'Year One' in the history of government and

I want to thank Harro Maas, Mary Morgan, Wade Hands, Annie Cot, and two anonymous referees for their comments on earlier drafts of this essay. I also thank Avi Cohen, Teresa Tomás Rangil, Tiago Mata, Craufurd Goodwin, Marcel Boumans, and the participants at the 2011 *HOPE* conference for valuable comments and discussion on topics related to this essay.

1. J. M. Converse's *Survey Research in the United States* (1987) is focused on the kinds of surveys that are the object of this essay (i.e., gathering subjective data). For a methodological account of the economic use of subjective facts, see Boulier and Goldfarb 1998; for accounts on the prehistory of the academic use of surveys and the development of sampling methods, see Bulmer et al. 1991, Desrosières 1991, and Duncan and Shelton 1992; for a focus on the history of social surveys, see Bateman 2001; and for accounts of surveys related to labor issues and poverty, see Rutherford, this volume, and Stapleford, this volume.

History of Political Economy 44 (annual suppl.) DOI 10.1215/00182702-1631815
Copyright 2012 by Duke University Press

behavioral expertise" (Herman 1995, 53). These two features relate to the two purposes of observation that are discussed in this essay: the use of attitudinal data for "understanding" aggregate consumption and their use for "predicting" durable goods sales as distinguished by George Katona (1901–1981), the main character in this study.

The following text explores a small part of the history of the economic use of subjective facts by presenting Katona's views and focusing on three different survey programs sponsored by the US Federal Reserve from the mid-1940s to the early 1970s: the Survey of Consumer Finances (SCF) conducted by the University of Michigan Survey Research Center (SRC), and the Surveys of Consumer Buying Intentions and Consumer Buying Expectations (SCBI and SCBE) conducted by the US Census Bureau. The failure of these programs contrasts with the success of the Surveys of Consumer Attitudes (SCAs) conducted by the SRC since the early 1950s and used to construct the widely used Index of Consumer Sentiment (ICS).

As shown below, the development of these surveys was intertwined with discussions about the purpose of the observations. According to Katona and his associates at the Economic Behavior Program of the SRC, sample interview surveys should be used to gather "clusters" of attitudes and financial variables in order to "understand" consumer behavior as suggested by gestalt-type theories of learning (Katona 1940). This view, which dominated the design of the SCF from the mid-1940s through the 1960s, was challenged by the SCBI and the SCBE. Opposing Katona's aim of understanding consumer behavior, these two surveys were designed to forecast durable goods sales.

Section 1 begins by presenting the theoretical underpinnings of the SCF. It introduces Katona's early work in his attempt to develop a program of "economic psychology" out of the analysis of interviews exploring the attitudes of businessmen and consumers. It presents Katona's original incursions into the analysis of economic subjects, as his interests switched from Gestalt psychology (*Organizing and Memorizing*, 1940) to the analysis of wartime inflation (*War without Inflation*, 1942) and the effects of price controls (*Price Control and Business*, 1945). It then focuses on the SCF as designed by Katona and his associates at the SRC (1946) and shows that the purpose of that project was to observe interactions between attitudes and financial variables, in order to explain aggregate consumption in the terms of Katona's gestalt theory of learning (i.e., not as an independent phenomenon but as part of more general configurations or "clusters").

Section 2 claims that, ironically for a psychologist of learning by understanding, Katona was arguably misunderstood by economists who focused on other aspects of consumption. During the mid-1950s, a consultant committee on consumer survey statistics evaluated the SCF at the request of the Federal Reserve Board. However, according to the committee's criteria, the SCF should be evaluated by testing the individual predictive power of the different attitudes, intentions, and expectations. The differences between the two views led to a controversy. The analysis of "clusters of attitudes" (SCF), on the one hand, and of "buying intentions" (SCBI) and "purchase probabilities" (SCBE), on the other, resulted in two different approaches, neither of which was successful.

The final section compares the history of the failure of the Federal Reserve programs presented throughout the essay to the success of the SCAs conducted also by the SRC since 1951, but under the auspices of private institutions like the Ford Foundation. Unlike the other survey programs, the SCAs were designed to gather general information on "consumer optimism and confidence" (Mueller 1963, 899) that served as raw data for producing the ICS. Interestingly, and despite Katona's downplaying of its importance, the ICS became "one of the most closely watched indicators of future economic trends" (Curtin 2004, 136).

1. From Gestalt Psychology to Katona's Program of Behavioral Economics

Katona's Gestalt Theory of Teaching and
Learning by Understanding

Basic knowledge of Katona's academic and professional background is necessary to clarify the main features of the project that generated the SCF. Born in Hungary in 1901, Katona moved to Germany in 1919, graduating in 1921 with a degree in experimental psychology from the University of Göttingen. During the 1920s and early 1930s he worked as an economic journalist in a context of hyperinflation that could not be accounted for by standard tools of economic analysis (Wärneryd 1982; Curtin 1983). After immigrating to the United States in 1933, Katona worked as an economic adviser for European investors in New York. It was only a serious illness that forced him back to academic work in psychology (1936–40) with the aid of a grant obtained by Max Wertheimer, his "beloved teacher and friend" who was also one of the founding fathers of the gestalt movement (Katona 1972, 13).

Organizing and Memorizing (1940), Katona's main contribution to the psychology of learning, was part of the gestalt movement in America, and as such it challenged the dominant learning theories of that time that were based on "behavioristic associationism" (Katona 1940, 25).[2] Unlike the behaviorist-type theories that used conditioning as "the fundamental principle of learning" (25), Katona thought that subject matter should be taught "as parts of whole processes" rather than as independent elements (26).

> The application of gestalt principles to the psychology of learning will lead to a fuller characterization of the learning process. We shall endeavor to accomplish this by analyzing the results, qualities, and laws of that kind of learning which consists of understanding organized wholes. (31)

The main argument of *Organizing and Memorizing* was that "learning by memorizing" was a "different process from learning by understanding" (53), and its main result was that pupils "should learn to learn by understanding" rather than "merely learn to memorize" (260). As shown below, Katona systematically applied this concept of understanding to economic subjects: in his New School course on the psychology of the war economy (1940–42), in his price control studies at the Cowles Commission (1942–44), and in the inception of the SCF at the US Department of Agriculture (1945).

From Psychology to Economics

War without Inflation (1942), Katona's first academic attempt to apply his theory of learning to economic subjects, came out of his economics and psychology course taught at the New School. It analyzed wartime inflation in the United States and stated that inflation was "not the auto-

---

2. With the advent of the Nazi regime in 1933, the departure of the gestalt theory leaders Max Wertheimer, Wolfgang Köhler, and Kurt Koffka led German experimental psychology to the United States at a time when behaviorism was "too new, too successful, too exciting an enterprise not to fight back spiritedly against the foreign invaders" (Mandler 2007, 143). According to historians of psychology, the gestalt approach was strongly resisted by American scholars, and the movement ended up being no more than a group of scholars who "might have fallen apart much faster had it not been held together by the common experience of the immigration" (163). The influence of the German approach became significant only in the long run, as it contributed to the "brew of information-processing, cognitive, and constructivist psychologies that made up the 'cognitive revolution' within a generation of their arrival" (164). For a detailed account of the reception of the main gestalt psychologists in America, see Sokal 1984.

matic effect of economic factors" (Katona 1942, 4). For Katona, the economic account was based on "an incomplete conception of the origins of inflation" (4). Instead of exclusively quantifying aggregates like "available income," "supply of civilian goods," and "armament production," Katona claimed that economists should incorporate elements such as the past inflationary experiences of the public and its understanding of the whole wartime setting:

> More money in the hands of the people, less merchandise in the stores, these are stimuli to which sellers as well as buyers respond. How they respond depends on many factors, among which are the past experience of the responding persons, the setting of the stimuli, and the way in which the stimuli are understood. . . . different behaviors in the same objective situation, are possible. This does not mean that there are no scientific laws of human behavior, but only that these laws are more complex than the mechanistic and invariable connection between a specific stimulus and a specific response. (6–7)[3]

Katona considered variations in economic aggregates as conditions for "potential inflation" (7) that would lead to "actual inflation" only if supported by "inflationary expectations" (14). Besides the usual price control policies of taxation and price-fixing, Katona thought that it was necessary for the authority to make the public understand the purposes of such measures. In line with his psychological theory of learning by understanding, Katona argued that governments should instruct people by playing active roles as announcers: "Government publicity . . . must be directed toward achieving the coöperation of the public. For that purpose the material must be presented to the people in such a way that they will be able to make up their own minds. The objective, then, is not to elicit thoughtless acceptance but to encourage thinking, to the end that the essential points of the situation may be grasped" (159–60).[4]

At this point, the main purpose of Katona's recommendations was to improve the effectiveness of wartime economic policies by encouraging a double understanding: not only of the attitudes, intentions, and

3. This argument is obviously related to the distinction advanced by gestalt psychologists between their own work and the behaviorist approach.

4. Wartime inflation, he claimed, was largely the outcome of expectations formed by the government and the media: "Government officials, politicians, newspaper editors and radio commentators have supplied much material for the creation of a framework from which inflationary expectations can be derived. . . . Without the existence of certain economic and political facts accounting for them, enduring expectations of inflation cannot emerge" (Katona 1942, 15).

expectations of the public but also of the purposes of the price control policies. The psychological approach was presented as a way to produce that missing and valuable information:

> To determine the best ways of insuring public coöperation with specific regulations and appeals, more accurate information about the attitudes of various population groups is desirable. Before private business enterprises introduce a new product or policy, psychological studies—market research—are frequently undertaken to determine the probable reception, as well as the best possible method for obtaining one. Government should be at least as much interested in the response to its measures as is business. (172)

Price Controls

From 1942 to 1944 Katona became a research associate at the Cowles Commission involved in a project organized by Theodore Yntema and supervised by Jacob Marschak, who was also a former member of the New School. The aim of that study was to analyze the "actions of American businessmen as affected by price regulations and other wartime conditions" by applying "psychological methods to economic research" (Katona 1945, viii).

Katona's monograph aimed not only at collecting data to support war planning but also at testing the method of interviews as a "legitimate tool of economic research" (5).[5] He used questionnaires designed to make businessmen interact with qualified interviewers who were granted a "relatively wide freedom" (8), and the study produced, for the most part, data on costs and prices, the analysis of which gave information about different pricing procedures for different types of business (i.e., "nonfood retailers," "nonfood wholesalers," "nonfood manufacturers," "food retailers," and "food processors and wholesalers"). The pricing procedures were divided into three categories: "direct price increases, indirect price increases, and price stabilities" (31).

As shown in figure 1, the pricing policies (A, B, C) differed for the different types of business. Further analysis of the data, however, showed that

5. For an analysis of different historical configurations of the collection of survey data, which are related to the different qualification degrees required in the interviewing process, see Stapleford, this volume. See also Stapleford's (2009) study on the production and analysis of cost-of-living statistics and the ensuing debates between the US Bureau of Labor Statistics and labor organizations during the 1940s for a complementary account of the importance of developing statistics for price control, especially during and after World War II.

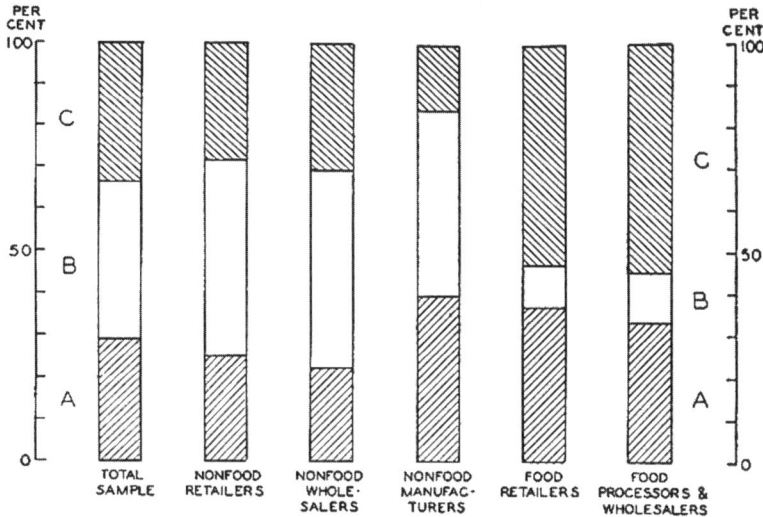

FIGURE 5. FREQUENCY OF DIFFERENT PRICING PROCEDURES
(in per cent of samples)

Procedure A: Keeping prices stable   B: Raising prices indirectly
C: Raising prices directly.

Figure 1 Graph from Katona's *Price Control and Business* showing different pricing procedures (A, B, C) for different kinds of businesses. Reproduced with the permission of the Cowles Foundation, which retains all rights under the original copyright

the pricing policies varied also within categories, and even for businessmen facing the same regulation conditions. To explain such differences, Katona turned to the analysis of attitudes that originated his program of economic psychology: "We must go further in the study of psychological factors by analyzing the businessmen's attitudes toward price control. Without them the list of variables that influenced pricing actions cannot be complete because the pricing decisions of different firms differed greatly even where the objective conditions (given type of regulation, certain supply and demand conditions, etc.) appeared to be the same" (157).[6]

Attitudes toward price controls were classified into three categories (cooperative, intermediate, hostile). Figure 2 shows the direct relation

---

6. For a methodological discussion about the subjectivity of different types of survey data, see Boulier and Goldfarb 1998.

	Fully Coopera-tive	Inter-mediate	Hostile	Total Number of Inter-views
ASSOCIATION BETWEEN ATTITUDES AND PRICING PROCEDURES				
A. ("Stability") --------------	57	62	6	125
B. ("Indirect Increases") ------	23	104	22	149
C. ("Direct Increases") -------	4	72	73	149
Total Number of Interviews--	84	238	101	423

Figure 2 Graph from Katona's *Price Control and Business* relating different pricing procedures (A, B, C) to different attitudes of businessmen toward price controls (Fully Cooperative, Intermediate, Hostile). Reproduced with the permission of the Cowles Foundation, which retains all rights under the original copyright

obtained between the attitudes and the pricing procedures: the more cooperative the attitudes, the more stable the prices.

Because the attitudes explained pricing procedures that affected the relative positioning of the firms, Katona concluded that the analysis of subjective facts was a worthwhile approach for studying economic phenomena. In line with his previous research, he concluded that the "understanding by both businessmen and consumers of the need for and the purposes of price controls" was among the main factors behind the success of the price regulation plan (217). The failure to "evoke full understanding of the functions of price control" was indeed claimed to be "largely responsible for occasional waves of hoarding and inventory accumulation and the resulting price increases" (221).

Observing Attitudes at the Survey Research Center

Right after his price control studies, Katona moved to the Division of Program Surveys of the US Department of Agriculture in 1945 where he directed the Survey of Liquid Asset Holdings, Spending and Saving (1946).[7] The aim of that survey, which used the sample interview method,

7. The first (and only) national Survey of Liquid Asset Holdings, Spending and Saving was conducted under the auspices of the Federal Reserve Board. The senior officials of the Division

was to collect both financial data on "individual economic units" and their "motives for, attitudes toward, and expectations of saving" (Katona and Likert 1946, 197). Its main purpose was to explore the household's plans for spending the considerable amounts saved during World War II (i.e., war bonds), which was one of the main uncertainties arising after the war's close, especially for Federal Reserve analysts studying inflation and willing to "assess the probability that consumers would attempt to purchase large amounts of consumer durable goods" (Likert 1972, 4).

But the postwar period was also characterized by the migration of survey research from government agencies to universities.[8] In 1946 Katona cofounded the SRC at the University of Michigan where the survey of liquid assets turned into the survey of consumer finances (SCF).[9] The design of the SCF (1947–71) was clearly influenced by Katona's background as a theorist of learning by understanding.[10] It encouraged the respondents' understanding of the questionnaires (Katona and Likert 1946, 197), and for that reason, it included personal questions that were initially discarded by the Federal Reserve, which was "not interested in the collection of data measuring consumer intentions to buy durable goods" but in financial variables only (Likert 1972, 5). That attitude changed, however, after Katona's successful challenge to forecasts showing that the US economy was headed for a "serious recession" in 1949 (5). Katona's prediction "impressed the [Federal Reserve's] research staff sufficiently so that, when planning the 1950 study, they asked to have the consumer intentions data made available to them as soon as possible" (7).

---

of Program Surveys were Angus Campbell, Katona, and Rensis Likert. It must be pointed out that the US Department of Agriculture (USDA) also hosted one of the main training programs in sampling techniques. For an account of the USDA graduate school training in statistics and economics (1921–1945), see Rutherford, forthcoming.

8. For an account of the migration of survey research from government agencies to universities like Columbia (Bureau of Applied Social Research), Michigan (Survey Research Center), and Chicago (National Opinion Research Center), see Converse 1987, 239–379.

9. The SRC was founded by Campbell, Katona, and Likert, and completed the first annual SCF in 1947. Sponsored by the Federal Reserve Board, the SCF was systematically (though only partly) published in the *Federal Reserve Bulletin*. The original version of the SCF was discontinued in 1971, which coincides with Katona's retirement year. For an account of the current design of the SCF, as conducted since 1992 by the National Opinion Research Center at the University of Chicago, see Kennickell and Starr-McCluer 1994.

10. For accounts of the design and inception of the SCF, see Katona and Likert 1946, 197–98, and Curtin 2004. For a detailed account of the different stages involved in this kind of survey research, see Didier, this volume.

It is worth noting that the Federal Reserve staff was impressed by the SCF potential as a forecasting tool, but not that interested in the role given to it by Katona (i.e., as a composing part of the SRC's Economic Behavior Program). Rather than merely collect consumer intentions data, the idea behind the design of the SCF was that, unlike "routine behavior," "genuine decisions" were made simultaneously by large numbers of both businessmen and consumers. The importance of empirically analyzing attitudes was justified by the fact that attitudes "bringing forth new economic decisions [were] not an everyday occurrence" (Katona 1946, 53). Attitudes tended to "change infrequently, radically, and simultaneously" for an important part of the population (54), and consequently, a theory of general attitude change was essential to explain shifts in aggregate consumption.

Katona's findings supposedly demonstrated that the "economics without psychology" approach was insufficient for studying aggregate consumer behavior. He claimed that just like psychology, "the study of behavior" (Katona 1947, 455), economic psychology, "the study of economic behavior," should be an empirical discipline producing "information concerning attitudes, motives, plans, intentions and expectations" to be used in conjunction with "micro-economic data on the distribution of income, savings, and liquid asset holdings" (456). The main aim of the SCF was to "determine the relation of attitudinal and financial data" (456) to supplement (not supplant) the analysis of traditional economic variables (459). It was not designed as a forecasting tool providing "measures of what will happen" but as a way "to obtain as complete an account as possible of the psychological field as it prevails at a given moment" (Katona 1951, 174).[11]

In his *Psychological Analysis of Economic Behavior* (1951), Katona presented the SCF as part of a research program that challenged the "widespread use" of equations like "$C = fY$ or $S = fY$" (172). Interestingly, Katona's critique of the use of consumption functions paralleled wider economic debates on the use of Keynesian-type approaches for forecasting postwar demand. Following Arthur Smithies (1945), Jacob Mosak (1945), and, especially, W. S. Woytinsky (1946), who claimed that there was "no positive correlation between the savings rate and real income"

---

11. It was also during the early 1950s that the Surveys of Consumer Attitudes (SCAs), discussed in the final section of this essay, began to be collected by the SRC on request of private institutions. Unlike the SCF, the SCAs were straightforwardly conceived as a way to predict trends in consumption.

(Woytinsky 1946, 10), there were many different attempts to decompose aggregate data on income, consumption, and savings, as, for instance, between different kinds of population groups (Bean 1946; Brady and Friedman 1947) and time periods of "prosperity" and "depression" (Friend 1946; Bennion 1946). Those studies, which aimed at accounting for apparently inconsistent observations of family budget data, generated a controversy about using regression formulas to estimate consumption.[12]

While the early economic discussion on the consumption function revolved around the "relative" versus "absolute" income interpretations (Duesenberry 1949; Tobin 1951; Reid 1952), the debate then generated an "intellectual tension between a liquidity and a wealth interpretation of income as the primary determinant of consumption" (Tobin 1972, 39). That tension led to adjustments in the mainstream approach, as evidenced in Franco Modigliani and Richard Brumberg's ([1954] 2005) "life-cycle" and Milton Friedman's (1957) "permanent income" hypotheses. Interestingly, none of the economic views in question were endorsed by Katona, who entered the dispute by bringing "quite a different bag of tools and insights from those of the technical economists" (Tobin 1972, 37).[13]

Katona's critique of the economic approach was directed against the exclusive use of regression formulas for estimating consumption. Such a method, he claimed, implied "projecting past relationships" to the analysis of current outcomes (Katona 1951, 172). Because shifts in aggregate consumption could not be explained without taking attitude changes into account, it was impossible to get "a correct picture of future relationships" by using regression formulas (172). Katona considered that the "preponderant use of the time-series approach" had "done disservice to economic research by impeding the study of the 'wanderings' of the consumption function" (173). It is worth noting at this point that even if Katona's approach failed to penetrate the economic theory of consumer behavior, "many of the kinds of survey and panel data in which Katona and his

12. For accounts of this controversy on the consumption function, see Cook 2000, Mason 2000, and Drakopoulos 2011.

13. There is an interesting opposition to draw between Katona's distinction between "understanding" and "predicting" consumer behavior and Friedman's (1953) essay on the methodology of positive economics. As shown in the next section, the economic reception of Katona's "tools and insights" seems to conform to Friedman's (1953, 8) claims that "theory is to be judged by its predictive power" and that a "hypothesis is important if it 'explains' much by little" (14). In *The Mass Consumption Society* (1964), Katona explicitly opposed Friedman's focus on the predictive power and simplicity of a theory rather than its "explanatory power."

organization pioneered" (Tobin 1972, 38) were subsequently explored by the federal government and other agencies.

2. Predicting Durable Goods Sales

The Smithies Report (1955)

In 1954 the Subcommittee on Economic Statistics of the US Congress requested that the Board of Governors of the Federal Reserve evaluate the "adequacy" of "statistical information in the fields of savings, business inventories and business and consumer expectations" (request letters in Smithies et al. 1955). In response to that request, the board organized a consultant committee aimed at exploring the "usefulness of consumer survey statistics in general" (Smithies et al. 1955, 1).[14] The committee focused mainly on the SCF and, to a lesser extent, on the "interim surveys" of attitudes (i.e., the SCAs) conducted by the SRC under the auspices of private institutions such as the Ford Foundation.[15]

In line with Katona's project, the Smithies report suggested that the "relatively expensive" SCF data should "supplement rather than replace the traditional kinds of information" (9).[16] However, instead of testing the survey according to its intended purpose (i.e., as being a composing part of the SRC's Economic Behavior Program), the committee proceeded by testing the individual predictive power of the different attitudes. In evaluating the attitudes collected in the SCF, the Smithies report was clear in stating that "buying intentions should be distinguished from less specific attitudinal data" (37), thus disregarding the theory supporting the SCF, which drew from Katona's holistic approach.

The report came to favorable conclusions about the predictive value of "buying intentions" data but disapproved of the "less specific" attitudes. That result was confirmed by comparing the buying intentions data with subsequent purchases of "automobiles," "furniture," "major household

14. The consultant committee, best known as the Smithies committee, was composed of Arthur Smithies (chairman), Hazel Kyrk, Guy Orcutt, Harold Passer, Bert Seidman, Samuel Stouffer, and James Tobin.

15. As shown below, unlike the SCF, the SCAs were developed as a way to gather general data to account for "'waves' of optimism and pessimism" affecting consumer behavior (Mueller 1963, 899).

16. According to the Smithies report, the annual budget for the SCF was $150,000 for three thousand interviews. The interim surveys were part of a study, "The Relation of Attitudes to Economic Actions," financed by the Ford Foundation at a cost of $148,500 (Smithies et al. 1955, 77).

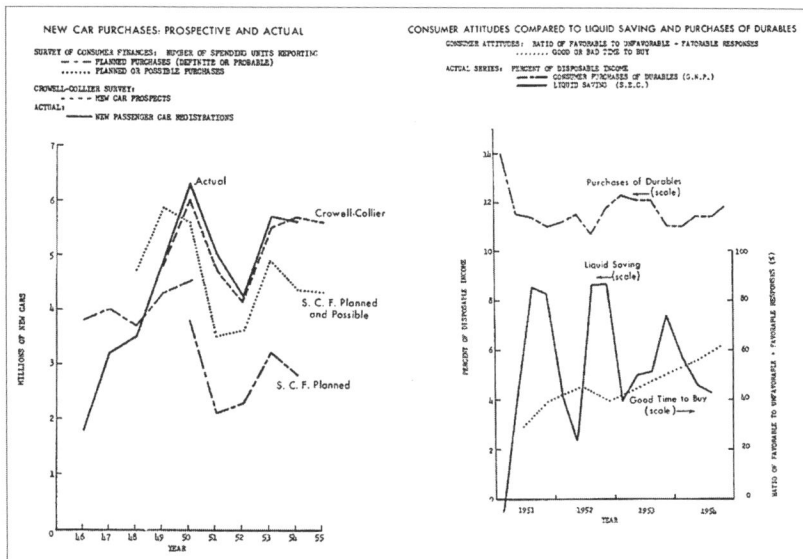

NEW CAR PURCHASES: PROSPECTIVE AND ACTUAL

CONSUMER ATTITUDES COMPARED TO LIQUID SAVING AND PURCHASES OF DURABLES

Figure 3 Two graphs from *Consumer Survey Statistics*, relating data obtained from the Survey of Consumer Finances to the Crowell-Collier Automotive Survey and actual car purchases (left-hand side), and to Purchases of Durables and Liquid Saving (right-hand side)

equipment," and "houses" (46–52) and by checking the accuracy of other projects gathering buying intentions, such as the "Crowell-Collier automotive survey": "The success of the Crowell-Collier survey argues strongly for the validity of intentions data as predictors. . . . a survey devoted entirely to one subject, as the Crowell-Collier survey is to automobiles, may be able to elicit more considered anticipations than a survey, such as the Survey of Consumer Finances, in which this is just one subject among many" (47).

Charts such as those in figure 3 supported the committee's analysis of the predictive power of buying intentions (left) versus that of the "less specific" attitudes (right). As shown in the left-side chart, the SCF data on "planned" and "planned or probable" car purchases (i.e., "buying intentions") were less accurate than those of the Crowell-Collier survey, but still considered appropriate for predicting changes in car purchase trends. Charts such as the one on the right side supposedly demonstrated the uselessness of the "less specific" attitudes ("Good Time to Buy," in this case) for predicting or even explaining changes in economic aggregates such as "Purchases of Durables" or "Liquid Saving": "No clear picture emerges from these [right side] Figures. On the whole, these attitudinal series conform less well to 'actual' series than do purchase intentions. It would be difficult to say whether there is more conformity of favorable attitudes to subsequent durable goods expenditure or to subsequent liquid saving" (53–54).

As a consequence of these kinds of tests, the committee concluded that the "less specific" attitudes were useless for predicting durable goods sales, however useful they were for noneconomic purposes such as building rapport between interviewers and respondents. These kinds of attitudes were supposed to have "considerable descriptive interest in themselves" as measures, for instance, of the "households' assessments of their own well-being" (66). However, they were not among the Federal Reserve's priorities in the subsequent design of its survey programs.

The Economic Expectations Controversy

In reviewing the Smithies report, Katona (1957, 40) claimed that the committee had overlooked the "socio-psychological" character of the SCF by comparing it to "more narrowly conceived economic studies." The report, he argued, was excessively focused on the use of attitudes as forecasting tools, without considering "explicitly the basic problems of cross-disciplinary or behavioral research" (40). By this, he meant that the committee had overlooked the use of the attitudes for understanding consumption, as it resulted from both the "ability" and the "willingness" to buy:

> The research work of the Survey Research Center on expectations is based on a psychological theory and is undertaken to develop further this theory. . . . Today in the United States consumer expenditures, and especially postponable expenditures are not rigidly tied to income. They are a function both of resources ("ability to buy") and of psychological factors ("willingness to buy"). Enabling conditions set more or less flexible limits to the rate of spending; the use consumers make of this latitude depends on their attitudes. (41)

As noted above, Katona's "attitudes" were considered current outcomes that had an influence on the agents' "perceptions, cognitions, and behavior" (41). Even expectations, a "subgroup of the more general concept of attitudes," were conceived as part of a program designed to understand consumers' current evaluations of their past, present, and future situations rather than as forecasting devices (41): "Expectations—intentions as well as other notions about the future—are current data which help to understand what is going on at the time when the expectations are held. Good diagnosis, of course, helps in making predictions. But forecasting remains a separate step, *additional to and different from* the measurement of prevailing expectations and intentions" (41; emphasis added).

In criticizing the atomistic viewpoint of the Smithies report, Katona argued that the charts presented (e.g., figure 3) were "based on the assumption that each individual attitude, taken in isolation, should have a specific relation, not changing over time, to action variables" (43). This was altogether different from Katona's aim in designing the SCF, which was of "clustering" attitudes to study the different possible configurations of them in conjunction with financial data gathered in the same surveys:

> The basic tenet of Gestalt psychology in which our studies originated is . . . that a part or item may change its meaning and function according to the whole to which it belongs. Thus, it is not at all surprising that expecting prices to rise was at certain times a factor promoting and at other times a factor retarding consumer purchases. . . . Instead of testing the predictive value of each attitude separately, the relation of clusters of attitudes to behavior should be studied. (43)

For Katona, the SCF was a way to develop a theory of economic psychology capable of generating an understanding of the prevailing attitudes in a given context. According to that view, attitudes such as "buying intentions" were not always to be considered data reflecting future purchases, but their function could be studied by taking them into account within the whole "cluster" of attitudes.

Katona's position generated a set of reactions by academic economists. James Tobin (1959, 1), for instance, replied with a new study on whether the answers to attitudinal questions provided "information of value in predicting the buying behavior of households."[17] Tobin compared the SCF

17. Other reactions to Katona's position may be found in the proceedings of the 1957 National Bureau of Economic Research (1960) conference "The Quality and Economic Significance of Anticipations Data." That conference was animated, namely, by Albert Hart, Franco Modigliani, Guy Orcutt, Katona, Eva Mueller, Irwin Friend, Robert Ferber, Thomas Juster, and Arthur Okun. Tobin's (1959, 5) paper drew largely on Okun's contribution to that conference, "The Value of Anticipations Data in Forecasting National Product," which claimed that the predictive success of the SCF was "due entirely to its buying-intentions components," while the "more diffuse attitudinal indicators, ma[de] no net contribution."

data with information on actual purchases gathered in reinterviews but insisted on separating buying intentions from the "less specific" attitudes. Besides replicating the Smithies committee's procedures, he literally did not see what Katona's aim was in designing the SCF, which demonstrates how different their views were about the purpose of the observations: "I do not see how the predictive value of these data can be adequately appraised without confronting the attitudes and intentions of individual households with the record of their subsequent behavior. But it is possible to interpret George Katona, the pioneer student and chief collector of consumer anticipations data, as challenging this point of view" (1).

In line with the Smithies report (of which he was a coauthor), Tobin (1959, 10) concluded that, unlike other attitudes, buying intentions did have "predictive value." By confirming the main conclusions of the report (10–11), he set in motion a sort of "official" position toward the collection of attitudes that had an impact in the subsequent development of the Federal Reserve survey programs.

Observing Intentions and Expectations at the US Census Bureau

In 1960 the Federal Reserve interrupted most of its funding for the SCF (Juster 1964), which was finally discontinued in 1971 (Curtin 2004). It sponsored instead the "Quarterly Survey of Consumer Buying Intentions," which was first conducted by the Census Bureau in 1959 (McNeil 1974). Unlike the SCF, which consisted of detailed interviews designed for collecting different kinds of attitudes, the SCBI adhered to the Smithies report's guidelines and collected only "buying intentions" through mailed questionnaires.[18] During the following years, Thomas Juster and James Byrnes from the Census Bureau recognized the existence of two different approaches to the analysis of attitudes: the SRC approach, on the one hand, and that of James Tobin, Arthur Okun, Lawrence Klein, John Lansing, Stephen Whitey, and Juster himself, on the other, that focused on the predictive power of the observations:

> One view is that consumer attitudes (thought of as generalized feelings of well-being reflecting relative optimism or pessimism) are fundamental determinants of spending and saving behavior and that both

18. Juster (1960) also analyzed an NBER study of attitudes using mail interviews that preceded the SCBI.

expectations (judgments about the course of events external to the household) and intentions (judgments about events internal to the household) are basically attitudes carrying a time dimension. . . . An alternative viewpoint is that attitudes, expectations, and intentions should be taken at face value. That is to say, expectations reflect the household's judgment about the future course of events external to the household; intentions, on the other hand, reflect tentative plans to undertake specified actions in the light of these judgments. (Juster 1964, 140–41)

Unlike Katona's (1951, 174) view, according to which the different attitudes were understood as indicators of "the psychological field as it prevails at a given moment," Juster and his associates considered the buying intentions of the SCBI as predictors of future purchases. But based on his own evaluations of the survey, Juster (1964, 1966) suggested a new method based on eliciting "subjective purchase probabilities" rather than on the yes/no replies of the buying-intentions questionnaires: "A reasonably good proxy for household purchase probability can be obtained from a survey of subjective purchase probabilities. The data indicate that a survey of buying intentions is simply a less efficient way of getting an estimate of purchase probabilities than a survey of explicit probabilities. Intentions seem to have no informational content that a probability survey does not also have, and the probability survey is able to extract information that is not obtainable from intentions surveys" (Juster 1966, 660–61).

Following Juster's studies, the Census Bureau discontinued the SCBI and replaced it with the Survey of Consumer Buying Expectations (SCBE) in 1966. Switching from the analysis of "buying intentions" to that of "subjective purchase probabilities," the Federal Reserve reaffirmed its aim of developing tools for predicting durable goods sales. Unlike the SCF, which drew from the SRC's program, the SCBE aimed at straightforwardly predicting purchase rates: "The objectives of a probability survey are, in principle, quite straightforward. An unbiased estimate of the future purchase rate is required, hence the survey should yield an estimate of mean probability which is on average equal to the observed purchase rate" (666).

However, the "legitimate reasons for optimism" that followed the first versions of the SCBE (McNeil 1974, 5) turned into suspicion during the late 1960s, especially after the "failure of the series to provide an advance signal or even to move with the decline in new car sales which began in late 1969" (5). Accordingly, the Census Bureau expressed its concern over the performance of the "expected car purchases" data, and in 1972 it discussed the "predictive value" of the survey together with "data users from industry, government, universities, and private research organizations" (5). The last SCBE was conducted in 1973, interrupting the Federal Reserve's attempts to collect data on attitudes, intentions, and expectations. According to McNeil's account, the Census Bureau program "survived for 15 years because the early part of that period was marked by a high correlation between plans and purchases" (McNeil 1974, 9). When the SCBE series "lost the strong trend factors which had been present for much of the 1960s," it "became apparent that aggregate purchase plans were not always a good predictor of aggregate purchase behavior," as it had been anticipated by Katona and his associates at the SRC (9).

3. Conclusions

Despite both the failure of the Economic Behavior Program in imposing Katona's behavioral economics (Curtin 2004) and the interruption of Katona's version of the SCF (now conducted by the National Opinion Research Center at the University of Chicago), attitudinal data are still produced by the SRC and used as composing parts of the widely used Index of Consumer Sentiment (ICS). Two main issues arise from the success of the ICS, as opposed to the failure of the survey programs presented above.

The ICS as a "Third Way"

The history presented throughout this essay is intertwined with that of the Surveys of Consumer Attitudes conducted by the SRC since 1951 under the auspices of private institutions like the Ford Foundation.[19] Unlike the SCF, the SCAs were straightforwardly conceived as tools for forecasting future economic developments, with the idea that consumers, like businessmen, were "subject to 'waves' of optimism and pessimism" (Mueller 1963, 899). The SCAs were initially used to construct the Index of Consumer Attitudes, first published in 1954. The ICA turned into the ICS during the 1960s (Curtin 1983), representing an alternative to both the study of the "clusters of attitudes" that characterized the SCF and the analysis of

---

19. For accounts of SCAs and their use for constructing the ICS, see Mueller 1963; Curtin 1982, 1983, 2004; Dominitz and Manski 2003; and Juster 2004.

intentions and expectations (SCBI and SCBE) as directly informing about future purchase trends. Unlike the observations obtained with the other survey programs, the ICS was conceived as summaries of a few attitudinal questions that were supposed to affect the "marginal buyer" (i.e., not all buyers) of durable goods (Mueller 1963). As noted by Eva Mueller (1963, 901), besides appropriately accounting for "*fluctuations* in durable goods sales," the ICS also revealed the inconsistency of the "buying intentions approach":

> Shifts in opinions and perceptions among consumers—such factors as concern about unemployment, cold war worries, satisfaction with prices—may induce "autonomous" shifts in consumer demand. . . . Consumer buying intentions appear to make a net contribution to the forecast in some of the regression equations examined, but these are largely equations not including the Attitude Index. When attitudes are also taken into account, the predictive performance of buying intentions is not consistent from one test to another. (916)

The SCF as Composing Part of Katona's Behavioral Economics

However, consequent with the development of his program of behavioral economics, Katona "believed that the use of the Index alone had limitations, since the surveys yield[ed] much more information than what was summarized in the Index" (Curtin 1983, 507). As noted throughout this essay, Katona clearly distinguished between "understanding" and "predicting" demand fluctuations, and he believed that "additional information was necessary for a complete understanding of the movements in the overall Index and its implications on spending behavior" (507). Katona (1967, 13) considered the ICS as just part of a program whose purpose was "not only to find out what [would] happen to discretionary demand, but also to find out *why*." In Curtin's (1983, 508) terms, to "place the entire empirical focus on predictive tests would ignore the importance Katona placed on the explanation and understanding of economic behavior."

For Katona (1967, 13), the "major task" of behavioral economics was the analysis of the "reasons for observed changes" in demand. This was a fundamental factor in the design of the SCF, and Katona considered that what both policymakers and the public opinion needed were not just the ICS prospects but also knowledge about the underlying forces explaining "large or small changes in the one or the other direction" (13). Katona maintained this position throughout his career, as evidenced in *Essays on Behavioral Economics* (1980), his last academic contribution. It is ironic that despite the effort invested in advancing the program, Katona's behavioral economics was overshadowed by the use of the ICS, which became "one of the most closely watched indicators of future economic trends" (Curtin 2004, 136).

"The lag in acceptance may be due to the stubbornness of economists; I prefer to attribute it to the originality of George's approach, which required a real restructuring of thought—a genuine paradigm shift—before it could begin to be assimilated" (Simon 1980, 12). This quote by Herbert Simon summarizes the difficulty met by Katona's project. Unlike the use of the ICS, understanding Katona's behavioral economics required knowledge of gestalt principles of psychology.

References

Arvidsson, A. 2004. "On the 'Pre-History of the Panoptic Sort': Mobility in Market Research." *Surveillance and Society* 1 (4): 456–74.

Bateman, B. W. 2001. "Make a Righteous Number: Social Surveys, the Men and Religion Forward Movement, and Quantification in American Economics." *HOPE* 33 (5): 457–85.

Bean, L. H. 1946. "Relation of Disposable Income and the Business Cycle to Expenditures." *Review of Economics and Statistics* 28 (4): 199–207.

Bennion, E. G. 1946. "The Consumption Function: Cyclically Variable?" *Review of Economics and Statistics* 28 (4): 219–24.

Boulier, B. L., and R. S. Goldfarb. 1998. "On the Use and Nonuse of Surveys in Economics." *Journal of Economic Methodology* 5 (1): 1–21.

Brady, D. S., and R. D. Friedman. 1947. "Savings and the Income Distribution." In *Studies in Income and Wealth*, 247–65. National Bureau of Economic Research.

Bulmer, M., K. Bales, and K. Sklar, eds. 1991. *The Social Survey in Historical Perspective, 1880–1940.* Cambridge: Cambridge University Press.

Converse, J. M. 1987. *Survey Research in the United States: Roots and Emergence, 1890–1960.* Berkeley: University of California Press.

Cook, S. 2000. "A Neglected Controversy in the Modeling of Consumers' Expenditure." *Cambridge Journal of Economics* 24 (2): 177–91.

Curtin, R. T. 1982. "Indicators of Consumer Behavior: The University of Michigan Surveys of Consumers." *Public Opinion Quarterly* 46 (3): 340–52.

———. 1983. "Curtin on Katona." In *Contemporary Economists in Perspective*, edited by H. W. Spiegel and W. J. Samuels, 495–522. New York: JAI.

———. 2004. "Psychology and Macroeconomics." In *A Telescope on Society: Survey Research and Social Science at the University of Michigan and Beyond*, edited by J. S. House, F. T. Juster, R. L. Kahn, H. Schuman, and E. Singer, 131–55. Ann Arbor: University of Michigan Press.

Desrosières, A. 1991. "The Part in Relation to the Whole: How to Generalise? The Prehistory of Representative Sampling." In *The Social Survey in Historical Perspective, 1880–1940*, edited by M. Bulmer, K. Bales, and K. Sklar, 217–44. Cambridge: Cambridge University Press.

———. 1998. *The Politics of Large Numbers: A History of Statistical Reasoning.* Cambridge: Harvard University Press.

Dominitz, J., and C. F. Manski. 2003. "How Should We Measure Consumer Confidence (Sentiment)? Evidence from the Michigan Survey of Consumers." NBER Working Paper No. 9926.

Drakopoulos, S. 2011. "The Neglect of Comparison Income: An Historical Perspective." *European Journal of the History of Economic Thought* 18 (3): 441–64.

Duesenberry, J. 1949. *Income, Saving, and the Theory of Consumer Behavior.* Cambridge: Harvard University Press.

Duncan, J. W., and W. C. Shelton. 1992. "U.S. Government Contributions to Probability Sampling and Statistical Analysis." *Statistical Science* 7 (3): 320–38.

Friedman, M. 1953. *Essays in Positive Economics.* Chicago: University of Chicago Press.

———. 1957. *A Theory of the Consumption Function.* Princeton: Princeton University Press.

Friend, I. 1946. "Relationship between Consumers' Expenditures, Savings, and Disposable Income." *Review of Economics and Statistics* 28 (4): 208–15.

Herman, E. 1995. *The Romance of American Psychology: Political Culture in the Age of Experts, 1940–1970.* Berkeley: University of California Press.

House, J. S., F. T. Juster, R. L. Kahn, H. Schuman, and E. Singer, eds. 2004. *A Telescope on Society: Survey Research and Social Science at the University of Michigan and Beyond.* Ann Arbor: University of Michigan Press.

Igo, S. E. 2007. *The Averaged American: Surveys, Citizens, and the Making of a Mass Public.* Cambridge: Harvard University Press.

Juster, F. T. 1960. "Prediction and Consumer Buying Intentions." *American Economic Review* 50 (2): 604–17.

———. 1964. *Anticipations and Purchases: An Analysis of Consumer Behavior.* Princeton: Princeton University Press.

———. 1966. "Consumer Buying Intentions and Purchase Probability: An Experiment in Survey Design." *Journal of the American Statistical Association* 61 (315): 658–96.

———. 2004. "Introduction to the Behavioral Study of Economics." In *A Telescope on Society: Survey Research and Social Science at the University of Michigan and Beyond*, edited by J. S. House, F. T. Juster, R. L. Kahn, H. Schuman, and E. Singer, 119–30. Ann Arbor: University of Michigan Press.

Katona, G. 1940. *Organizing and Memorizing.* New York: Columbia University Press.

———. 1942. *War without Inflation: The Psychological Approach to Problems of War Economy.* New York: Columbia University Press.

———. 1945. *Price Control and Business: Field Studies among Producers and Distributors of Consumer Goods in the Chicago Area, 1942–44.* Bloomington, Ind.: Principia.

———. 1946. "Psychological Analysis of Business Decisions and Expectations." *American Economic Review* 36 (1): 44–62.

———. 1947. "Contribution of Psychological Data to Economic Analysis." *Journal of the American Statistical Association* 42 (239): 449–59.

———. 1951. *Psychological Analysis of Economic Behavior.* New York: McGraw-Hill.

———. 1957. "Federal Reserve Board Committee Reports on Consumer Expectations and Savings Statistics." *Review of Economics and Statistics* 39 (1): 40–45.

———. 1964. *The Mass Consumption Society.* New York: McGraw-Hill.

———. 1967. "Anticipations Statistics and Consumer Behavior." *American Statistician* 21 (2): 12–13.

———. 1972. "Reminiscences." In *Human Behavior in Economic Affairs: Essays in Honor of George Katona*, edited by B. Strümpel, J. N. Morgan, and E. Zahn, 11–14. Amsterdam: Elsevier.

———. 1980. *Essays on Behavioral Economics.* Ann Arbor: University of Michigan Press.

Katona, G., and R. Likert. 1946. "Relationship between Consumer Expenditures and Savings: The Contribution of Survey Research." *Review of Economics and Statistics* 28 (4): 197–99.

Kennickell, A. B., and M. Starr-McCluer. 1994. "Changes in Family Finances from 1989 to 1992: Evidence from the Survey of Consumer Finances." *Federal Reserve Bulletin* 80 (10): 861–82.

Likert, R. 1972. "Courageous Pioneer: Creating a New Field of Knowledge." In *Human Behavior in Economic Affairs: Essays in Honor of George Katona*, edited by B. Strümpel, J. N. Morgan, and E. Zahn, 3–9. Amsterdam: Elsevier.

Mandler, G. 2007. *A History of Modern Experimental Psychology: From James and Wundt to Cognitive Science.* Cambridge: MIT Press.

Mason, R. 2000. "The Social Significance of Consumption: James Duesenberry's Contribution to Consumer Theory." *Journal of Economic Issues* 34 (3): 553–72.

McNeil, J. 1974. "Federal Programs to Measure Consumer Purchase Expectations, 1946–1973: A Post-Mortem." *Journal of Consumer Research* 1 (3): 1–10.

Modigliani, F., and R. Brumberg. (1954) 2005. "Utility Analysis and the Consumption Function: An Interpretation of Cross-Section Data." In *The Collected Papers of Franco Modigliani*, 3–46. Cambridge: MIT Press.

Mosak, J. L. 1945. "Forecasting Postwar Demand: III." *Econometrica* 13 (1): 25–53.

Mueller, E. 1963. "Ten Years of Consumer Attitude Surveys: Their Forecasting Record." *Journal of the American Statistical Association* 58 (304): 899–917.

National Bureau for Economic Research (NBER). 1960. *The Quality and Economic Significance of Anticipations Data: A Conference of the Universities–National Bureau Committee for Economic Research.* Princeton: Princeton University Press.

Reid, M. G. 1952. "Effect of Income Concept upon Expenditure Curves of Farm Families." National Bureau of Economic Research, *Studies in Income and Wealth* 15:131–74.

Rutherford, M. Forthcoming. "The USDA Graduate School: Government Training in Statistics and Economics, 1921–1945." *Journal of the History of Economic Thought.*

Simon, H. A. 1980. "Behavioral Research: Theory and Practice." In *The 1979 Founders Symposium, the Institute for Social Research: Honoring George Katona,* edited by M. Kallick and J. N. Morgan. Ann Arbor: University of Michigan Press.

Smithies, A. 1945. "Forecasting Postwar Demand: I." *Econometrica* 13 (1): 1–14.

Smithies, A., H. Kyrk, G. H. Orcutt, H. C. Passer, B. Seidman, S. Stouffer, and J. Tobin. 1955. *Consumer Survey Statistics: Report [submitted to] the Subcommittee on Economic Statistics of the Joint Committee on the Economic Report.* Washington, D.C.

Sokal, M. 1984. "The Gestalt Psychologists in Behaviorist America." *American Historical Review* 89 (5): 1240–63.

Stapleford, T. 2009. *The Cost of Living in America: A Political History of Economic Statistics, 1880–2000.* New York: Cambridge University Press.

Strümpel, B., J. N. Morgan, and E. Zahn, eds. 1972. *Human Behavior in Economic Affairs: Essays in Honor of George Katona.* Amsterdam: Elsevier.

Tobin, J. 1951. "Relative Income, Absolute Income, and Saving." In *Money, Trade, and Economic Growth,* 135–56. New York: Macmillan.

———. 1959. "On the Predictive Value of Consumer Intentions and Attitudes." *Review of Economics and Statistics* 41 (1): 1–11.

———. 1972. "Wealth, Liquidity, and the Propensity to Consume." In *Human Behavior in Economic Affairs: Essays in Honor of George Katona,* edited by B. Strümpel, J. N. Morgan, and E. Zahn, 37–56. Amsterdam: Elsevier.

Wärneryd, K. 1982. "The Life and Work of George Katona." *Journal of Economic Psychology* 2 (1): 1–31.

Woytinsky, W. S. 1946. "Relationship between Consumers' Expenditures, Savings, and Disposable Income." *Review of Economics and Statistics* 28 (1): 1–12.

Navigating the Shoals of Self-Reporting: Data Collection in US Expenditure Surveys since 1920

Thomas A. Stapleford

If there is one domain of economics grounded in direct observations, it would seem to be economic statistics. For more than a century, quantitative data have provided raw material for debates about political economy and economic theory. But describing economic statistics as "observations" is misleading: strictly speaking, many economic data—unemployment rates, wages, national income, consumer expenditures—are not based on observations at all. Rather, they are derived from self-reporting by the original participants, whether businesses or households.

Alongside the familiar methodological quandaries that accompany the practice of observation in general (such as the role of theory in guiding observation or the concern that observational practices may alter the phenomena under study), self-reporting raises a new dilemma: How can we know that self-reported data are accurate, that is, that the data match what the survey's designers would have recorded had they been directly privy to the transactions in question?

Deliberate deception is a serious issue, especially when participants have incentives to provide misleading information (e.g., during surveys of workplace safety or employment practices). Many statisticians in the nineteenth and early twentieth centuries wrestled mightily with the problem of deception, especially from employers suspicious of government

History of Political Economy 44 (annual suppl.) DOI 10.1215/00182702-1631824
Copyright 2012 by Duke University Press

intrusion.[1] Deception was not the only threat to accurate self-reporting, however: potential subjects might refuse to participate because of privacy concerns or lack of time; they might misunderstand the queries and hence answer incorrectly; or they might simply lack the knowledge needed to provide accurate information.

This essay examines how economists have responded to the challenges posed by self-reporting in economic statistics. My focus is on the major surveys of household income and expenditures administered by the US government during the twentieth century, especially those coming from the US Bureau of Labor Statistics (BLS). Statisticians and labor activists began conducting expenditure surveys in the late nineteenth century to document the typical living conditions of working-class families.[2] In the 1930s, however, federal expenditure surveys expanded to encompass a new goal that soon came to dominate the projects: providing empirical data for the study of consumer demand (Stapleford 2007). Over the next few decades, this shift prompted a twofold change in the focus of BLS expenditure surveys: from the working class to all American consumers and from families to all households (including single individuals).

Expenditure surveys provide a valuable case study in the problems of self-reporting because, unlike businesses, households do not employ accountants and rarely keep even minimally detailed records. As a result, expenditure surveys face numerous challenges: households lack the expertise that can ameliorate the risk of miscommunication with investigators seeking financial data; they are forced to rely more heavily on memory; and their response to inquiries can take a substantial amount of time (because the requisite information is not readily at hand). The efforts of BLS statisticians to wrestle with these obstacles form a particularly attractive topic because the bureau operates the most prominent expenditure surveys in the United States, has a long tradition of running such surveys (see table 1), and is far more open about its methods than are private firms devoted to market research.

1. See the frequent discussions of this issue at the annual conventions of the National Association of Bureaus of Labor Statistics, especially the tenth convention (1894). For concerns about deception in the twentieth century, see Marcel Boumans's essay on Oskar Morgenstern, this volume.

2. Since all major surveys of household expenditures conducted by the US government also covered household income, I refer to these studies simply as "expenditure surveys," with the income component being implied.

Table 1 Major Expenditure Surveys of the US Bureau
of Labor Statistics

Date	Cooperating Agencies	Coverage
1888–1890		8,544 families of urban wage-earners in select industries in the US and several European countries
1901–1902		25,440 families of urban wage-earners and low-salaried clerical workers
1917–1919		12,096 families of white, urban wage-earners and low-salaried clerical workers
1934–1936		12,903 families of urban wage-earners and low-salaried clerical workers
1935–1936	US Bureau of Home Economics	~60,000 families, urban and rural, all occupations and income levels
1950		12,489 households (single individuals or families) in urban areas, all occupations and income levels
1960–1961	US Agricultural Research Service	13,728 households in urban and rural areas, all occupations and income levels
1972–1973	US Bureau of the Census	Partial information (in different forms) from ~70,000 households in urban and rural areas, all occupations and income levels
1980–	US Bureau of the Census	Continuing survey of households in urban and rural areas, all occupations and income levels. As of 2005, ~45,000 households participate each year.

Sources: Lamale 1959; BLS 1971, 1978, 2007.

The Evolution of Data-Collection Methods: An Overview

A simple history of BLS survey procedures does not present a clear teleology: some practices that were once rejected as inefficient or misleading were later readopted, while other long-favored strategies were subsequently critiqued. To some degree, this lack of teleology reflects the changing context for expenditure surveys: as I discuss in the conclusion, both funding constraints and changes in the structure of households and the consumer economy have necessarily shaped BLS survey methods. Yet it also reflects conceptual shifts in which new approaches to survey research came to supplement or even supplant earlier practices.

The first change was the gradual rationalization of survey procedures, that is, an increasing reliance on highly standardized rules. From the late nineteenth century into the early decades of the twentieth, the BLS confronted the difficulties of self-reporting by relying on the personality, charisma, and social skills of its field agents to elicit the most accurate answers from respondents. By the early 1930s, however, the bureau had followed other federal agencies in shifting its focus to standardized rules and formal procedures, encompassing both survey design and the training and oversight of field agents. In a classic pattern of Weberian rationalization, BLS staff began to treat survey methodology as an object for scientific observation and experimentation in its own right, taking these results and feeding them back into bureau practices. In this framework, each survey became a double-experiment, yielding information about both economic activity and the survey's methodology. The goal of this process was to elicit the most accurate and complete responses for a given household, an objective that in principle could be reached after a sufficient number of refinements.

By the 1960s, however, BLS survey methodology was in crisis, as conflicting results and the inherent limitations of self-reporting suggested that no single set of procedures would result in consistently accurate and complete responses for a full range of households. At this stage federal statisticians developed a simple yet (in context) radical solution: rather than collect complete expenditure data from each household in the sample, the survey would be split into two components, with each household reporting only part of its annual expenditures. While a logical step, this change forced statisticians to abandon certain tests for internal coherence and consistency that had previously been viewed as critical tools for filtering out sloppy or inaccurate survey responses. I argue that the new procedures therefore reflected a growing confidence in the bureau's research on survey methodology. In essence, the BLS trusted that research would reveal and eliminate systematic response errors, while residual (random) inaccuracies would disappear when combined into average values. As a result, survey responses no longer had to be discarded if they were incomplete or contained suspected mistakes; indeed, the BLS even began to "correct" incomplete survey responses based on typical patterns.

Rationalizing Household Interviews

During the first several decades after the founding of the BLS in the late nineteenth century, the bureau treated its field agents as highly skilled workers who could be granted a relatively substantial amount of autonomy. The success of survey research thus rested on the agents' charisma, social intuition, and previous experience in fieldwork. This labor model encountered problems, however, as the geographic scope of BLS surveys expanded, and especially when the bureau had to hire large numbers of temporary workers for intermittent projects. Accordingly, the BLS began to impose tighter supervision and oversight on its agents in the early decades of the twentieth century (Stapleford 2010). Nonetheless, the agency retained its emphasis on natural abilities and social skills as the key to successful interviews for household surveys.

The persistence of that tradition is evident in the description of an ideal field agent for expenditure surveys given by BLS commissioner Ethelbert Stewart in the mid-1920s. According to Stewart, "a careful high school education and mathematical accuracy or ordinary intelligence as applied to the mathematical side" would be sufficient for a field agent. The keys to success lay elsewhere: "Kindness and a knack at making friends, ability to state her mission in perfectly simple, impressive and appealingly argumentative language, and pleasing personality are the basic requirements of a good agent, when it comes to getting the basic information from the housewife herself." By use of her persuasive powers, a good agent could turn the housewife into a strong ally, making her "really interested for her own sake in working out an itemized statement of the quantities and cost of things she consumes in her household."[3] Likewise, draft instructions for an

---

3. Ethelbert Stewart to Secretary of Labor, November 25, 1927, folder 2, box 1, Correspondence of the Commissioner with the Secretary of Labor and Units of the Labor Dept., 1925–1929, Records of the US Bureau of Labor Statistics, Record Group 257, US National Archives II, College Park, Maryland.

uncompleted expenditure survey encouraged field agents to rely on their social skills and intuition to pry information from recalcitrant subjects:

> The agent should work on the assumption that there are no facts called for on the schedule which cannot be determined if properly sought after. To this end she should use patience, perseverance, tact, and skillful and ingenious questioning. She should determine by experimentation the best order in which to take up questions so as to avoid tiring the housewife so quickly that the schedule cannot be completed accurately.[4]

As the gendered pronouns in these descriptions implied, the BLS typically hired women for expenditure surveys in the early twentieth century, in part (one suspects) because they were thought to be more effective dealing with housewives and in part because the emphasis on "kindness," "patience," and conversational acumen resonated with twentieth-century conceptions of feminine characteristics.[5]

Even during this period, of course, BLS staff recognized that proper technique could improve survey results, and indeed that some social skills could be explicitly *taught* to agents. For example, the draft instructions reminded agents that "in questioning a family as to surplus and deficit, it is sometimes advantageous to avoid the use of the words, 'Surplus, deficit, savings, and debt,' and to approach the subject in a more tactful way by asking such questions as, 'Were you able to put aside or invest anything for a rainy day?', 'Were you able to meet all of the year's expenses with the year's earnings?', etc."[6] Likewise, the bureau instructed agents to be cognizant of typical prices and quantities consumed for basic household goods in the cities under study and "to call [the housewife's] attention in a kindly way to what seems to be an unusual statement." Yet even here, the field agent's judgment and social graces took a central role: Ethelbert Stewart insisted that agents who encountered apparent discrepancies should utilize "common sense, but above all kindness," since "it very often happens that these unusual statements are true."[7]

4. "Instructions, Family Budgets, July 1931," pp. 2–3, Instructions for Future Study—Developed from 1918 Survey, box 1, Records of the Consumer Expenditure Survey Program and Predecessors, 1933–1971, Records of the US Bureau of Labor Statistics, Record Group 257, US National Archives II, College Park, Maryland.

5. That trend continued in later years as well, though the bureau relied on men for nighttime interviews and visits to "less desirable areas of the cities" (Lamale 1959, 64).

6. "Instructions, Family Budgets," 11.

7. Stewart to Secretary of Labor.

By contrast, during the major expenditure surveys conducted by the BLS in the mid-1930s, the previously explicit emphasis on "kindness," "pleasing personality," and social acumen largely disappeared. Though charisma and conversational skill were probably factors in hiring decisions and undoubtedly affected the success of various agents in the field, they were no longer discussed in BLS documents. Job descriptions during the 1930s emphasized professional qualifications ("preferably . . . should have college training in economics or sociology and research experience or comparable business experience"); the only social skill listed was a vague reference to "good judgment in making contacts."[8] Likewise, for the next major survey (1950) staff screened applicants through a standardized federal aptitude test that measured "(1) general intelligence; (2) verbal ability; (3) numerical ability; and (4) clerical perception." Field supervisors did interview prospective agents in part to assess their "personality traits," but the latter referred primarily to factors that might *distort* the results, such as "class consciousness" or a tendency "to become emotionally involved in the personal lives of the respondents" (Lamale 1959, 63).

Instead of the charisma and "ingenious questioning" of field agents, BLS staff members from the 1930s on placed their faith in proper survey design, detailed procedural guidelines, and close oversight of field agents. As far as possible, the entire survey process would be tightly specified and regulated by the staff in Washington, who would plan and administer the investigation based on the best, empirically tested strategies for maximizing accurate returns.[9] The process paralleled the kind of Weberian rationalization that occurred in manufacturing, where Taylorist disciples codified procedures as a way to standardize production, often leading to a deskilling of the workforce in the process. Not surprisingly, the drive toward rationalization was partly a response to the labor problems created by intermittent, large-scale surveys. Such projects required high numbers of temporary workers and (just as occurred with the US census) had been leading the BLS to increase its oversight of field agents since the turn of the century (Stapleford 2010). The New Deal accelerated this process across the federal bureaucracy as administrators used large,

8. "Description of Positions Open to Persons on Relief Rolls in the Study of Urban Consumer Purchases," p. 1, 1934–36 Field Procedures, box 1, Records of the Consumer Expenditure Survey Program and Predecessors, 1933–1971, Records of the US Bureau of Labor Statistics, Record Group 257, US National Archives II, College Park, Maryland.

9. For a more detailed examination of this transformation in the BLS during the 1930s, see Stapleford 2003, 322–58.

short-term statistical surveys as white-collar relief projects in the early years of the Roosevelt administration, creating more than 2.5 million temporary positions for field agents in just a few years and producing what Emmanuel Didier (2011) has called the "industrialization" of statistical field agents.

Yet the renewed push to rationalize BLS fieldwork in the 1930s also reflected a change in the ethos of the bureau's top staff. Prior to the New Deal, the BLS had been run largely by self-styled "practical statisticians" who had little advanced academic training and who often regarded effective data collection as an art learned through practical experience. The arrival of the Roosevelt administration brought a wholesale overhaul of the bureau's top staff, with the older generation replaced by a young cadre of social scientists (primarily economists) who shared the common belief that empirically grounded procedures could lead to a more rigorous, scientific knowledge about American society (Stapleford 2009, 145–69). Rationalization offered the alluring promise of ever-increasing accuracy and detail made possible by refinements in method, refinements that were largely under the purview of the top staff members who designed the survey forms, devised the overall methods for each investigation, and wrote the instruction manuals. Rules and procedures became a focus, in other words, partly because they were something that managerial staff could control.

One component of the new strategy involved crafting formal guidelines and training procedures for interview techniques that (ideally) would compensate for any deficiencies in a field agent's personality or social expertise. Agents participating in a housing survey in the late 1940s, for example, received a three-page sheet describing "Interview Technique[s]." Some were basic social skills, adapted for an effective sales pitch: "Look at respondent"; "Talk slowly"; "Sell, don't order." Agents were told to take control of the conversation and to have "a ready answer for every objection." To that end, the staff provided seven common objections with recommended responses.[10] Likewise, the training regimen for field agents in the 1950 BLS expenditure survey included a battery of practice interviews as well as a cartoon film titled "Some Helpful Guides for Interviewing" (Lamale 1959, 63, 65).

10. "Interview Technique—Personal Contact," BLS—Price Subcommittee of LRAC, 1948–1949, box 7, file C, Files of the Economist of the AFL (Series 5), Records of the American Federation of Labor, Wisconsin State Historical Society, Madison.

Yet the effort to rationalize charisma and conversational acumen was never entirely successful, in the BLS or elsewhere. After several decades of research by psychologists and other social scientists, two experts in the 1970s concluded that although "rapport" was universally regarded as critical to the success of any survey interview, the concept could not be rigorously defined for experimental purposes and hence could not be studied effectively (Goudy and Potter 1975). Likewise, another scholar acknowledged that "though rapport-building techniques are an essential part of the data-collection process," they were also inherently limited. Accordingly, "many investigators prefer to seek more mechanical methods of controlling extraneous variables that do not depend so heavily on *ad hoc* procedures and unspecifiable skills" (Scott 1968, 239).

For the BLS, as for other survey researchers, these limitations led to a greater emphasis on the aspects of the survey process that could be controlled, tested, and refined: the frequency of interviews, procedures for handling nonresponses, the structure of the survey form and the interview itself, the phrasing of questions, strategies for evaluating the accuracy of responses, and so forth. As a result, the BLS began to spell out proper survey procedures in immense detail. Whereas draft instructions to field agents from the 1920s staff totaled only twenty-eight pages, the 1930s version was nearly three times as long, and that was only one of many new instruction manuals produced by 1935. Meanwhile, the staff created an extensive system for training and monitoring field agents, including exams, closely guided reviews of completed "schedules" (survey forms), and regular "check-interviews" in which supervisors revisited homes and reinterviewed housewives to double-check an agent's report.[11] For the 1950 expenditure survey, basic training for field agents took a full seven days and included an assortment of "audio-visual aids" to supplement the lengthy manuals (Lamale 1959, 65). Not surprisingly, BLS staff approvingly cited a 1956 British study that concluded that field agents who returned schedules with the smallest response errors were those who had the ability and willingness to follow complicated rules; by contrast, poor field agents manifested "an impatience with a formal system of collecting facts" (Cole 1956, 58; cf. Lamale 1959, 28). Indeed, following the rules

11. Compare "Instructions, Family Budgets, July 1931" to "Instructions to Field Agents" (January 1936), Instructions—1934–36, box 1, Records of the Consumer Expenditure Survey Program and Predecessors, 1933–1971, Records of the US Bureau of Labor Statistics, Record Group 257, US National Archives II, College Park, Maryland. More generally, see Stapleford 2003, 332–40.

had become the major desideratum: as the BLS explained, "the techniques for hiring and training the interviewers" for the 1950 expenditure survey "were designed to reduce the interviewer variability as much as possible" by ensuring that agents would follow instructions precisely (Lamale 1959, 29). In 2003 the rationalization of survey work reached its next natural terminus with the introduction of the Computer Aided Personal Interview, a software package that permits direct data entry and guides field agents through the interview process (BLS 2007, 3).

Rationalization—with its emphasis on rules and procedures—led BLS staff to envision expenditure surveys as double-experiments: studies of the economy and studies of how to collect data. If the accuracy of a survey depended solely on the formal procedures and tools used to gather data (survey forms, instructions to field agents, etc.), then one could test the efficacy of different procedures experimentally. Though BLS staff had always learned from past experiences and used previous surveys as models, that viewpoint became far more formal and deliberate after 1933. Thus, for example, the 1940s staff described innovative survey schedules as "experimental in character" and explained that "in a very real sense, each survey constitutes a methodological test for the one that follows it" (Brady and Williams 1944, 341, 333). In turn, this view of surveys as methodological experiments led to new practices. Previously, BLS staff rarely archived any survey documents beyond a few blank schedules and (occasionally) the completed forms for major surveys (such as the 1917–18 national expenditure survey). The 1930s brought a radical leap in archival record-keeping, as staff preserved instruction manuals, memos to and from the field, minutes and memos from the planning and tabulation processes, a broad range of sample forms, and extensive documentation of methodological discussions. The organization and labeling of these materials strongly suggests that they were preserved as references for future expenditure surveys.[12] Not surprisingly, BLS publications on the next major expenditure survey (1950) included a volume on methodology in which BLS staff member Helen Humes Lamale (1959, 1–40, 174–233) provided a historical overview of expenditure survey methodology, including detailed information on previous BLS projects. Indeed, the very existence of Lamale's monograph reflected the rise of rationalization: alongside other volumes in the series that sketched a history of family incomes

12. Records from the 1930s, for example, were housed in a separate subcollection, eventually titled "Records of the Consumer Expenditure Survey Program and Predecessors, 1933–1971."

and expenditures, the BLS offered a history of the surveys themselves, one that highlighted the refinement of survey procedures and the current state of the art.

The most striking innovation that accompanied rationalization, however, was the rise of small-scale, experimental surveys that were designed primarily to test methodology rather than collect data per se. In the late 1920s the Bureau of Home Economics (BHE) in the Department of Agriculture ran a small test survey intended to compare the accuracy of family "accounts" or diaries (when families recorded daily purchases on a standardized form) and responses from an interview (when a field agent asked families to recall what they had purchased over a set period, ranging from one month to a year) (Williams 1932, 3). When the BHE's supervisor of family expenditure surveys, the economist Faith M. Williams, moved to the BLS in 1934, she continued to explore the possibilities of experimental surveys. As a result, the BLS ran several independent experiments on data-collection techniques during the 1940s and began to incorporate carefully designed "pilot surveys" into every major project so that staff could test "the phrasing of the questions, the selection of details to be recorded, and the inclusion of probes and check questions" (Brady and Williams 1944, 332–33; Lamale 1959, 6, 19). In later decades, the BLS established the Statistical Methods Division to oversee research on data collection, and by the early 1990s this had been supplemented by the Collections Procedures Research Laboratory that performed "cognitive testing" of questions and survey forms on small groups of subjects (Dippo 1987; Jacobs and Shipp 1993, 71).

The Results and Crisis of Midcentury Methodological Research

Results

Since the BLS had begun to see its surveys as experiments in methodology, understanding the subsequent history of that methodology requires exploring the results of the bureau's "experimental" research. BLS studies of survey methodology during the middle third of the twentieth century seemed to converge on several major results. The first and perhaps most durable finding was that human memory is more effective when given specific prompts. BLS experiments during the early 1940s revealed that checklists (where subjects were asked about specific items) led to more self-reported purchases than "free-listing" (when subjects were asked to write down purchases in general categories); likewise, more detailed lists tended to produce correspondingly more complete reports of expenditures (Brady and Williams 1944, 331–32; Lamale 1959, 18–19). Accordingly, BLS survey forms rapidly ballooned. The standard "schedule" for the 1917–19 BLS expenditure survey was eleven pages, which expanded to twenty pages in the 1934–36 version. By 1950 the length had jumped to fifty-nine pages, and by the 1990s it was over one hundred pages (Lamale 1959, 189, 208, 261–304, 321–35; Jacobs and Shipp 1993, 62).

The second major conclusion, albeit one that proved far more controversial, was that expenditure surveys should be based primarily on an interview format (in which field agents asked subjects to recall purchases over different periods, usually the previous week and the previous year) rather than the "diary" method (in which subjects recorded purchases as they occurred). US statistical agencies had a long tradition of favoring interviews for expenditure surveys dating back to the first federal surveys in the 1890s (see, e.g., US Commissioner of Labor 1891). However, the diary method was much more popular outside the United States and was also a common component of American market research (International Labour Office 1939, 671; Lamale 1959, 4, 6). Not surprisingly, in light of this divergence, survey format became a focus for federal research in the 1930s and 1940s (including the BHE's first survey experiment, discussed above).

By 1934 BLS staff had developed a provisional view that was reinforced by subsequent research over the next two decades. The diary method, Faith Williams conceded in 1935, "would seem to be the logical one to use, as a record of events made day by day as they occur should be more accurate than a report of these same events from memory several months later" (Williams and Zimmerman 1935, 45). Nonetheless, that abstract advantage was undercut by critical weaknesses in practice. First, statisticians wondered if the need to record expenditures would alter family purchasing habits, a speculation that was apparently confirmed by research showing that families asked to track food expenditures tended to report total costs that were lower than those obtained through interviews (Cornfield 1942, 67–68). Second, American statisticians worried that the extra burden of keeping diaries would skew the sample of families participating in a survey. To provide a complete picture of expenditures, surveys needed to cover a lengthy period; the International Labour Office, for example, recommended gathering "daily records of income and expenditure . . . for a period of 12 months" (International Labour Office 1926, 110n40). But how many families would be willing to undertake such a project, and would they be representative of Americans as a whole? Williams was skeptical (Williams and Zimmerman 1935, 46), and again, subsequent research suggested that diary-based surveys suffered from high refusal rates and samples that overrepresented families with (relatively) higher incomes, more education, and greater community involvement (Lamale 1959, 7–12). Finally, diaries seemed to promise higher costs. Not only would tabulation be more expensive (because of the need to aggregate numerous daily entries), but an early BHE study demonstrated that accurate results required "frequent visits to the family or a continuous editing and correspondence," thereby leading Williams to conclude that the costs would be substantially higher than for a comparably sized survey based on interviews (Brady and Williams 1944, 329–30).

Despite these concerns about diaries, Williams and her colleagues also recognized the potential weaknesses of an interview that required participants to recall their annual expenses in a full range of categories (including food, clothing, shelter, furnishings, appliances, medical care, insurance, etc.). Accordingly, the BLS adopted a hybrid procedure for its major surveys from the mid-1930s through the early 1960s. The main survey remained an interview that covered annual expenses across the full range of expenditure categories. In addition, however, the bureau asked respondents to record expenditures during the last seven days for a subset of frequently purchased goods (notably food, drugs, and personal care items), and the agency occasionally supplemented that portion with one or more weekly expenditure diaries recorded by the family (cf. Lamale 1959; BLS 1971).

Finally, continued experience with expenditure surveys in the years after 1930 (with a concerted focus on technique) revealed systematic biases in subjects' responses. Many of these biases became apparent as the bureau sought to evaluate the accuracy of its data by cross-checking individual responses for internal consistency and comparing aggregate results with data from other sources. For example, during the 1917–19 survey, the BLS told field agents that if the total income and total expenditures (including savings) did not match for a given respondent, then "the figures of one item or the other must be revised" before the schedule was submitted. As Williams put it dryly, "This procedure seems to encourage 'adjustments' in the figures provided by the family to a dangerous point" (Brady and Williams 1944, 340). For the 1934–36 survey, agents were asked to reinterview families with substantial imbalances between income and expenditures, but not to force the matter; instead, the BLS just discarded schedules where the final imbalance between overall money receipts and money expenditures exceeded 5.5 percent.[13] Likewise, housewives had to give both an annual expenditure estimate for food and a detailed account of the last week; fifty-two multiplied by the one-week total had to come within 15 percent of the annual estimate for the schedule to be tabulated.[14]

These new procedures allowed BLS statisticians to begin studying patterns in schedule imbalances, which proved to have certain tendencies. Overall, Lamale could report in 1959 that "average family income is usually understated; average family expenditures are also understated but somewhat less; and average savings are greater or dissavings less than shown by the reported changes in assets and liabilities" (22). Comparing BLS data with aggregate data from other sources (such as tax returns or sales figures from the Department of Commerce) gave the agency confidence that these imbalances represented true errors rather than legitimate trends in income and expenditure patterns. Such comparisons became possible only after the 1930s, when the BLS expanded its expenditure survey program to encompass all urban consumers and partnered with the Department of Agriculture to collect data on rural families as well, thereby providing comprehensive coverage that could readily be extrapolated to national aggregates.

These comparisons allowed the identification of more specific problems. Total expenditures ran (on average) about 10 percent less than Department of Commerce figures, with the largest shortfalls coming in food and clothing (especially for luxury goods such as jewelry, where survey results were "strikingly low"). These underestimations were partly offset by higher survey results for housing, fuel, light, and refrigeration (though the BLS had no solid explanation for the discrepancy). Most of the income shortfall, meanwhile, arose from undercounting interest and dividends. Finally, the effort to survey all Americans revealed systematic sampling problems: families at both ends of the income spectrum (but especially the higher end) were much more likely to refuse to participate in the survey (Brady and Williams 1944, 326–28, 341–43).

13. "Instructions to Field Agents," 5–6, 76.

14. "Instructions to Editors," February 1936, p. 8, Instructions—1934–36, box 1, Records of the Consumer Expenditure Survey Program and Predecessors, 1933–1971, Records of the US Bureau of Labor Statistics, Record Group 257, US National Archives II, College Park, Maryland.

In principle, most of these problems could be addressed by further refinements in procedures. Oversampling could offset higher refusal rates among certain population segments, for example, and staff hoped that more-detailed survey questions would reduce underreporting by improving recall (see, e.g., Brady and Williams 1944, 328). For suspected cases of "intentional bias," as when consumers understated expenditures on alcohol or luxury items such as jewelry, the bureau developed new interviewing strategies that promised more accurate estimates (Lamale 1959, 20). Given these possibilities, there seemed no reason to doubt that researchers would continue to improve the accuracy of individual household reports well into the future.

A Growing Crisis

By the late 1960s, however, any such optimism had dissipated. In part, some of the mandates developed through rationalization pulled the bureau in opposite directions. For example, as I have shown, the most basic lesson of methodological experiments was that the accuracy of individual returns increased when interviewers asked more-detailed questions. However, more-detailed questions also required more time, potentially reducing participation rates or skewing samples. Already in the 1930s, one experienced market researcher warned that the bureau's survey questions were "so detailed, so numerous, and so inquisitorial that no ordinary person will care to answer them"; indeed, he suggested, only "abnormal" people would even know the relevant information (White 1936, 23). By 1950, when the average interview took eight hours to complete, such fears seemed increasingly plausible. Responding to "widespread concern about the length of the interview" and its potential consequences for response rates and "inaccuracy . . . because of fatigue," the BLS sought to shorten the interview time for the 1960 survey by eliminating duplication and consigning some peripheral questions to other surveys. Nonetheless, the drive to improve accuracy led to expansions in other areas. As a result, the net reduction was minimal, with the average interview still lasting just under seven hours (BLS 1971, 6, 17, 24).[15]

A similar conflict occurred over the bureau's various requirements for internal consistency within a given schedule, such as the balance between

15. For the 1960 survey, the bureau insisted that tests indicated no substantial increase in refusal rates between an interview requiring four hours and one requiring seven hours; still, interview time clearly remained a concern. Today the typical interview for the BLS consumer expenditure survey lasts just over one hour (BLS 2007, 2).

total income and expenditures or the comparison of annual and weekly food estimates. The 1930s staff had used these tests to gauge the accuracy of results, using them to trigger second interviews and excluding schedules with imbalances above certain levels. However, by emphasizing the importance of consistency, the bureau also risked pressuring agents and families to make artificial adjustments merely to conform to expected standards. Already in 1936, a young Milton Friedman (working for a federal agency overseeing a major expenditure survey) had warned supervisors that his visits to field offices had revealed "a danger of a tendency to 'force a balance'" in order to make schedules acceptable.[16] Indeed, after a pilot study in 1949, the bureau itself highlighted "the danger of placing too much emphasis on a balancing criterion," and it weakened the criterion for the 1950 study, using imbalances as prompts for revisiting families but not as an eligibility requirement (Lamale 1959, 25). That policy mitigated the threat of overenthusiastic editing, but at the cost of what earlier staff members had considered a basic safeguard. For the 1960 survey, the BLS retained the same general procedure but added a "professional review" of all schedules by highly trained staff members who scrutinized schedules for internal consistency and attention to detail. Most schedules were accepted; some were rejected; and a few (roughly 1 percent) were "improved" when reviewers felt that they could clearly identify missing items (BLS 1971, 29–33, esp. 33). Balancing criteria thus hovered uneasily between being essential guides to accuracy and sources of distortion.

The most serious issues, however, involved the growing evidence that a single interview of a household (the bureau's preferred method) might not be able to capture a complete record of expenditures.[17] The BLS, for example, acknowledged that different goods and services were best captured by recall periods of different lengths: annual, monthly, or weekly (Lamale 1959, 19). Yet extrapolating annual totals from monthly or weekly estimates required either assuming that there was no seasonal variation or undertaking continuous sampling over an entire year. Meanwhile, multiple studies during the 1950s and 1960s illuminated new problems such as telescoping—a phenomenon (common with large expenditures) in which

16. Milton Friedman to Day Monroe, August 22, 1936, folder 705.1, box 1734, Central Office Records, Records of the National Resources Planning Board, Record Group 187, US National Archives II, College Park, Maryland.

17. "Single interview" is understood here to also encompass a small set of interviews that all deal with the same time period. Completing a schedule sometimes did require multiple visits to a family over successive days.

consumers mistakenly attributed purchases from earlier periods to a later period covered by the survey (Neter and Waksberg 1964, esp. 43–49).

Even as statisticians confronted the limitations of interviews, the debate over the value of diaries reignited when a major, unpublished study of expenditure survey methodology from the US Census Bureau drew attention once again to the contrast between American reliance on annual recall and European use of diaries (Pearl 1968). New experiments on diaries versus recall yielded mixed results, but nonetheless indicated that diaries could have real advantages over recall methods in certain circumstances (Neter 1970, 23–24; Sudman and Ferber 1971). The controversy was made more acute by the context: The study from the Census Bureau came as US statisticians were planning for a new nationwide survey (eventually conducted in 1972–73) and as the BLS (which had long favored recall interviews) was handing responsibility for administering the survey over to the Census Bureau as a cost-saving measure. The result was a sharp dispute that exemplified the broader tensions emerging from BLS research.

Abandoning the Complete Household Survey

Following their existing strategies, US government statisticians sought to resolve the impasse by appealing to experiment: in this case, two test surveys that would compare diary and recall methods. Before the results were analyzed, however, the US Office of Statistical Standards (OSS, housed within the Office of Management and Budget) imposed its own solution. The OSS was responsible for coordinating all federal statistics and therefore had final responsibility for approving survey methods, which in turn gave it the power (when necessary) to settle conflicts. In this case, according to two observers, it acted on "*a priori* statistical and logistical grounds" (Jacobs and Shipp 1993, 67) to develop a novel and elegant strategy that broke with previous tradition.

Rather than continue to tinker with the standard, annual recall interview, the OSS replaced it with two separate surveys: a quarterly interview panel survey and a diary survey. Households participating in the panel survey were interviewed every three months over a fifteen-month period and asked about their expenditures. Households in the diary survey recorded their purchases for two weeks. Not only were the two surveys entirely separate, with independent questionnaires and samples, but they each covered only part of the full range of expenditures, with the panel survey emphasizing more expensive, less frequent expenditures while the diary survey focused on smaller, frequently purchased items (BLS 1978, 2).

The new design alleviated many of the tensions that had come to plague BLS methodology. For example, splitting the survey into two parts made it easier to ask more-detailed questions without overwhelming respondents. Moreover, with the quarterly panel survey divided into five visits, the bureau could distribute topics across different visits, allowing some information (such as demographic characteristics, housing costs, appliance purchases, or insurance premiums) to be gathered annually or semiannually. As a result, average time for a single interview plunged to one and a half hours (Jacobs and Shipp 1993, 67), and official response rates rose from roughly 80 percent in 1950 and 1961–62 to 89 percent (BLS 1978, 4). In fact, the true rise in response rates was substantially higher. The earlier surveys had substituted alternates when the initially contacted household refused to participate (a procedure that "violated strict probability selection" according to later staff members [Jacobs and Shipp 1993, 65]), and the BLS did not count these refusals in the official response rates.[18]

The flexibility of the panel survey–diary combination also mitigated the weaknesses of the recall method that had been identified over the previous three decades. For example, it allowed the bureau to design appropriate recall periods (daily, quarterly, semiannually, etc.) for different goods. Moreover, by using the first interview of the panel survey to take an inventory of the household's current durable goods, the bureau was able to recognize (and eliminate) much of the "telescoping" that might occur in future interviews (BLS 1978, 2). Most obviously, of course, the new procedures ended the long-standing conflict over the interviews versus diaries.

The shift to the new format, however, required a fundamental reconceptualization of the framework for the surveys. The previous approach assumed that the proximal objective was to gather complete expenditure information from individual households that had been randomly selected so as to represent the distribution of American households overall. By contrast, the new strategy dispensed with the focus on individual households; instead, it aimed directly at gathering average expenditures for groups with different socioeconomic characteristics (defined by income,

18. If one did count initial refusals, the response rate for urban households would have been about 75 percent in 1961–62 per data supplied by the bureau (BLS 1971, 25).

race, geographic location, etc.), a goal that could be reached without having a complete record for any given household.[19]

In principle, the new approach was perfectly compatible with the overall goals of expenditure surveys. From the nineteenth century onward, statisticians had conducted surveys to learn about the characteristic behaviors of different socioeconomic groups, and the emphasis on correlating expenditures with economic and demographic variables had only grown over time (cf. Stapleford 2007). The spending patterns of individual households were of no interest per se; they were only means to the larger end. In that light, one might have expected American statisticians to drop the focus on obtaining complete household records much earlier. In one sense, they did: as early as 1945, BLS staff discussed the possibility dividing a full expenditure survey into multiple, independent components, and both the BLS and the US Department of Agriculture conducted small-scale tests of "split-schedule" surveys that same year (Brady and Williams 1944, 337–38; Lamale 1959, 16–18). In both cases, however, the format was rejected, and that decision tells us much about the different conceptual framework that guided American statisticians' methodological choices at midcentury.

Higher costs were a very important, and very legitimate, concern. (Adding the diaries to the interviews in 1972–73 almost tripled the number of families visited, and the panel survey required multiple visits over fifteen months.)[20] Yet BLS staff also worried about reduced accuracy, and specifically about "the loss of the general criterion of acceptability of a report in the reasonable balance of income, expenditures, and savings" (Brady and Williams 1944, 338). The loss of the balance criterion continued to be mentioned in subsequent years as a significant black mark against the "split-schedule" method, and the results of test surveys failed to demonstrate significant advantages to the format even as they reinforced fears that the absence of checks for internal consistency would leave results liable to what the Department of Agriculture called "considerable field error" (Lamale 1959, 16–17; BLS 1971, 3).

19. For example, one sample of households could provide information on food purchases, while a different sample provided information on clothing purchases. As long as the sampling procedures matched, each average could be regarded as truly representative of the population from which the samples were drawn, and therefore the averages could be combined to yield information about average total expenditures on food and clothing.

20. The full increase was even higher, since the 1972–73 survey expanded the overall sample size, but this does not seem to be related to the new format.

Indeed, the adoption of the panel survey–diary combination led directly to the abandonment of balancing criteria altogether. Since each quarterly interview covered only a portion of a household's expenditures, there was no way to analyze internal consistency by comparing expenditures and income, and subsequent BLS staff members dismissed such analyses as "judgmental" anyway (Jacobs and Shipp 1993, 68). Of course, BLS staff members continued to worry about the accuracy of their results, but they now relied primarily on comparisons with other sources of aggregate data and on experimental research into survey methodology rather than on the consistency of individual returns, trusting that the former strategies would provide general guarantees, while any real problems in individual returns would have minimal effects on the final tables. As the bureau rather dryly explained, "The data base [for 1972–73] may contain unusual entries"; nonetheless, the staff remained confident in the verity of its group averages (BLS 1978, 18).

In essence, therefore, federal statisticians abandoned the balancing criteria (making it possible to split the survey into multiple components) because they now were worried less about the accuracy of individual returns. Implicitly, they expected their methodological research to uncover any systematic biases in interview responses while unsystematic (random) errors would cancel each other out in the process of computing an average. The balancing criteria were thus unnecessary. We can see a similar transformation in the bureau's increased willingness to "correct" incomplete responses on individual schedules. This trend had begun with the 1960–61 survey, in which staff allocated some expenditures from broad categories into smaller subcategories according to typical patterns if the original family had been unable or unwilling to do so (BLS 1971, 31). During and after the 1972–73 survey, this process was dramatically expanded and automated through computer processing (cf. BLS 1978, 18–19). Today, these post hoc adjustments take three forms: imputing data for "missing and invalid entries" in all fields other than assets (including income and demographic characteristics); allocating expenditures from general categories to more specific subcategories; and classifying expenditures by month to calculate calendar-year totals (BLS 2007, 4). These procedures reflect an increased trust in the verity of BLS averages such that (somewhat paradoxically) one need fret less about the accuracy of the individual returns used to construct those averages. Whereas many of the issues listed above would have once been viewed as signs of sloppy or inaccurate reporting that might merit disqualification from the survey, these schedules are now readily accepted and "corrected" based on typical patterns.

Evolution without Teleology

I suggested at the outset of this essay that the history of methodology in BLS expenditure surveys did not present a clear teleology. In part, that judgment rests on the noncumulative nature of shifts in BLS practices. The balancing criteria that were initially introduced as crucial bulwarks against error-prone schedules, for example, were later discarded as unnecessary and perhaps even as distorting. Likewise, the diary methods that were eschewed in the 1930s and 1940s subsequently became a basic component of the survey program, indeed perhaps the more reliable of the two methods (Jacobs and Shipp 1993, 70). It would be naive to think evaluations of survey methodology will not be subject to similar fluctuations in the future; conceivably, a new generation of statisticians will decide that the bureau has become overly lenient in its willingness to accept schedules that evince signs of careless reporting.

More generally, though, the nonteleological nature of a history of survey methodology reflects a factor that limited space has prevented me from exploring here: the changing context for survey work. It should be obvious, for example, that funding levels can determine the range of viable methodological options. Though the move to the split panel survey–diary format required a conceptual shift, and came only after a vigorous theoretical debate, it would have been impossible to implement (and thus impossible to consider seriously) had the survey program not received substantially more funding. Likewise, the bureau was fortunate (in a peculiar way) that the 1970s oil shock and subsequent economic upheaval came right after it had completed its 1972–73 survey, since the poor timing provided the political impetus (and thus the funding) for a continuous survey beginning in 1980 (Jacobs and Shipp 1993, 68–69).

Yet equally important, though more readily overlooked, are changes in the subjects of expenditures, that is, American households and their economic activity. If one considers the radical changes over the last century in household composition, employment patterns, retail practices, financial tools, government interventions (including tax laws), and modes of economic exchange (e.g., credit cards), it becomes evident that even if statisticians have maintained the same abstract goals, they have not been facing the same practical challenges. Why should a set of strategies that worked well in the past continue to function with the same effectiveness in the future? To take but one example, response rates for expenditure surveys (indeed, most government surveys) have suffered from continual decline since the 1970s: the response rate for the 1972–73 survey was nearly 90 percent; today (with less time-consuming schedules), it is roughly 70–75 percent (BLS 2007, 5). A history of survey methodology must be nonteleological, in other words, because the surveys themselves are aiming at moving targets. What I have sketched above is therefore only an outline; we await a deeper, richer narrative that will unite the intellectual history of survey methodology with an appropriately dynamic view of American social, economic, and political life.

References

Brady, Dorothy S., and Faith M. Williams. 1944. "Advances in Techniques of Measuring and Estimating Consumer Expenditures." *Journal of Farm Economics* 27 (2): 315–44.

Cole, Dorothy E. 1956. "Field Work in Sample Surveys of Household Income and Expenditure." *Journal of the Royal Statistical Society*, ser. C (Applied Statistics) 5 (1): 49–61.

Cornfield, Jerome. 1942. "On Certain Biases in Samples of Human Populations." *Journal of the American Statistical Association* 37 (217): 63–68.

Didier, Emmanuel. 2011. "Counting on Relief: Industrializing the Statistical Interviewer during the New Deal." *Science in Context* 24 (2): 281–310.

Dippo, Cathryn S. 1987. "A Review of Statistical Research at the U.S. Bureau of Labor Statistics." *Journal of Official Statistics* 3 (3): 289–97.

Goudy, Willis J., and Harry R. Potter. 1975. "Interview Rapport: Demise of a Concept." *Public Opinion Quarterly* 39 (4): 529–43.

International Labour Office. 1926. *The Third International Conference of Labour Statisticians Held at Geneva, 18 to 23 October 1926*. International Labour Office, Studies and Reports, series N (Statistics), no. 12. Geneva: International Labour Office.

———. 1939. "An International Survey of Recent Family Living Studies: I." *International Labour Review* 39 (5): 662–705.

Jacobs, Eva, and Stephanie Shipp. 1993. "A History of the Consumer Expenditure Survey: 1935–36 to 1988–89." *Journal of Economic and Social Measurement* 19: 59–96.

Lamale, Helen Humes. 1959. *Methodology of the Survey of Consumer Expenditures in 1950*. Study of Consumer Expenditures, Incomes and Savings. Philadelphia: University of Pennsylvania.

Neter, John. 1970. "Measurement Errors in Reports of Consumer Expenditures." *Journal of Marketing Research* 7 (1): 11–25.

Neter, John, and Joseph Waksberg. 1964. "A Study of Response Errors in Expenditures Data from Household Interviews." *Journal of the American Statistical Association* 59 (305): 18–55.

Pearl, R. 1968. "Methodology of Consumer Expenditure Surveys." US Bureau of the Census. Working Papers, No. 27. Washington, D.C.: US Government Printing Office.

Scott, William A. 1968. "Attitude Measurement." In *Handbook of Social Psychology.* 2nd ed. Reading, Mass.: Addison-Wesley.

Stapleford, Thomas A. 2003. "'The Most Important Single Statistic': The Consumer Price Index and American Political Economy, 1880–1955." PhD diss., Harvard University.

———. 2007. "Market Visions: Expenditure Surveys, Market Research, and Economic Planning in the New Deal." *Journal of American History* 94:418–44.

———. 2009. *The Cost of Living in America: A Political History of Economic Statistics, 1880–2000.* New York: Cambridge University Press.

———. 2010. "The Labor History of U.S. Labor Statistics, 1880–1930." Unpublished working paper. February.

Sudman, Seymour, and Robert Ferber. 1971. "Experiments in Obtaining Consumer Expenditures by Diary Methods." *Journal of the American Statistical Association* 66 (336): 725–35.

US Bureau of Labor Statistics (BLS). 1971. *Consumer Expenditures and Income: Survey Guidelines.* Bulletin of the U.S. Bureau of Labor Statistics 1684. Washington, D.C.: US Government Printing Office.

———. 1978. *Consumer Expenditure Survey: Integrated Diary and Interview Survey Data, 1972–73: Total Expenditures and Income for the United States and Selected Areas.* Washington, D.C.: US Government Printing Office.

———. 2007. Consumer Expenditures and Incomes. In *BLS Handbook of Methods.* Washington, D.C. www.bls.gov/opub/hom/pdf/homch16.pdf.

US Commissioner of Labor. 1891. *Seventh Annual Report.* Vol. 2. Washington, D.C.: US Government Printing Office.

White, Percival. 1936. "New Deal in Questionnaires." *Market Research* 4 (June): 23.

Williams, Faith M. 1932. *Bibliography on Studies of Costs and Standards of Living in the United States.* Washington, D.C.: US Government Printing Office.

Williams, Faith M., and Carle C. Zimmerman. 1935. *Studies of Family Living in the United States and Other Countries: An Analysis of Material and Method.* USDA Miscellaneous Publication 223. Washington, D.C.: US Government Printing Office.

Part 3
Relocating Vision

Field, Undercover, and Participant Observers in US Labor Economics: 1900–1930

Malcolm Rutherford

Over the period considered in this essay, American work in labor economics focused overwhelmingly on various aspects of the "labor problem." This was the problem of industrial relations, of union and anti-union activity, of strikes and violence, of "yellow-dog" contracts and court injunctions.[1] This led the first few generations of American labor economists to direct their studies to the labor movement and its motivations and goals, the working and living conditions experienced by working people, the managerial and workplace practices that might affect productivity and morale, and possible ways to improve relations and mediate conflict. As the theory of competitive labor markets was not seen as a useful guide to the realities involved, the approach taken by these labor economists was strongly empirical in nature. There was little relevant official data,[2] and labor economists, of necessity, became field observers and data collectors of various types. The use of methods of field observation linked economics to other social science disciplines, especially sociology and anthropology, and also to government commissions of inquiry, to social work, and to muckraking journalism.

Three examples are examined here. The first is a study of steelworkers, done as part of the Pittsburgh Survey, by John Fitch, a student of

---

1. Yellow-dog contracts were employment contracts that forbade membership in a union.
2. Some data were available from the US Census and from state and federal bureaus of labor.

History of Political Economy 44 (annual suppl.) DOI 10.1215/00182702-1631833

John R. Commons, published in 1910. The second is the work done on migrant labor and the Industrial Workers of the World (IWW) in California by F. C. Mills and Paul Brissenden under the supervision of Carleton Parker for the California Commission on Immigration and Housing and the US Commission on Industrial Relations, completed between 1914 and 1916. The third is a study of workplace practice among nonunion workers done by Stanley Mathewson, a student of William Leiserson,[3] completed in 1930 and published a year later. Each of these cases involves the study of a specific problem, but they encompass different observational techniques. It is also possible to examine the extent to which these studies fed into more theoretical formulations.

In these various observational endeavors one can discern a typology based on two oppositions: open versus covert observation, and participant versus nonparticipant observation. Labor economists did not always have the cooperation of management or of any of the trade unions involved. Both sides could be suspicious of the investigator, and investigators sometimes feared that their presence, if known, might change the behavior of their research subjects. So in some instances the observation was covert. In other instances the observer made no effort to conceal his or her identity and purpose, but sought in various other ways to gain trust. Participant observation involves actually taking on the role of the individuals one is studying, joining the group and living and working as a member of the group. This is a method designed to generate a deeper understanding of the group, its functioning, and its norms than could be achieved by a nonparticipant who observes without joining in the life of the group. Participant observation can be open, as in anthropology where the observer normally cannot conceal his or her outsider status, or covert if the observer can and does pass as an insider. The first of the studies examined here used open nonparticipant observation, the second used covert observation with aspects of participant observation, and the third used covert participant observation. Most observational work in economics belonged to the open observation, nonparticipant type.

There is also an important distinction to be drawn between surveys that are essentially quantitative, designed to collect statistical information on such factors as housing conditions, expenditures, or unemployment, and fieldwork with broader purposes such as the development of a picture of a

3. Leiserson was a student of John R. Commons and had also been McCarthy's assistant on the US Commission on Industrial Relations.

workplace, a community, a way of life, or a set of practices that goes beyond numbers. None of the studies discussed here were purely or even predominantly statistical or quantitative in nature, although data were collected in various ways. In the years that followed, surveys in economics became increasing statistical and "objective" in nature, and the types of field research outlined here fell out of favor.

The Steelworkers

Fitch's study of steelworkers was a part of the Pittsburgh Survey conducted in 1907 and 1908 under the direction of Paul U. Kellogg and funded by the Russell Sage Foundation. The survey produced six volumes: Fitch (1910) on steelworkers; Crystal Eastman (1910) on work accidents and the law; Elizabeth Butler (1909) on women and the trades; Margaret Byington (1911) on the households of Homestead, a mill town just outside Pittsburgh itself; and two volumes of essays on various topics edited by Kellogg (1914a, 1914b). The methods employed had their origins in the surveys conducted by Charles Booth in London[4] and by the social work researchers at Hull House[5] in Chicago.

At the time of the survey, Pittsburgh was a heavily industrial city dominated by iron and steel companies, the largest of which was the US Steel Corporation, formed in 1901. There had been violent strikes, notably the Homestead strike of 1892, in which the union (the Amalgamated Association of Iron and Steel Workers) had been defeated. Another failed strike occurred in 1901, and the union effectively driven out of the industry, so that "since that time the employers have again been free to work out their own policies" (Fitch 1910, 5). What Fitch was investigating, then, was what he called the "labor policy of unrestricted capital" (192).

Fitch's book does not give much detailed information about his observational methods. There is, for example, no list of plants visited or of the number of visits, no reporting of the number of men interviewed at work or at home, no list of company officials interviewed, and little information

---

4. Booth's (1902–3) work was a survey of living and working conditions in London. The first edition was published in 1889 and featured maps of poverty and living standards by street. Many of Booth's research assistants came from Toynbee Hall, where young reform-minded intellectuals could live and experience life in the East End of London.

5. Hull House was a community of university women, founded by Jane Addams, modeled on Toynbee Hall, and dedicated to providing educational and other opportunities and services to the people of Chicago's Near West side, a poor immigrant population. Their work included investigations of working and living conditions in the Hull House neighborhood.

on the exact sources of data. Even in cases where sources are given, they may be informal (e.g., from a letter written by a worker to a union newspaper). It is clear that Fitch did a great deal of work in attempting to check his information, but the book is full of what are inevitably subjective estimates of reliability.

Fitch spent ten months in the Pittsburgh district, visiting every large mill there, and most he visited "repeatedly." He visited mills in the company of regular mill guides, officials of the steel companies, men "well acquainted with steel manufacture but now in no way connected with the industry," and skilled workers who volunteered their services and "explained the part played by labor in the process of iron and steel manufacture" (9). These visits and discussions form the basis of the bulk of the book's early chapters on the work of the blast furnace crews, the puddlers and iron rollers, the steelmakers, and the men of the rolling mills. Fitch watched the work under all sorts of conditions and talked to the men as they rested between tasks:

> To understand these men you must first of all see them thus at their work; you must stand beside the open-hearth helper as he taps fifty tons of molten steel from his furnace; you must feel the heat of the Bessemer converters as you watch the vesselmen and the steel pourer; and above the crash and roar of the blooming mills you must talk with rollers and hookers, while five- and ten-ton steel ingots plunge madly back and forth between the rolls. You must see the men working in hoop mills and guide mills, where the heat is intense and the work laborious; you must see them amid ladles of molten steel, among piles of red hot bars, or bending over straightening presses at the rail mills. (10)

Fitch also visited and interviewed workingmen in their homes, something he thought was also vital to an understanding of them. In these cases he was initially given introductions to "leading steel workers" by friends, and these people in turn furnished him with the names of others. In this manner Fitch claims he was able to get close to the lives of "typical" skilled and unskilled men, even though he was often suspected of being a company spy attempting to find out about attitudes toward the union or the company. The steel companies did employ numerous spies, and men found to be union organizers were routinely discharged. Despite this atmosphere of intimidation, Fitch claims he was able to get some degree of cooperation, provided he could show his letters of introduction, explain his purpose, and promise not to reveal names (215–16). Fitch indicates he talked at length with over one hundred men, but it is impossible to say how representative a sample Fitch obtained of the roughly seventy thousand men employed in the industry in Pittsburgh and the surrounding towns. In chapter 2 Fitch gives excerpts from his interviews with nine men and says that he "tried to introduce the leading types—the twelve hour man, the eight hour man, the church member, the man who is at outs with the church, the union man and the socialist" (21), but throughout the book Fitch draws on his interviews with workers, foremen, and superintendents. The interview with John Griswold (the twelve-hour man) is reported in direct quotation:

"Mighty few men have stood what I have, I can tell you. I've been twenty years at the furnaces and been workin' a twelve hour day all that time, seven days a week. We go to work at seven in the mornin' and we get through at night at six. We work that way for two weeks and then we work the long turn and change to the night shift of thirteen hours. . . . Now, if we had eight hours it would be different . . . after dinner me and the missus could go to the park if we wanted to, or I could take the childer to the country where there ain't any saloons." (11)

Direct observation of the workplace and interviews were not the only sources of information for Fitch. Chapter 7 discusses health and accidents in steelmaking, with data drawn primarily from the companion volume by Eastman (1910). Chapters 8 to 10 discuss the history of unionism in the industry, the policies of the Amalgamated Association, and the "great strikes." Fitch draws on trade union newspapers, union circulars, union constitutions and bylaws, and other union-provided documents and data. Chapters 11 to 16 detail employer practices and policies, including issues of wage scales, cost of living, the working day and week, speeding up, and the bonus system. These chapters made use of Bureau of Labor bulletins, data provided by the steel companies, company policy documents about seven-day labor, profit-sharing plans, accident relief plans, and Carnegie pension plans, information taken from previous investigations of strikes, congressional testimony, labor newspapers, data from other Pittsburgh Survey volumes, and data classifying employees according to skill level, citizenship, and language, which appear to have come from company sources. The last two chapters on citizenship in the mill towns and the spirit of the workers are again based largely on Fitch's own observations and interviews.

In addition to all of this material, the Pittsburgh Survey employed an artist and a photographer. This was not an unconsidered matter. Kellogg himself was editor of the *Survey* and the *Survey Graphic*, and the latter

Figure 1 *At the Base of the Blast Furnace: Pittsburgh*, by Joseph Stella. Carnegie Library of Pittsburgh, all rights reserved

publication especially made a feature of the use of photographs and other graphic material (see Charles and Giraud 2010). The artist was Joseph Stella and the photographer was Lewis Hine. Stella was an accomplished artist later associated with the futurist and precisionist movements. Hine later became deeply involved in the campaign against child labor, a campaign in which his photographs played a key role (Freedman 1994). Examples of their work are included here. Stella's drawing *At the Base of the Blast Furnace* is reproduced as figure 1; Hine's photograph *Pouring Steel Old Fashioned Way* is reproduced as figure 2.

Fitch's commentary, and the thrust of the book, relates to certain key conditions of work, the steady increase in mechanization, the speeding up of work, the exploitation of ethnic divisions, and most of all the twelve-hour day and seven-day-week schedule followed in most of the mills. This schedule gave a man one twenty-four-hour period off work every two weeks when shifts changed. On the other side, this required one twenty-four-hour shift every two weeks. This work pattern was found by Fitch to be at the heart of most of the labor problems of the steel industry. Fitch also detailed the dangers of the steelworker's jobs, the lack of a state

Figure 2 *Pouring Steel Old Fashioned Way, Small Pittsburgh Mill, 1908–9*, by Lewis W. Hine. Courtesy of George Eastman House, International Museum of Photography and Film

factory-inspection system or workmen's compensation laws, the low and declining real wages paid to most of the workers, and the attempts by the steel companies to influence the political activities and votes of their employees. For Fitch, all of this indicated the desirability of union representation and collective bargaining. Fitch (1910, 206) argued employers had utilized their freedom from restraint to introduce "negative and destructive policies." For Fitch, a union has a "clear moral right to a voice in determining labor conditions" (205).

It has been argued that the Pittsburgh Survey and other similar surveys had little influence on the later development of American social science, either because the social survey movement was more social work than social science or because the later development of social science moved toward more "objective" quantitative work as exemplified by Wesley Mitchell in economics and William Ogburn in sociology (Greenwald and Anderson 1996). On the other hand, Mary Furner (2000, 409–11) has argued that the successors of the survey movement can be found in "the Labor, Children's and Women Bureau's work," in the investigations of the

US Commission on Industrial Relations, in "the New Deal–era studies of migrant communities," and in the work on labor economics and industrial relations being conducted at the University of Wisconsin by Commons and his students. These points are worth emphasizing. The approach taken by Fitch in the steelworkers book is strikingly similar to that taken in a great deal of the work on unions and industrial relations undertaken by Commons and his students. Most of this work relied heavily on document collection and interviews and is not primarily quantitative or statistical. Commons (1934, 106) described "the constructive method of interviewing" as the "prime method of investigation,"[6] and the economics department at Wisconsin regularly offered a course on the techniques of field investigation at least through the later 1920s (Rutherford 2006). As with Fitch's book, this work provided a basis not only for the advocacy of collective bargaining and other reforms to labor law as a substitute for industrial unrest but also for more general and theoretical discussions of unionism, in the form of the development of a social-institutional approach to union history that, in the American case, presented unions as primarily concerned with the protection of job opportunities (Perlman 1928; Kapuria-Foreman and McCann 2010). It is true, however, that after 1945 work of this type tended to move from economics departments to schools of industrial relations.

The California Casual and the IWW

In November 1913 Carleton Parker, a labor economist at the University of California at Berkeley, was appointed executive secretary of the California Commission on Immigration and Housing. Part of Parker's job was to investigate the causes of the Wheatland Hopfield riot. This riot, which involved migratory hop pickers in the summer of 1913, resulted from the appalling conditions in a labor camp on the Durst hop ranch. The ranch had advertised for many more workers than were required, and part of the wages was withheld to be paid as a bonus to those who remained for the whole picking season. The camp was a barren field, with severely inadequate sanitation and water supply. Temperatures were over 100 degrees Fahrenheit. Water and supplies could not be brought in, as Durst was profiting from the only store on the ranch, and his cousin had a lemonade concession. The protest reached a head at a rally called by the Industrial

---

6. Commons (1934, 106) gives a number of references to works on interview methods.

Workers of the World. The local sheriff arrived with a posse to arrest the ringleaders, and in the ensuing riot four people died (including the district attorney and a deputy sheriff), and many were wounded. The National Guard was called in, IWW members were arrested all over the state, and the two IWW leaders at the camp (Richard Ford and Herman Suhr) were eventually sentenced to life in prison. Concerns over migrant labor were heightened even more by the episode of "Kelly's Army," a march of unemployed seasonal workers in the fall of 1913 that was eventually broken up by force (Woirol 1992, 5–11). In the spring of 1914 Parker was also deputized to investigate the Wheatland Hopfield riot for the US Commission on Industrial Relations.

Parker's report on the Wheatland riot provides a considerable amount of information on his methods of investigation. In Parker's (1920, 174) words:

> This report is founded on a careful personal investigation of the physical facts by all the investigators employed by the commission; upon a close study of the trial of Ford, Suhr, Beck and Bagan at Marysville; upon interviews with witnesses at the trial and with pickers who were present on the ranch during the days before August 3rd and who were not present at the trial, but scattered throughout the state; and upon interviews with residents of Yuba County.

Parker and his investigators took sixty-seven written statements and affidavits, and an additional thirty oral interviews. Of the witnesses who made written statements, fifty-seven are classified as "perfectly reliable" and ten as of "doubtful reliability." The oral interviews included Durst and his regular employees. The investigators also examined the job advertisements placed by Durst and inspected Durst's books. The investigation was able to document the numbers of people in the camp, the wages paid, the misleading nature of the job advertisements, the extremely poor conditions in the camp, the questionable arrangements relating to the lemonade and store concessions, and the numbers and actions of the IWW members present on the ranch. Parker's primary recommendation was to properly enforce the state regulations on conditions in labor camps, condemning both the attitudes of the employers who would allow substandard conditions and the violent strike methods of the IWW.

Parker's job was made difficult both by the interest of the employers of seasonal labor in concealing the true working and living conditions and by the suspicion of IWW members of any "official" investigation of their activities. In the spring of 1914 Parker hired two of his former

Berkeley students, F. C. Mills and Paul Brissenden, to conduct under-cover investigations of the conditions in various labor camps, gather information on migrant life, and assess the presence of, and attitudes toward, the IWW. Thanks to Gregory Woirol (1992), substantial information is available on Mills's work.

Mills embarked on his investigation, posing as a hobo, in May 1914. He dressed the part, took an assumed name, joined the IWW, worked in various camps, traveled on foot or rode the rails (including "riding the rods" under boxcars), slept rough in hobo "jungles" or in haystacks or boxcars, and washed at roadside hydrants or in irrigation ditches. He worked packing oranges in the San Joaquin valley, as a laborer in a Sierra lumber camp, and on a road construction project at Sand Creek. He wrote two reports on conditions in the orange-picking industry, one each on his lumber camp and Sand Creek experiences, and several items on life "on the road." He also made observations about the opinions held by various groups of workers on the IWW and on the general level of IWW activity, and he kept a detailed diary. Brissenden wrote a report on the IWW in California. Mills's travels lasted two months, after which he spent another year working for Parker and the California Commission on Immigration and Housing, but did not go on the road again.[7]

In his first job, packing oranges, Mills reported that the advertisements for workers had far overstated the requirements and that he had found "idle men on every street corner" (Woirol 1992, 23). The workplace conditions he found satisfactory, but the work itself strenuous. For the hardest jobs, the rate of turnover of labor was extremely high. Many of the workers boarded at local lodging houses, but Mills had difficulty finding places to sleep. On one occasion he was given meal tickets in place of wages. In the lumber camps he found workers living in tents and cabins, four together, in one case with no toilets initially, the men using the nearby hillside instead. Otherwise he found conditions satisfactory. His report detailed the types of work, the numbers of men employed, the ethnic composition of the workforce, the wages paid, and the living and working conditions. On the Sand Creek project Mills visited two camps, one of which had very poor conditions and employed mostly immigrant labor. Mills suspected the employer in this camp to be colluding with an employment agency in Fresno. The men were charged a fee by the agency and a fee for transportation to the camp. The employer received part of these

---

7. There is a suggestion that both Mills and Brissenden contracted malaria.

fees. As many as a dozen men arrived each day for a work crew of about twenty or thirty. Workers frequently quit because of the conditions, were forced out, or were fired on some pretense to make room for new arrivals (25–75). Later in his travels Mills was to make further investigations of employment agencies (104).

His reports on life on the road were based more on conversations and subjective impressions, and contain many descriptions of individuals he met. Mills, here, was attempting to provide a picture of "the general character of the men studied and their attitude toward certain things, in a way that mere statistical data cannot do" (quoted in Woirol 1992, 88). In this aspect of Mills's work, his procedure moves more fully into a participant-observer mode, in which his own participation in the life of the itinerant worker is key to the research effort and to his ability to gain an understanding of the men and their attitudes. Mills's reports contain some lengthy descriptions of individuals he met on the road and in the camps:

> "Tony" as he told me to call him, was a fellow worker in the grading crew at Hume. Twenty-three years old, he was born in the island of Sardinia. . . . Hearing wonderful tales of the amount of work in California, Tony came out last March, leaving his brother in New York. For two months he stayed in San Francisco and could get no work. . . . Tony is unmarried, and says that practically all Italians who work as he does from place to place are also unmarried, as a settled life is impossible. . . . His ambition is to save enough to get a small farm or store and bring out a wife from Italy and settle down. (quoted in Woirol 1992, 50–51)

Mills's work added to the substantial collection of life histories of itinerant workers being collected by Parker. What became clear to Mills was that the itinerant life was easy to fall into but difficult to escape. Most of the jobs he encountered, with the exception of some of the lumbering jobs, did not allow the worker to save a large enough amount to escape the casual life. Once workers had a history of temporary jobs, they were not considered for permanent positions. Life as a casual was inconsistent with any settled family life and often led to a pattern of periods of work punctuated by bouts of "dissipation" (Woirol 1992, 60–64).

Mills also observed attitudes toward the IWW, finding little sympathy among the more skilled workers in the packing plants or among the better-paid lumberjacks, but much more, if not universal, sympathy with the IWW in the case of the less skilled and more itinerant part of the labor force. Although Mills was not himself sympathetic to the IWW's methods, he found it easy to understand the organization's appeal to the itinerant class of labor. He reported that "the evidences of a social unrest, of a growing dissatisfaction with their lot in life, are not lacking among this class." The IWW "is the most alluring of all the voices that offer a way out, and there is a wide-spread knowledge of and sympathy with the activities of that organization" (Woirol 1992, 120). Many men had come to accept the idea of direct action: "In city squares the thought is applauded; in hobo jungles it is endorsed. Upton Sinclair and Jack London are preaching it" (128). Paul Brissenden, in his report on the IWW, reached a similar conclusion: that the appeal of the IWW was a reaction to the "socially antiquated" system of treating itinerant labor (122).

The impact of Mills's and Brissenden's undercover work was both practical and theoretical. On the practical side, the California Commission on Immigration and Housing, in its December 1914 *Report on Unemployment*, recommended the creation of state labor exchanges and more regulation of private agencies. On the more academic side, Brissenden (1919) went on to write his Columbia University PhD thesis on the IWW. Brissenden opposed the extreme and wholly negative view of the IWW that was commonly held. His book is largely a discussion of the evolution of the IWW and its organization, membership, policy positions, and internal disputes, but he clearly does see some positive aspects to the IWW views on industrial democracy. Brissenden's book became the standard reference on the IWW.

Carlton Parker also made considerable use of the reports provided by his various investigators. In a 1915 paper on the California Casual, he talks of "schedules" describing 222 "typical migratory workers" whom he used to provide a profile. He reports on the inspection of 867 camps and provides data on the living and working conditions found, a data set supplemented by information taken from the books of the Southern Pacific and Northwestern Pacific about labor turnover in their railway construction camps. To this he adds information from the reports of two investigators who spent "weeks among the casuals" (Parker 1920, 74–79).

More significantly, Parker (1920, 59) combined the information he had gained about the life of the casual into a theory of labor unrest based on the idea of a maladjustment between human nature and "a carelessly ordered world." Human activity is "actuated by the demand for realization of the instinct wants," but the economic environment faced by many, and particularly the casual, is such as to thwart these instincts and to result in a "psychic revolt" that can express itself either as a loss of interest or as antagonism or violence: persistent unrest, dissatisfaction, and decay of morale (161–64).[8] Parker included the IWW in the scope of this thesis. The usual condemnations of the IWW as unlawful in its actions, unpatriotic, and un-American Parker saw as completely ignoring the conditions that gave rise to the movement: "The casual migratory labourers are the finished product of an economic environment which seems cruelly efficient in turning out human beings modeled after all the standards which society abhors. . . . The I.W.W. has importance only as an illustration of a stable American economic process" (123).[9] As indicated by Pier Francesco Asso and Luca Fiorito (2004), Parker's approach had an influence on early industrial sociologists such as Ordway Tead (1918) and Helen Marot (1918), and even found a highly sympathetic audience in Irving Fisher (1919).

Workplace Norms and Nonunion Workers

The final study considered here was conducted by Stanley Mathewson, a student at Antioch College, under the supervision of William Leiserson. Mathewson's study concerned restricting output among nonunion workers, a phenomenon that had originally come to his attention as a freshman on a five-week co-op work placement. Although the practice of output restriction had been frequently observed, it had usually been associated with the presence of unions, on the grounds that it was the union organization that provided the means for such collective action. As Leiserson pointed out: "Until the present investigation was undertaken no one . . . had attempted to inquire thoroughly and at first hand into the practice of restriction of output among non-union workers." In addition, no one had "described the methods by which individual employees limit their output, and no systematic study of the circumstances that lead to such limitation had been made" (quoted in Mathewson 1931, 160).

The approach taken by Mathewson was to conduct a covert participant-observation study, which was a pathbreaking application of the method to

---

8. Parker did not limit his thesis to the casual laborer but applied it generally. See Parker 1920, 125–65.

9. Particularly because of its antiwar attitudes, the IWW increasingly became the subject of governmental efforts at active suppression. Mills always denied that he had in any sense been a "labor spy" (Woirol 1992, 133). Parker resigned from the commission in October 1914, possibly because of frustration with political appointments and interference in his research (Parker 1919, 88).

industrial sociology. Mathewson (1931, 7) "worked as a labourer, machine operator, bench assembler, conveyor assembler, and skilled mechanic." He held eleven different jobs in two industrial centers, worked day, afternoon, and night shifts, and lived "with working people in their home environment." To aid him in his work, he recruited six workers who held various jobs in other industrial centers. Records were produced in the form of letters written after each working day and mailed to an associate. In total, reports of restriction of output were obtained from 105 establishments in forty-seven localities. In addition, interviews were conducted with approximately 350 workers and 65 executives. Some of these interviews were "systematic," with those interviewed "informed of the purpose," while others were "informal conversations with fellow workers." As a final step, "after many workers' experiences were recorded, a random sampling was made in order to verify through executives the accuracy of the workers' reports" (8). There is little detail given of the precise conduct of the research or the criteria of selection used. It is stated that the cases "finally selected for study" were of two types: "those in which output was reduced and those in which the intent to reduce output was clearly evident, whether or not actual restriction resulted" (10).

The book's first part is devoted to reporting various aspects of "the practice of restriction." Mathewson found that the pressure for restriction came from the workers themselves, from their bosses, from wage payment plans and time studies, or from fear of being laid off. All of these aspects are dealt with by the reporting of a large number of specific instances from different industries and locations. Among the workers themselves, the group norms for the pace of work were rapidly communicated and enforced by social pressure to conform. The usual motivation was to maintain a certain piece or bonus rate for the job, which would be cut if it became known that higher production levels could be readily achieved. An example is given in the case of Tex, who was given a job running a coil-winding machine:

> He had never run such a machine, but found it quite easy to operate after he had been "shown how." The average output of the coils he was running had been 72 a day . . . but at the end of the second day he found he had turned out 90 coils. If a new boy could produce as many as that on his second day, a much larger number might have been possible as he became better acquainted with his machine. Tex never found out what he might have done, however. He was frightened out of such an effort by two of the older workmen who approached him at the end

of that second day and demanded, in a threatening manner, that he cut down his production. (17–18)

One of Mathewson's more surprising findings was that pressure for restriction came from above, usually from foremen attempting to protect the jobs and earnings of the workers under them or to protect their own earnings. If the foreman became known as a rate cutter, his men would become uncooperative and his own job would be at risk. Foremen also participated in efforts to mislead the time-study men. Outside factory production, and in cases where pay was by the hour, in construction, for example, restriction would take the form of delaying the completion of projects to lengthen the time of employment.

Among the executives interviewed, about 20 percent considered restriction a negligible problem, while about 60 percent stated that restriction had been eliminated by the introduction of payment systems such as group bonus plans. Of course, much of the case material on restriction had been gathered from plants using exactly such systems of pay. In one case where an executive claimed that restriction had been practically eliminated, Mathewson went to check by striking "up an acquaintance with the first workman he saw near this plant" and obtaining from him a detailed account of "his own restrictive practice and that of the workers about him" (135). Moreover, the man testified that both his foreman and general foreman "had not only approved, but had helped the workers figure out exactly how much each man should do on each shift 'so that our efficiency won't run high enough to get our rate cut'" (136). Two other men confirmed this story. For Mathewson, "the belief held by executives, namely that various incentive-wage-payment plans tend to lessen restriction, was one of the most puzzling things in the whole investigation" (137). The executives also held that it was not their practice to cut rates, a view directly contrary to that held by their workers.

Mathewson's conclusions were that restriction was widespread, that scientific management had failed to resolve the problem or foster a spirit of confidence, that management attempts to speed up work had been offset by the ingenuity of workers in developing restrictive practices, that management had given only superficial attention to the problem, and that the practices of management had "not yet brought the worker to feel that he can freely give his best efforts without incurring penalties" (146–47). In commentaries at the end of the book, Leiserson suggests some form of joint worker-management committees to decide on reasonable standards, while Mathewson and Henry Dennison express faith in applying scientific methods in the form of experimental and laboratory methods. Interestingly, Mathewson's study was conducted at the same time as Elton Mayo was carrying out his Hawthorne experiments. Mathewson's book preceded the first of Mayo's (1933) major publications on the Hawthorne experiments by two years, but Mayo's findings were that the experiments themselves changed the behavior of the workers.[10]

The participant-observation methods used by Mathewson did not become a significant part of labor economics in the post-1930s period, but such methods did become well established in industrial sociology. In a reissue of Mathewson's book, published in 1969, the famous industrial sociologist Donald Roy (1969, xv) speaks of Mathewson's work being "essential reading" during the 1940s for those involved in human relations in industry, and a direct inspiration of his own work on output restriction.

Conclusions

In all of the cases examined here, it is claimed that the methods employed provided information that would have been impossible to obtain in other ways, either because the information required direct observation and experience of the working or living conditions involved, or because of disincentives to be truthful on the part of the subjects of the investigation, or both. In all cases the investigators were aiming not just at quantitative data but at an understanding of their subjects, and they were clearly deeply impressed by what they witnessed or experienced. These pieces of work all contributed to generating improved social knowledge for social policy purposes, which was an outstanding characteristic of American social science of the time. Moreover, the information gained did feed into more general or theoretical treatments of the issues involved.

Such field studies were far from unusual in American labor economics, and in social science more generally, from the 1890s through the 1930s. Most fieldwork in this period conformed to the type of open observation combined with interviews and collection of documentary evidence, as in the Fitch study. A large number of Commons's students did this type of work.[11] These methods of observation were also used widely in sociology:

10. The Hawthorne experiments and the effects on the workers involved have been the subject of a great deal of discussion. See Adair 1984.

11. It is not difficult, however, to find cases of economists who drew from their own direct observation of factories or firms but who never included explicit reports of their observational activities in their published work. Alfred Marshall and Ronald Coase are only two of many possible examples.

Robert and Helen Lynd's famous *Middletown: A Study of Modern American Culture* (1929) used direct observation, interviews, questionnaires, and collection of documents. The methods the Lynds used clearly link back to those of the social survey movement, and their book became a paradigm of sociological research (Igo 2007).

The use of photographic evidence also continued, perhaps the best example being the work of Dorothea Lange and Paul Taylor (1939) on the dust bowl migration to California. In her commentary on Lange and Taylor, Anne Spirn (2008, xi–xii, 20) talks about "seeing as a way of knowing," of unearthing what has been "neglected or not known," and of "daring to look."

Participant-observation studies (covert or not) were much less common in economics, but some other examples can be found. From 1890 through the early part of the twentieth century, various undercover reporters made attempts to report on working-class life, but these were often aimed at a more popular audience.[12] For example, Carleton Parker's widow, Cornelia Parker (1922), wrote a series on working women based on her own experiences of adopting the persona of and living as a working woman with a variety of jobs. These were originally published in *Harper's* and later as a book. It has been claimed that participant-observation is a method that is characteristic of institutional economics (Wilber and Harrison 1978), but apart from the work reported here I have not found any clear examples.[13]

There were also links to more popular forms of literature. Publications such as Kellogg's *Survey Graphic* linked the academic literature in labor economics to a broader reform-minded audience. Mills's reference to the novels of Jack London and Upton Sinclair indicate the link to muckraking journalism and to exposé fiction. The novels of Frank Norris discussed by Craufurd Goodwin in this volume provide a further example.

Despite all of this, direct observational work of the type discussed here fell out of favor in economics. A number of lines of criticism raised concerns about reliability, especially the question of the accuracy of the information gained from interviews and statements. Fitch had to deal with the atmosphere of intimidation that made his subjects cautious about speaking out, and find ways of gaining trust. Parker had to judge the reliability

12. Mark Pittenger (1997) discusses a large number of these works and their role in constructing the progressive concept of the underclass.

13. There are many studies of government agencies by individuals who worked for the organization concerned, but most of these stay on the level of the formal organization and are not considered participant-observation studies here.

of his witness statements. Participant observation studies have also been subject to sharp debates over the reliability of the information gained.[14] Covert methods, and particularly covert participant observation, are perhaps less subject to these lines of criticism, but in all the cases considered here there is a heavy reliance on the investigator's judgment and expertise, and more or less reliance on subjective impressions. In addition, the collections of field observations and reports have to be aggregated and analyzed in various ways, and as the information was not limited to the quantitative, this was often done in terms of attempting to generate a picture of what was "typical" or of the various leading "types" to be found. The issues of how representative the samples were and how the typology was arrived at are obvious ones. Finally, there was often a lack of information on the methods and procedures used, although not all studies were equally deficient. The Lynds' *Middletown* study (1929) contains a seven-page appendix on method, but according to Igo (2007, 57), this was "a much praised innovation."[15]

With the advent of the New Deal and World War II, the available sources of official data relating to labor increased significantly. Labor economics, like many other areas of economics and sociology, moved increasingly to more "objective" surveys, focused on collecting statistical data, and to the use of statistical methods, and moved away from broader and more subjective social observation. This is not to say that issues of bias and representativeness disappeared, especially in those cases where data were collected by enumerators who might have had to use judgment. What one can trace is a movement from surveys based on expert judgment to more formalized techniques and rules for data collection (Didier 2011; Stapleford, this volume). It has been a long time since students in economics were provided training in methods of field research or in methods of interviewing.

Despite these difficulties, field studies remained much more a part of the other social sciences than economics, and this raises the question of why economics lost an important fieldwork component. This might be because fieldwork, especially of the type discussed here, focuses on the specific, while neoclassical theory, which came to dominate American economics after 1945, focuses on the general, diminishing the signifi-

14. Notably the debate over Margaret Mead's work on Samoa.

15. Booth's study of London did provide details of how data were gathered in some of the volume introductions.

cance given to the particular, the historical, and the contingent. Quantitative and econometric work also fit well with new methodological ideas, such as those expressed in Milton Friedman's 1953 essay, with its emphasis on the empirical testing of predictions. Both of these tendencies were stronger in economics than in other social sciences.

There are, however, some interesting recent exceptions to the relative neglect of the methods of field research in economics. The National Bureau of Economic Research/Sloan project on industrial technology and productivity begun in 1994 explicitly included plant visits and interviews. A session containing papers from the project was included in the 2000 American Economic Association meetings. Martin Feldstein (2000) argues that these methods can provide insights and suggest hypotheses in ways that go beyond more conventional approaches, and Susan Helper (2000) specifically mentions the advantages of being able to ask people directly about their objectives and constraints, to explore areas where little or no data exist, and to gain insights into what data might be collected. She also argues that the problems raised previously about objectivity and ability to generalize can be overcome with improved research design. One good example is the work on factory organization and productivity in India by Nicholas Bloom, John Roberts, and their colleagues (2011). This is designed as a field experiment with treatment and control groups, but direct observation (and even photographs) still clearly plays a role.

References

Adair, John G. 1984. "The Hawthorne Effect: A Reconsideration of the Methodological Artifact." *Journal of Applied Psychology* 69 (2): 334–45.

Asso, Pier Francesco, and Luca Fiorito. 2004. "Human Nature and Economic Institutions: Instinct Psychology, Behaviorism, and the Development of American Institutionalism." *Journal of the History of Economic Thought* 26 (December): 445–78.

Bloom, Nicholas, Benn Eifert, Aprajit Mahajan, David McKenzie, and John Roberts. 2011. "Does Management Matter? Evidence from India." NBER Working Paper No. 11658, January.

Booth, Charles. 1902–3. *Life and Labour of the People in London*. 17 vols. London: Macmillan.

Brissenden, Paul. 1919. *The I.W.W.: A Study of American Syndicalism*. New York: Columbia University Press.

Butler, Elizabeth Beardsley. 1909. *Women and the Trades*. New York: Russell Sage Foundation.

Byington, Margaret. 1911. *Homestead: The Households of a Mill Town.* New York: Russell Sage Foundation.

California Commission on Immigration and Housing. 1914. *Report on Unemployment.* Sacramento, Calif.: Government Printing Office.

Charles, Loïc, and Yann Giraud. 2010. "Economics for the Masses: The Visual Display of Economic Knowledge in the United States (1921–1945)." Mimeo.

Commons, John R. 1934. *Institutional Economics: Its Place in Political Economy.* New York: Macmillan.

Didier, Emmanuel. 2011. "Counting on Relief: Industrializing the Statistical Interviewer during the New Deal." *Science in Context* 24 (2): 281–310.

Eastman, Crystal. 1910. *Work-Accidents and the Law.* New York: Russell Sage Foundation.

Feldstein, Martin. 2000. "The NBER-Sloan Project on Productivity Change." *NBER/Sloan Project Report.* www.nber.org/sloan/project_report.html.

Fisher, Irving. 1919. "Economists in Public Service." *American Economic Review* 9 (March): 5–21.

Fitch, John A. 1910. *The Steel Workers.* New York: Russell Sage Foundation.

Freedman, Russell. 1994. *Kids at Work: Lewis Hine and the Crusade against Child Labor.* New York: Clarion.

Friedman, Milton. 1953. "The Methodology of Positive Economics." In *Essays in Positive Economics*, 3–43. Chicago: University of Chicago Press.

Furner, Mary O. 2000. "Seeing Pittsburgh: The Social Survey, the Survey Workers, and the Historians." *Journal of Policy History* 12 (3): 405–12.

Greenwald, Maurine W., and Margo Anderson, eds. 1996. *Pittsburgh Surveyed: Social Science and Social Reform in the Early Twentieth Century.* Pittsburgh: University of Pittsburgh Press.

Helper, Susan. 2000. "Economists and Field Research: 'You Can Observe a Lot Just by Watching.'" *American Economic Review* 90 (May): 228–32.

Igo, Sarah E. 2007. *The Averaged American.* Cambridge: Harvard University Press.

Kapuria-Foreman, Vibha, and Charles R. McCann. 2010. "An Appreciation of Selig Perlman's *A Theory of the Labor Movement.*" Mimeo.

Kellogg, Paul U., ed. 1914a. *The Pittsburgh District: Civic Frontage.* New York: Russell Sage Foundation.

———, ed. 1914b. *Wage Earning Pittsburgh.* New York: Russell Sage Foundation.

Lange, Dorothea, and Paul Taylor. 1939. *An American Exodus: A Record of Human Erosion.* New York: Reynal and Hitchcock.

Lynd, Robert S., and Helen M. Lynd. 1929. *Middletown: A Study in Modern American Culture.* New York: Harcourt, Brace.

Marot, Helen. 1918. *The Creative Impulse in Industry.* New York: Dutton.

Mathewson, Stanley B. 1931. *Restriction of Output among Unorganized Workers.* New York: Viking.

Mayo, Elton. 1933. *The Human Problems of an Industrial Civilization.* New York: Macmillan.

Parker, Carleton H. 1920. *The Casual Laborer and Other Essays*. New York: Harcourt, Brace and Howe.

Parker, Cornelia S. 1919. *An American Idyll: The Life of Carleton H. Parker*. Boston: Atlantic Monthly Press.

———. 1922. *Working with the Working Woman*. New York: Harper.

Perlman, Selig. 1928. *A Theory of the Labor Movement*. New York: Macmillan.

Pittenger, Mark. 1997. "A World of Difference: Constructing the 'Underclass' in Progressive America." *American Quarterly* 49 (March): 26–65.

Roy, Donald. 1952. "Quota Restriction and Goldbricking in a Machine Shop." *American Journal of Sociology* 57 (March): 427–42.

———. 1969. Introduction to *Restriction of Output among Unorganized Workers*, by Stanley B. Mathewson, xv–lii. Carbondale: Southern Illinois University Press.

Rutherford, Malcolm. 2006. "Wisconsin Institutionalism: John R. Commons and His Students." *Labor History* 47 (May): 161–88.

Spirn, Anne W. 2008. *Daring to Look: Dorothea Lange's Photographs and Reports from the Field*. Chicago: University of Chicago Press.

Tead, Ordway. 1918. *Instincts in Industry: A Study of Working Class Psychology*. Boston: Houghton Mifflin.

Wilber, Charles K., and Robert S. Harrison. 1978. "The Methodological Basis of Institutional Economics: Pattern Model, Storytelling, and Holism." *Journal of Economic Issues* 12 (March): 61–89.

Woirol, Gregory R. 1992. *In the Floating Army: F. C. Mills on Itinerant Life in California, 1914*. Urbana: University of Illinois Press.

Observation through Fiction: Frank Norris and E. M. Forster

Craufurd D. Goodwin

The modern novel has roots in romances of the Middle Ages that told about the death of King Arthur or heroic characters in search of ideals or pursuit of an enemy. Picaresque novels contained absurd characters such as Don Quixote mocking the heroes of the romances. Modern novels appeared in the eighteenth century and from the start had economic ideas embedded in them. *Robinson Crusoe* (1717) and *Gulliver's Travels* (1726) may be seen as reflections of a debate over the costs and benefits of an integrated global market system (Goodwin 2011). In the nineteenth century, "economic novels" were used to represent and explore through their characters the behavioral postulates of Enlightenment economists such as Adam Smith and later interpreters such as James Mill and John Stuart Mill. To a degree, these novels reflected their predecessors. The characters in Jane Marcet's *Conversations on the Nature of Political Economy* (1810) and Harriet Martineau's fictional *Illustrations of Political Economy* (1834) are pursuing the heroic goal of economic rationality and its consequence, the efficient competitive market. Critical responses came from Thomas Love Peacock in *Crochet Castle* (1831) and Charles Dickens in *Hard Times* (1854), who conjured up absurd and heartless economic automatons with few redeeming human qualities. In neither of these fictional forms was actual observation of the economy a serious objective.

Later in the nineteenth century and into the twentieth, "realist novels," as they came to be known, provided a much richer and deeper understand-

History of Political Economy 44 (annual suppl.) DOI 10.1215/00182702-1631842

ing of the economy resulting from serious observation by the authors using methods not unlike those of the American institutional economists of the time (see Rutherford 2011 and this issue). Novelists in this tradition include Elizabeth Gaskell (*North and South*), William Makepeace Thackeray (*Vanity Fair*), George Eliot (*Middlemarch*), and Anthony Trollope (*The Way We Live Now*). Two prominent novelists of this period are examined here: an American, Frank Norris, and an Englishman, E. M. Forster. They are discussed together because they both set out to analyze problematic economic phenomena that were rooted in the complex behavior of economic actors, and because they started out with some understanding of contemporary economic theory.

Frank Norris: Action on the Frontier and in the Commodities Markets

Troubling economic circumstances in England and the United States were pushed to the fore in the 1890s, which the new marginal economics could not, or did not wish to, take into account. Most prominent were depression and the social costs of unemployment, secular deflation, the growth of trusts and monopolies, the increasing power of global market institutions, and the neglect of resources both natural and built by developers and other entrepreneurs. At the same time, new and radical economic theory was proposed that rejected the rational man even as a tool of analysis and insisted on exploring human behavior more widely and deeply. The most challenging new works of economic theory were by Thorstein Veblen: *The Theory of the Leisure Class* (1898), which dealt mainly with market demand, and *The Theory of Business Enterprise* (1904), on supply. Instead of picturing rational man as populating both sides of the market, Veblen postulated various kinds of economic actors, each one driven by complex internal motivations akin to instincts that he called, variously, the pecuniary bent, the impulse to purposive behavior, the instinct of workmanship, the pugnacious bent, the desire for conspicuous consumption and leisure, and other terms. Veblen's challenge went to the heart of marginal economic theory, and it was carried quickly from the United States to Britain; probably it was known by both Norris and Forster. If in fact the economy was driven by complex rather than simple forces, how could it be understood, and modeled? One way might be to use the discipline of psychology, which made substantial advances during the early decades of the twentieth century. Another could be through storytelling. Two of the most powerful fictional narratives on economic subjects were parts of a trilogy, planned in 1899 by Frank Norris, a young American intellectual, journalist, and novelist, to focus on American economic expansion westward, called *The Epic of the Wheat*. Only two of the volumes were published, *The Octopus* (1901) and *The Pit* (1903). The third was not completed before Norris died in 1902 at age thirty-two. That Norris was motivated to understand the economy in his novels can be discerned from his description of the trilogy as concerned with the familiar divisions of an economics textbook: "(1) the production, (2) the distribution, and (3) the consumption of American wheat" (Norris 1903, frontispiece).

Norris died just at the moment when he was recognized as one of America's leading novelists (McElrath and Crisler 2006). His career began with training in studio art in Paris and literature at Berkeley and Harvard. He worked for several publishers and wrote widely for newspapers and magazines. He was a pioneer war correspondent and covered the Jameson raid in South Africa and the US invasion of Cuba. He worked for *McClure's Magazine*, one of the most prominent publishers of "muckraking" articles about the economy. He is not thought of primarily as a writer of economic novels. Most often he is categorized as a pioneer literary naturalist and "the American Zola." But he was fascinated by the economy in the widest sense, and economic questions loom large in his novels. There is no evidence that he had any training in formal economics, except perhaps through an introductory college course, or that he actually read Veblen, but he did precede the writing of his books with serious library research, interviews, and consultation with experts (341). To understand life on a ranch, he spent time there, and to make sense of the Chicago commodities exchange he moved to Chicago. There are historical figures and events that correspond to many of the characters and stories in Norris's novels (11). Norris's methods were those of the well-informed investigative journalist rather than the traditional economist, but he made available for hundreds of thousands of his readers a detailed level of economic observation that was seldom provided by the professional economist.

If before World War I one wished to understand how some of Veblen's abstractions might look in real life, one could do no better than to read Norris. The novels deal primarily with personal morality, but they are not intended to be didactic like the work of Peacock and Dickens. There are no lists of obvious good people and bad, as there are in *Crochet Castle* and *Hard Times*; indeed most of the characters are tragic figures not easily identified as either heroes or villains. Categories of economic actor can be discerned in Norris's work, including some of those identified by Dickens, but here they are far more nuanced. *The Octopus* revolves around the interactions between a set of agricultural entrepreneurs and the local railroad company (the octopus of the title) that together have opened up for development the fertile San Joaquin Valley of California. In one sense the big ranchers are heroic figures like those from the early romances, who take large risks for the possibility of great gain. But in another sense they are dangerously irrational in that they fail to attend to their insecure land tenure and dependence on adjustable freight rates until it is too late. Moreover, they operate with exceptionally short time horizons: they wish to make big money quickly at the expense of the land and the water and the wildlife that they exploit to the full. The description of a roundup and slaughter of jackrabbits that Norris witnessed in his research is especially chilling.

The ranchers in *The Octopus* are not uniform in character or behavior as they might have been in earlier economic novels. The leading family is the Derricks. The patriarch, Magnus, is a statesmanlike man of high principle—until he cannot resist bribing a politician. His cavalier attitude to the land may have come from his experience as a gold rush miner in the 1840s; his approach is not rational but "haphazard" and "unscientific," with the land essentially chips in a casino. "It was the true California spirit that found expression through him, the spirit of the West, unwilling to occupy itself with details, refusing to wait, to be patient, to achieve by legitimate plodding; the miner's instinct of wealth acquired in a single night prevailed, in spite of all. It was in this frame of mind that Magnus, and the multitude of other ranchers of whom he was a type, farmed their ranches. They had no love for their land. They were not attached to the soil. They worked their ranches as a quarter of a century before they had worked their mines. To husband the resources of their marvelous San Joaquin, they considered niggardly, petty, Hebraic. To get all there was out of the land, to squeeze it dry, to exhaust it, seemed their policy. When at last the land, worn out, would refuse to yield, they would invest their money in something else; by then they would all have made fortunes. They did not care. 'After us the deluge'" (208). Magnus Derrick's son Lyman, by contrast, is from a new breed of politician who sees the marketplace as a source of wealth more through corruption and manipulation than exploitation. Yet not all the ranchers are like the Derricks. Their neighbor Buck Annixter is a very different type: a master tactician with college education in finance, political economy, scientific agriculture, and engineering (24).

He is neurotic and has intellectual pretensions and can be found reading *David Copperfield* when not managing the ranch. Although brilliant on many dimensions, Annixter is unreliable and leads the other ranchers to disaster and his own death.

Other kinds of market participant are described by Norris, especially the small farmers, sometimes the tenants of the ranchers, and often recent immigrants, who cannot make sense of the circumstances in which they find themselves. One is Hooven, a German veteran of the Franco-Prussian War, who lives with the foggy memory of his heroism at Sedan. Another is Dyke, an idealist who gives up his job with the railroad to become a hop farmer. All of these farmers are fair game for various kinds of predators. Dyke makes careful cost-revenue calculations for his hop farm only to discover that if he does well the railroad will raise the freight rates on his product so as to extract all his profit; ultimately he is driven to bankruptcy and a life of crime, all because he could not comprehend the behavior of his nemesis the railroad. "Under his feet the ground seemed mined; down there below him in the dark the huge tentacles went silently twisting and advancing, spreading out in every direction, sapping the strength of all opposition, quiet, gradual, biding the time to reach up and out and grip with a sudden unleashing of gigantic strength" (240).

As sort of hangers-on in the drama of agricultural development are the women of the ranchers and farmers, often in contrast with their husbands because of experience in the arts and literature. They have difficulty comprehending the seeming mania of their husbands, but are powerless to control it. Magnus Derrick's wife grew up in eastern Ohio "where the farmers loved the land, caressing it, coaxing it, nourishing it as though it were a thing almost conscious. . . . But this new order of things—a ranch bounded only by the horizons, where as far as one could see, to the north, to the east, to the south and to the west, was all one holding . . . troubled her, and even, at times, filled her with an undefinable terror" (47). The women because of their powerlessness in the end suffer most from the catastrophes that ensue, one driven to prostitution and another to death by starvation. Mrs. Derrick goes on reading Walter Pater as her world collapses around her.

In roughly the same category as the women are a few intellectuals and artists who remain in the shadows of the development activity, trying to make sense of what is happening, without much success. Vanamee, a college graduate who prefers the life of a laborer, recognizable today as like someone from the 1960s, is a mystic who never escapes the memory of his murdered fiancée. Modeled perhaps on Henry David Thoreau, "he was, as he desired, close to nature, living the full measure of life, a worker among workers, taking enjoyment in simple pleasures, healthy in mind and body. He believed in an existence passed in this fashion in the country, working hard, eating full, drinking deep, sleeping dreamlessly" (32). Presley, another college graduate, perhaps modeled on Norris himself, is a rather effete poet who has come to California for his health and in his views seems reminiscent of Walt Whitman. He is a man of big ideas that never seem to lead anywhere:

> He flung aside his books of poems—Milton, Tennyson, Browning, even Homer—and addressed himself to Hill [Mill?], Malthus, Young, Pushkin, Henry George, Schopenhauer. He attacked the subject of social inequality with unbounded enthusiasm. He devoured rather than read, emerged from the affair his mind a confused jumble of conflicting notions, sick with over effort, raging against injustice and oppression, and with not one sane suggestion as to remedy or redress. (214)

Finally, if there is anything like an evil force operating in the San Joaquin, it is the railroad, based in San Francisco. But those who run this railroad are not simply villains. They are agents of a large corporation that thrives playing mainly by the rules, and since they are usually the ones that make the rules they win most disputes and conflicts. Unlike the swashbuckling ranchers, they have good lawyers and abundant experience with how to play the game of business. There were two layers of decision making in this large corporation. The chief executive is Shelgrim, living in San Francisco, a legendary financier, philanthropist, and sophisticated patron of the arts. He is modeled on Collis B. Huntington of the Southern Pacific Railroad. Despite his enormous power, he explains to Presley that he is only a pawn in a large chess game and should not be taken too seriously. "You are dealing with forces, young man, when you speak of wheat and the railroads, not with men. There is the wheat, the supply. It must be carried to feed the people. There is the demand. The wheat is one force, the railroad another, and there is the law that governs them—supply and demand. Men have little to do with the whole business" (396). This sounds like Andrew Carnegie speaking: "Here was the man not only great, but large; many sided, of vast sympathies, who understood with equal intelligence the human nature in an habitual drunkard, the ethics of a masterpiece of painting, and the financiering and operation of ten thousand miles of railroad" (395). Nevertheless, Shelgrim holds the interests of his shareholders to be his primary concern, and he is unwilling to contemplate any other norm for his corporation than profit. At the lower levels of management are less-appealing characters, such as S. Behrman in charge of the San Joaquin operation, required to apply the rules sent down from on high with no questions asked. When invited to spell out his operating principle, Behrman says, "All-the-traffic-will-bear" (242). He dies in the end when he falls into wheat being loaded for export.

The plot of *The Octopus* is that of an ultimatum bargaining game, one of the earliest experiments in game theory where the outcome is inconsistent with the economist's expectation (Carter and Irons 1991). The railroad develops its original large land grant by selling some parcels at low prices and intimating informally that ranchers and farmers who purchase may use adjacent parcels over which it retains ownership with the expectation that the railroad will sell these properties to them at some time in the future at below market prices. This assurance leads the farmers and ranchers to make improvements through clearing and irrigation on the railroad property. But when the time comes to sell, the offer by the railroad (the "allocator" in the bargaining game) is for sale of the land at current market prices. The ranchers (the "receivers" in the game) protest bitterly that they are the ones who caused the appreciation in land value and should receive the increment rather than the railroad. But they have no documentary proof of a promise or of ownership claims. Their legal case is weak and is rejected all the way to the Supreme Court. The only rational action for the ranchers and farmers, at this point, is to accept the best offer made to them by the railroad, which now has the full force of government behind it. But just as in the classic ultimatum bargaining game, they refuse to do so because they perceive such an offer to be unfair, and they precipitate a violent confrontation that leads to loss of life on both sides and tragedy for all concerned.

Norris is not sympathetic to the work of radical pamphleteers and agitators who call for conflict and peddle utopian economic schemes, in this case to the ranchers and farmers. In *The Octopus* an anarchist saloon-keeper, who "knew something of Mill and Bakounin" (320), calls for violence but is nowhere to be found when the violence breaks out. Perhaps with Henry George in mind Presley remarks sarcastically: "The social reformer writes a book on the iniquity of the possession of land, and out of the proceeds buys a corner lot. The economist who laments the hardships of the poor allows himself to grow rich upon the sale of his book" (261).

Nevertheless, Norris calls eloquently for some kind of market reform. He warns that if workers are consistently treated unfairly in the marketplace through the prices they pay for goods and receive for their labor, social stability is impossible. The response of the people of California to news of the death of the San Joaquin farmers and ranchers should be taken as an omen. "And from all this throng, this single unit, this living, breathing organism—the people—there rose a droning, terrible note. It was not yet the wild, fierce clamor of riot and insurrection, shrill, high-pitched; but it was a beginning, the growl of the awakened brute feeling the iron in its flank, heaving up its head with bared teeth, the throat vibrating to the long, indrawn snarl of wrath" (374–75). The poet Presley, enraged by the loss of so many friends, tells the railroad that it must change its ways of dealing with "the man in the street" and introduce some sort of commutative justice, or else face catastrophe. "Take care, oh, as you love your lives, take care, lest someday calling upon the Lord his God he reach out his arms for the pillars of your temples. . . . They [the railroads] swindle a nation of a hundred million and call it financiering; they levy a blackmail and call it commerce; they corrupt a legislature and call it politics; they bribe a judge and call it law; they hire blacklegs to carry out their plans and call it organization; they prostitute the honor of a state and call it competition" (379). To those who called for free markets rather than for reform, Presley reminds them: "Freedom is *not* given free to any who ask; Liberty is not born of the gods. She is a child of the people, born in the very height and heat of battle, born from death, stained with blood, grimed with powder. And she grows to be not a goddess, but a fury, a fearful figure, slaying friend and foe alike, raging, insatiable, merciless, the Red Terror" (380).

As sort of a transition from the first volume in his trilogy about the American West to the second, Norris has a San Francisco businessman remark in *The Octopus*: "The great word of the nineteenth century has been production. The great word of the twentieth century will be—listen to me, you youngsters—markets" (213). This second volume, *The Pit*, tells a story that is relatively familiar today but was unexplored at the time, that of the addictive gambler and the consequences the addiction has for the gambler, his family and close associates, the market in which he gambles, his society, the nation, and the world. The story is rather simple. A typical American country boy, Curtis Jadwin, a wheat farmer from the Midwest modeled on the notorious speculator Joseph Leiter (McElrath and Crisler 2006, 11), moves to Chicago so that he may play the commodities markets where he has become adept, and especially the wheat market called The

Pit. He does well, marries the love of his life, a country girl from Massachusetts, and settles into a relatively conservative career as a grain trader. He is amiable and public spirited and rescues bankrupt Sunday schools as a hobby. With his own and his wife's wealth, everything is open to them. They purchase a mansion in the city, a country home, a pipe organ, and a steam yacht. But, before long, the lure of gambling becomes too much. He tells his wife, "Oh, it's not the money. It's the fun of the thing; the excitement" (Norris 1903, 231). He muses: "What are we fellows who have made our money to do?" And he concludes: "Speculating seems to be about the only game, or the only business that's left open to me—that appears to be legitimate" (232). His wife, Laura, who married Jadwin instead of a promising artist, joins enthusiastically in the orgy of consumption: "The figure that held her imagination and her sympathy was not the artist, soft of hand and of speech, elaborating graces of sound and color and form, refined, sensitive, and temperamental; but the fighter, unknown and unknowable to women as he was; hard, rigorous, panoplied in the harness of the warrior" (65). Yet in time she becomes disillusioned with consumption for its own sake, and like the women in *The Octopus* she struggles to understand what drives her husband. Like Veblen, whose first book had just been published, she asked what led to the insatiable search for more. "A whole new order of things was being disclosed, and for the first time in her life she looked into the workings of political economy" (130).

One of Jadwin's friends warns him about gambling addiction. "I tell you the fascination of this Pit gambling is something no one who hasn't experienced it can have the faintest conception of. I believe it's worse than liquor, worse than morphine. Once you get into it, it grips you and draws you and draws you, and the nearer you get to the end the easier it seems to win, till all of a sudden, ah! There's the whirlpool" (131). The Chicago trading pit became for Jadwin a medieval bear pit or jousting ring. It was all about sport and armed conflict where only the strong bulls or bears could survive, and certainly not lambs, the common citizens. "The Lambs! Such a herd, timid, innocent, feeble, as much out of place in La Salle Street [the location of the commodity exchange] as a puppy in a cage of panthers; the Lambs, whom Bull and Bear did not so much as condescend to notice, but who, in their mutual struggle of horn and claw, they crushed to death by the mere rolling of their bodies" (81). Jadwin had all the wealth he could possibly want, but he could not resist wagering everything for the thrills. The economists of the day might see the Pit as a place where differing expectations were reconciled and where equilibrium prices were established; by contrast, the war correspondent Norris explains, it was the place where "contending armies" met and where gamblers got their daily fix (105).

As a grand gesture, Jadwin decides to corner the world market in wheat, an adventure his associates know to be extremely foolhardy and unlikely to succeed, but one that seemed increasingly possible in the integrated global economy. The story is based on an actual incident in the history of the Pit that played out in much the same way as in the novel. The addiction is strong, and Jadwin sets out to purchase all wheat futures contracts. During the wild speculation that follows, he neglects his family and his close associates. He is like a man possessed. Economists might see his actions as the exercise of clever reasoning. He knows better. "Often he acted upon what he knew to be blind, unreasoned instinct. Judgment, clear reasoning, at times, he felt forsook him" (350). Over time the market defeated him. The supply of wheat was far more elastic than he had guessed; as the price rose he was inundated with wheat, and he and everyone around him were ruined. "Why the Wheat had grown itself; demand and supply, these were the two great laws the Wheat obeyed. Almost blasphemous in his effrontery, he had tampered with these laws, and had roused a Titan" (374).

The consequences of Jadwin's mania and ultimate bankruptcy are that he and Laura must give up their conspicuous consumption and return to a simple life. But there are also external effects. Kansas farmers and European peasants experience first a boom in the price of wheat, a boon for the producing farmers, a catastrophe for the consuming peasants, and then a collapse with the opposite effects. The question may naturally be asked from this tale, Should the addiction of a single speculator be allowed to wreak this havoc on the world? Norris did not answer the questions he raised, but he asked them very clearly. When he was criticized for this stance, he said, "One should turn to a political economist and not a literary man for a comprehensive proposal for a solution of the 'present discontent'" (McElrath and Crisler 2006, 12).

In these two novels Norris tapped into the country's growing interest in exciting economic developments after the Civil War: completion of westward expansion and closing of the frontier, anchored by extension of the great transcontinental railways; growth of enormous corporations dominated by swashbuckling entrepreneurs; a major depression in the 1890s, with attendant unemployment and human suffering; and globalization of trade with commodity markets centered for the first time in America. In most cases Norris's fictional narratives simply record events in the manner of an investigative reporter, with particular attention to the behavior of key economic actors such as farmers, ranchers, lawyers, and bankers. For the most part there are few surprises as the actors pursue their self-interests; there is no suggestion that Norris is testing a rival hypothesis or developing a new theory of human behavior. But the complexity of human responses to stimuli is a constant source of interest. Sometimes he deals with apparent anomalies that puzzled thoughtful observers of the time. He explored the manic pursuit of wealth by monopolists, speculators, and public officials that was attracting attention from muckraking journalists like Ida Tarbell and Lincoln Steffens in magazines like *McClure's*. Through the use of fiction Norris was able to speculate more than the journalists about the reasons for this behavior.

Norris also reported the surprising mistreatment of the natural environment of the West that was of increasing concern at this time to thoughtful observers such as the pioneering ecologist Aldo Leopold (Goodwin 2008). Destruction of the land and slaughter of the wildlife seemed inconsistent with the fond hopes in the Homestead Act and other legislation that a responsible and contented peasantry could be settled permanently on the land. Norris looked for an explanation in the behavior of those who pushed into the frontier initially and prospected for minerals.

Through his novels Norris responded to the concerns of readers to understand what was happening in the American West and what policy changes might be implemented. The economics discipline did not supply much that was easily accessible or digestible. Before the appearance of think tanks such as the Brookings Institution (1916) and the National Bureau of Economic Research (1920), economic novels and articles by muckrakers remained the main sources to which interested citizens might turn for information and interpretation of some pressing issues. Indeed, the popularity of these "undisciplined" sources may have inspired the development of those more respectable institutions.

The practice in which Norris was a pioneer, of combining investigative reporting on the economy with storytelling, grew through the twentieth century in the works of Theodore Dreiser, Sinclair Lewis, Scott Fitzgerald, Upton Sinclair, Virginia Woolf, Tom Wolfe, and many others. So long as the economics profession recoiled from micro-level observation of this kind, novelists took on a role as observers by proxy.

E. M. Forster and the Social Economy

The economic subjects observed by Forster in his works of fiction are in some respects quite similar to those explored by Norris, but in other respects different. Forster, like Norris, came from a comfortable upper-middle-class family, and except for an accident would have been named "Henry" after his wealthy economist ancestor Henry Thornton (Moffat 2010, 26, 27). *The Octopus* and *The Pit* deal with two distinct market phenomena peculiar to the United States and hardly dealt with in the professional economics literature of the time: tension between the railroads and the farmers and ranchers in the settlement of the West, and establishment of world prices for agricultural products in the great commodity exchanges. Forster's interests were broader and related to the intersection of economic activity with the social and political context of national development. These interests grew out of Forster's membership in a small, informal association of friends who began to meet while students at Cambridge University around the turn of the century and continued when they lived in London and, with an enlarged membership, became known as the Bloomsbury group. Two of its core members were John Maynard Keynes and Leonard Woolf, both intensely interested, like Forster, in a wide range of social and economic questions. Most of the issues explored in Forster's novels were high on the agendas of Keynes and Woolf: tensions between economic classes and how to reduce them, prejudice in the workplace against women and minorities, mass unemployment and its impact, the comparative performance of public charity and private philanthropy in dealing with social problems, the consequences of empire, and destruction through economic development of the natural and built environment. All of these issues were raised in Forster's first major novel *Howards End* (1910). It is certainly not suggested that these topics were assigned to Forster by his Bloomsbury friends to examine in his novels. Rather, it seems likely that Forster, a quiet participant, listened to the excited talk and then explored these issues in his stories. It is likely also that he was well aware of the research that had been undertaken recently by Charles Booth on the British working class, published in seventeen volumes as *Life and Labour of the People in London* (1902–3) and that it had engendered in him a sense of "the class consciousness of sin" that it had in others. Like Norris, Forster did not propose solutions to economic and social problems. His style, too, was to observe the world around him, set forth issues, reflect on them in his novels, and consider thoughtfully and openly policy proposals that were in the air at the time.

There are areas of overlap between Norris and Forster, though there is no evidence that Forster read Norris's work, and Norris died before Forster's work appeared. Perhaps the most obvious similarity is in their nuanced treatment of the businessman-entrepreneur, in contrast to the demonization of this figure by socialist and other radical reformers of the day. The entrepreneur is treated antiseptically in the marginal economics literature of the turn of the century as the coordinator and integrator of inputs and the source of new ideas for the productive process. By contrast, Norris and Forster portray their entrepreneurs as colorful and tragic figures, with deep character flaws that lead ultimately to their downfall. But the novelists remain respectful of entrepreneurial achievements. One of Forster's characters says about the entrepreneurs: "They keep a place going, don't they? Yes, it is just that. They keep England going, it is my opinion" (216). A rancher like Annixter in *The Octopus* is shown by Norris to bring engineering, scientific agriculture, finance, and the law to bear on agricultural development. Similarly, Henry Wilcox in *Howards End*, a flawed human being in his personal life, has responded to the world's demand for rubber by mobilizing a multinational corporation that answers the need. Both Norris and Forster are dismissive of the radical reform proposals of the nineteenth century that, they imply, may make the reformers feel virtuous but often do more harm than good. They both muse over the problem of how to integrate women into the economy. They illustrate how women are excluded from decision making and are prevented from intervening in matters where clearly their inclusion would be socially beneficial. Finally, they both observe, long before professional economists, how cavalier decision makers in England and America were about preserving their environmental heritage.

Impermeable barriers between social classes, and the labor market stratification that these created, are a main concern for Forster. *Howards End* is substantially about Leonard Bast, a lower-middle-class clerk in a London insurance company who is trying desperately to climb the social ladder by copying the intellectual and artistic interests of those above him. He is patronized by two young emancipated women, the misses Schlegel, independently wealthy, with a well-developed social conscience, and modeled it seems after two Bloomsbury group members Forster knew well, the daughters of the great literary figure Sir Leslic Stephen, Vanessa Bell and Virginia Woolf. The Schlegel sisters are involved earnestly in a range of public policy discussions, except for the contentious foreign policy debates of the time:

In their own fashion they cared deeply about politics, though not as politicians would have us care; they desired that public life should mirror whatever is good in the life within. Temperance, tolerance, and sexual equality were intelligible cries to them; whereas they did not follow our Forward Policy in Thibet [*sic*] with the keen attention that it merits, and would at times dismiss the whole British Empire with a puzzled, if reverent, sigh. (21)

They engaged in intense debate in a reading group over the wisdom of conditioning welfare payments to the poor. Margaret Schlegel, reflecting the venerable liberal tradition, insisted No! "Give them a chance. Give them money. Don't dole them out poetry-books and railway-tickets like babies. Give them the wherewithal to buy these things. When your Socialism comes, it may be different, and we may think in terms of commodities instead of cash. Till it comes, give people cash, for it is the warp of civilization, whatever the woof may be" (100). Welfare of all kinds is rejected by the businessman Henry Wilcox with an argument that sounds like that of Vilfredo Pareto. "You do admit that, if wealth was divided up equally, in a few years there would be rich and poor again just the same. The hardworking man would come to the top, the wastrel sink to the bottom" (122). Indeed, argument of this kind is so intense among the sisters and their friends that when an aunt comes for a visit she feels it necessary soon to find "relief from the politico-economical-aesthetic atmosphere that reigned at the Schlegels" (43).

Henry Wilcox attacks all of the "Schlegel fetiches" with the strong assertion "that Equality was nonsense, Votes for Women nonsense, Socialism nonsense, Art and Literature, except when conducive to strengthening the character, nonsense" (17). Yet increasingly the Schlegel sisters express the uncomfortable acknowledgment that they (and Forster) live off the surplus generated by the business elite, represented by Wilcox, with whom they are often engaged in argument, and business must not be just dismissed. Margaret notes: "If Wilcoxes hadn't worked and died in England for thousands of years, you and I couldn't sit here without having our throats cut. There would be no trains, no ships to carry us literary people about in, no fields even. Just savagery. No—perhaps not even that. Without their spirit, life might never have moved out of protoplasm. More and more do I refuse to draw my income and sneer at those who guarantee it" (137–38). Margaret even speaks respectfully of a Schlegel son who has gone to Nigeria on a colonial mission. "He doesn't want the money, it is work he wants, though it is beastly work—dull country, dishonest natives, an eternal fidget over fresh water and food. A nation who can produce men of that sort may well be proud. No wonder England has become an Empire" (87).

The Schlegel sisters take on Leonard Bast as a philanthropic project, rather in the manner prescribed under the first President Bush's program for "a thousand points of light." The intent was to help Bast rise on the social and economic ladder, as he wished to do. The result was what they all agreed became a terrible "muddle." To begin, Bast could not make sense of the postimpressionist cultural theory explained to him by the sisters. "With an hour at lunch and a few shattered hours in the evening, how was it possible to catch up with leisured women who had been reading steadily since childhood? His brain might be full of names, he might have even heard of Monet and Debussy; the trouble was that he could not string them together into a sentence" (30). Forster applied to the fictional Leonard Bast a theory often propounded by Leonard Woolf, that the political doctrine of equality, made popular by the French Revolution and the American Declaration of Independence, had severely destabilized the competitive labor market that inevitably reflected inequality. The doctrine of equality had made Bast and his colleagues dissatisfied and impatient for change:

> His mind and his body had been alike underfed, because he was poor, and because he was modern they were always craving better food. Had he lived some centuries ago, in the brightly coloured civilizations of the past, he would have had a definite status, his rank and his income would have corresponded. But in his day the angel of Democracy had arisen, enshadowing the classes with leathern wings, and proclaiming: "All men are equal—all men that is to say who possess umbrellas," and so he was obliged to assert gentility, lest he slipped into the abyss where nothing counts and the statements of Democracy are inaudible. (35)

The consequences of this private philanthropy for Leonard Bast are that he receives disastrous labor market advice to give up his job on an ill-founded rumor about the instability of his employer, he cannot find new employment, and absent any kind of safety net for such conditions he sinks into poverty and accidental death at the hands of a Wilcox son. Shortly before his death, Bast explains the consequences of unemployment for the working class, results that can hardly be imagined by those with wealth.

"I shall never get work now. If rich people fail at one profession, they can try another. Not I. I had my groove, and I've got out of it. I could do one particular branch of insurance in one particular office well enough to command a salary, but that's all. Poetry's nothing, Miss Schlegel. One's thoughts about this and that are nothing. Your money, too, is nothing, if you'll understand me. If a man over twenty once loses his own particular job, it's all over with him. I have seen it happen to others. Their friends gave them money for a little, but in the end they fell over the edge. It's no good. It's the whole world pulling. There always will be rich and poor." (179)

It may be significant that Maynard Keynes read these words in his youth and participated in the discussion that led up to them and to his pioneering search for a solution to unemployment.

Forster's observations and reflections in *Howards End* on the consequences for the environment of increasing economic activity were more like those of Rachel Carson in *Silent Spring* a half-century later than those of a proto-environmental economist. But in attitude they resonate with Norris's account of the jackrabbit slaughter. Forster, like Norris, is sounding the alarm, not proposing specific policies. He wrote about London: "And month by month the roads smelt more strongly of petrol, and more difficult to cross, and human beings heard each other speak with greater difficulty, breathed less of the air, and saw less of the sky. Nature withdrew: the leaves were falling by midsummer; the sun shone through dirt with an admired obscurity . . . those who care for the earth with sincerity may wait long ere the pendulum swings back to her again" (84). Forster saw the prospect of increasing global economic integration as a continuing threat to the environment. "Under cosmopolitanism, if it comes, we shall receive no help from the earth. Trees and meadows and mountains will be only a spectacle, and the binding force that they once exercised on character must be entrusted to Love alone. May love be equal to the task!" (205).

It was not only classical economics that made an appearance in *Howards End*. Roger Fry brought back to the Bloomsburys from New York, where he worked at the Metropolitan Museum of Art, news of the revolutionary economic theory of Veblen, and Veblen's ideas can be seen throughout Bloomsbury writings. Forster describes the young feminist Helen Schlegel "preparing a speech about political economy," wherein she relates the problem of women in the economy to what sounds very much like Veblen's instinct of workmanship. She says: "I believe that in the last century men have developed the desire for work, and they must not starve it. It's a new desire. It goes with a great deal that's bad, but in itself it's good, and I hope that for women, too, 'not to work' will soon become as shocking as 'not to be married' was a hundred years ago" (86).

The nearest thing to a reform program in *Howards End* is a plea for better human relations. "Only connect" is the motto of the book, similar to an appeal heard often in the nineteenth century for "cooperation" to complement or replace competition. Margaret Schlegel makes the case thus: "Only connect the prose and the passion, and both will be exalted, and human love will be seen at its height. Live in fragments no longer. Only connect, and the beast and the monk, robbed of the isolation that is life to either, will die" (147). Forster sees the difficulty of achieving successful interpersonal relations to be increasing with the growth of the market system. Economic actors were becoming less and less sensitive to the implications of isolation. Toward the end of the book Margaret Schlegel delivers a heated soliloquy on the subject to Henry Wilcox, who is now her husband. "It was spoken not only to her husband, but to thousands of men like him—a protest against the inner darkness in high places that comes with a commercial age. Though he would build up his life without hers, she could not apologize. He had refused to connect, on the clearest issue that can be laid before a man, and their love must take the consequences" (262).

Howards End, E. M. Forster's first great novel, is about large questions in economic development: labor market complexity, environmental externalities, and the failure to reconcile economic forces with social realities such as entrenched social classes. Forster, like Norris, does not recommend specific reforms for the problems he uncovers, but he does appeal for a greater sense of community to deal with social and economic problems. His second and last major work, *A Passage to India* (1924), was published after the trauma of World War I and after Forster had traveled widely through the Middle East and Asia. He worked for a welfare agency in Alexandria and as a temporary bureaucrat in India. The book is mainly about the future of the British Empire, a topic that had become urgent and about which Forster had become increasingly uneasy. There remained many in Britain who pictured the empire as boon to the metropolis and colonies alike. Shouldering the white man's burden would bring trade, investment, good government, and civilization to benighted parts. One objective of this second novel was to cast doubt on this claim. Forster observed that the authoritarian dominance of any one nation over another was not viable in the long run, an assertion enthusiastically shared by his Bloomsbury friends. The roots of the problems in India, he concluded, were a lack of sensitivity and understanding among the British rulers and a universal human yearning to be free among the Indians. It was striking to Forster that after two centuries the British administrators continued to see themselves as little more than jailers. One junior officer in the Indian civil service, Ronny, tells his mother, Mrs. Moore, visiting from England: "I am out here to work, mind, to hold this wretched country by force. I'm not a missionary or a Labour Member or a vague sentimental sympathetic literary man. I'm just a servant of the Government; it's the profession you wanted me to choose myself, and that's that. We're not pleasant in India, and we don't intend to be pleasant. We've something more important to do" (44). Forster's observation of India was that the imperial authority had learned through experience how to keep the peace most of the time. The human agents involved were not capable of more. This was only a short-term equilibrium, and an alternative set of relationships among the nations of the world must be contemplated and introduced before long. A new global system after the end of empire was a subject pursued vigorously over the next decades by Forster's friends Leonard Woolf and Maynard Keynes. These early observations by their close friend Morgan Forster may have played a role in their thinking.

Conclusion

Observation of the economy is not simply like measuring physical or biological phenomena in the laboratory. As with the "harder" sciences, certain variables in economics have been determined to be of special significance and can be estimated and interpreted using accepted theory. In this way the explanatory power of economics has been increased through observation. An examination of the wider interaction of economic theory with observation suggests, however, that the impact may be far more complex. The two novelists examined here began as faithful to the doctrine with which they were familiar and which they mainly accepted. Nevertheless, they were led to raise issues not much attended in the professional literature. Their observations were simply delivered in fictional form.

In Norris and Forster we see two contrasting approaches to the use of fiction as a vector for observing the economy. For Norris, fiction was a natural extension of his career as an investigative reporter. Forster, by contrast, had led a rather sheltered life before writing *Howards End*, living in suburbia with his mother and in contact with a narrow group of intellectual and artistic friends. He did spend time in London and taught at a working men's college where the picture of Bast may have been developed. He never had a close engagement with the economy like Norris. Forster's fiction was much more the product of his imagination, and through this he dealt with various components of the evolving market economy not touched by Norris: the would-be socialists, the do-gooding middle class with money, the wastrel children of the hardworking entrepreneurs.

By presenting their findings in such an arresting form, both Norris and Forster contributed to economic understanding. They explored various economic phenomena that they could see were becoming important for society yet were neglected, for several reasons, by the economics profession. They were both successful and respected novelists, and their observations of human behavior are likely to have affected both the professional practice of economics and the use of economics in government and public debate. They contributed to an understanding of the tensions present in westward expansion in North America, price determination in global commodity markets, the complex consequences of unemployment, the effectiveness of public and private programs of welfare, and environmental degradation from economic activity. This kind of observation was stimulated by contemporary economics and, in return, may have had an effect on that same economics, at least in the long run.

References

Booth, Charles. 1902–3. *Life and Labour of the People in London*. London: Macmillan.

Carter, John, and Michael Irons. 1991. "Are Economists Different and If So Why?" *Journal of Economic Perspectives*, no. 2 (Spring): 171–77.

Defoe, Daniel. (1717) 1927. *The Life and Surprizing Adventures of Robinson Crusoe of York, Mariner*. 3 vols. Oxford: Blackwell.

Dickens, Charles. (1854) 2003. *Hard Times*. London: Penguin Books.

Forster, E. M. (1910) 1985. *Howards End*. New York: Bantam Books.

———. (1924) 1984. *A Passage to India*. New York: Harcourt Brace Jovanovich.

Goodwin, Craufurd D. 2008. "Ecologist Meets Economics: Aldo Leopold." *Journal of the History of Economic Thought* 30 (4): 429–52.

———. 2011. "The First Globalization Debate: Crusoe vs. Gulliver." *QA-Rivista dell'Associazione Rossi-Doria* 3

Marcet, Jane. 2009. *Conversations on the Nature of Political Economy*. New Brunswick, N.J.: Transaction Publishers.

Martineau, Harriet. 1834. *Illustrations of Political Economy*. Vol. 2. London: Charles Fox.

McElrath, Joseph R., Jr., and Jesse S. Crisler. 2006. *Frank Norris: A Life.* Urbana: University of Illinois Press.

Moffat, Wendy. 2010. *A Great Unrecorded History: A New Life of E. M. Forster.* New York: Farrar, Straus and Giroux.

Norris, Frank. (1901) 1969. *The Octopus.* New York: Airmont Publishing.

———. 1903. *The Pit: A Story of Chicago.* New York: Doubleday, Page.

Peacock, Thomas Love. (1831) 1893. *Crochet Castle.* London: J. M. Dent.

Rutherford, Malcolm. 2011. *The Institutionalist Movement in American Economics, 1918–1947.* Cambridge: Cambridge University Press.

Swift, Jonathan. (1726) 2005. *Gulliver's Travels.* New York: Oxford University Press.

Observing Shocks

Pedro Garcia Duarte and Kevin D. Hoover

1. The Rise of Shocks

Macroeconomists have observed business cycle fluctuations over time by constructing and manipulating models in which shocks have increasingly played a greater role. *Shock* is a relatively common English word, used by economists for a long time and to a large extent, much as other people use it to refer to external influences: small or large, frequent or infrequent, regularly transmissible or not. Over the past forty years or so, economists have broken ranks with ordinary language and both narrowed their preferred sense of *shock* and promoted it to a term of econometric art. A search of the economics journals archived in the JSTOR database shows that the use of the term *shock* has risen from about 3 percent of all articles in economics up to the 1960s to more than 23 percent in the first decade of the new millennium. If we restrict attention to macroeconomics, the proportion of articles that use *shock* rises to 44 percent. Year-by-year analysis of the 1960s and 1970s localizes the take-off point to 1973.

How can we account for the rise of the language of shocks? Our answer consists of a story about how the meaning of *shock* became

A longer version of this essay is available on SSRN (papers.ssrn.com/sol3/papers.cfm?abstract_id=1840705). Pedro Duarte gratefully acknowledges financial support from FAPESP and CNPq (Brazil). Kevin D. Hoover acknowledges the support of the US National Science Foundation (grant no. NSF SES-1026983).

History of Political Economy 44 (annual suppl.) DOI 10.1215/00182702-1631851

sharpened and how shocks themselves became the objects of economic observation—both shocks as phenomena observed using economic theory to interpret data and shocks themselves as data that become the basis for observing phenomena that were not well articulated until shocks became observable.

What does it mean to be observable? We do not want to get sidetracked into the difficult issues in the philosophy of science, yet the philosophers James Bogen and James Woodward do provide a useful framework for discussing the developing epistemic status of shocks in (macro)economics that will enrich our historical account. They distinguish between *data* and *phenomena*:

> Data, which play the role of evidence for the existence of phenomena, for the most part can be straightforwardly observed. However, data typically cannot be predicted or systematically explained by theory. By contrast, well-developed scientific theories do predict and explain facts about phenomena. Phenomena are detected through the use of data, but in most cases are not observable in any interesting sense of that term. (Bogen and Woodward 1988, 305–6)

Cloud-chamber photographs are an example of data, which may provide evidence for the phenomena of weak neutral currents. Quantum mechanics predicts and explains weak neutral currents, but not cloud-chamber photographs.

We can see immediately that Bogen and Woodward's distinction is not unproblematic. Surely, individual price information gathered by the US Bureau of Labor Statistics is data, something identified independently of the observational apparatus. But is then the price index—a theoretically informed construction based on those data—a phenomenon, or is it, as macroeconomists typically treat it, itself data?[1] But, then, are those data "straightforwardly observed"? Does the quantity theory of money explain the phenomenon of the price level or the inflation rate, or are they the data it uses to explain the phenomenon of the proportionality of money and prices?

The ambiguity between data and phenomena, an ambiguity between the observable and the inferred, is recapitulated in the ambiguity in the

---

1. For further discussion on compromises made in data collection, see Stapleford, this volume; and Didier, this volume.

status of shocks, which shift from data to phenomena and back depending on the target of theoretical explanation. Our major goal is to explain how the changing epistemic status of shocks and the changing understanding of their observability account for the massive increase in their role in macroeconomics.

The roots of the rise of shocks can be found in two critical developments in the earliest days of modern macroeconomics and econometrics. The first is Ragnar Frisch's (1933) characterization of business cycle models as divided into impulse and propagation mechanisms: the shocks that perturbed the economic system away from equilibrium, and the structural properties of this system. The second is Trygve Haavelmo's (1944) division of econometric models into a deterministic component and a random component, which could be characterized by a well-behaved probability distribution. The random component could be seen as a mixture of "error" and Frisch's "impulses." The word *shock* frequently encompassed them both. Macroeconometric modeling used the terminology of shocks more frequently, characterizing them as phenomena (thus inferred and not observed): phenomena that were described only to be set aside as of secondary interest. Our story addresses the breakdown, beginning in the early 1970s, of the strategy of treating shocks as secondary phenomena.

2. Impulse and Error

Although the business cycle was a central target of economic analysis and observation in the early twentieth century, shocks first came to prominence in the late 1920s and early 1930s. Frisch's (1933) distinction between propagation and impulse problems became a key inspiration for later work on business cycles. Frisch represented the macroeconomy as a deterministic mathematical system of equations. *Propagation* referred to the time-series characteristics of this system, or "the structural properties of the swinging system" (171), which he characterized by a system of deterministic differential equations. Frisch argued that "a more or less regular fluctuation may be produced by a cause which operates irregularly" (171): he was principally interested in systems that displayed intrinsic cyclicality—that is, systems of differential equations with imaginary roots. He conjectured that damped cycles corresponded to economic reality.

Frisch drew on Knut Wicksell's (1907) metaphor of a rocking horse hit from time to time with a club: "The movement of the horse will be very different to that of the club" (quoted in Frisch 1933, 198). The role of the *impulse* is as "the source of energy" for the business cycle: an exterior shock (the club striking) pushes the system away from its steady state, and the size of the shock governs the "intensity" of the cycle (its amplitude), but the deterministic part (the rocking horse) determines the periodicity, length, and the tendency or not toward dampening of the cycle. Frisch referred to impulses as "shocks" and emphasized their erratic, irregular, and jerking character, which provide "the system the energy necessary to maintain the swings" (197).[2]

Frisch's own interest is principally in the propagation mechanism, and in 1933 he does not give a really distinct characterization of shocks. Frisch (1933, 198–99) credits Eugen Slutsky ([1927] 1937), among others, as a precursor in the "mathematical study [of] the mechanism by which . . . irregular fluctuations may be transformed into cycles." Where Frisch's focus was primarily on the deterministic component and not the shocks, Slutsky's was the other way round—focusing on the fact that cumulated shocks looked rather like business cycles without giving much explanation for the economic basis of the cumulation scheme or investigating the properties of its deterministic analogue.

Neither Frisch nor Slutsky was engaged in measuring the business cycle. The target of the analysis was not the impulse itself but the business cycle phenomenon. They sought to demonstrate in principle that, generically, systems of differential (or difference) equations subject to the stimulus of an otherwise unanalyzed and unidentified impulse would display behavior similar to business cycles. Shocks or other impulses were a source of "energy" driving the cycle, yet what was tracked were the measurable economic variables.

Shocks were not observed. But they could have been measured inferentially as the "'errors' in the rational behavior of individuals" (Frisch 1939, 639). A shock could then be defined as "any event which contradicts the assumptions of some pure economic theory and thus prevents the variables from following the exact course implied by that theory" (639). A practical implementation of that approach was available in the

---

2. Impulse is not a synonym for shock in Frisch's view. Impulses also include Schumpeterian innovations that are modeled as "ideas [that] accumulate in a more or less continuous fashion, but are put into practical application on a larger scale only during certain phases of the cycle" (Frisch 1933, 203). However, he leaves to further research the task of putting "the functioning of this whole instrument [i.e., innovations] into equations" (205).

form of the residual error terms from regression equations in structural equation models (640).[3] Frisch understood that the error terms of regression equations were not pure measures but a mixture of "stimuli" (the true impulse, the analogue of the club) and "aberrations" (Frisch [1938] 1948; see Qin and Gilbert 2001, 428–30).

Frisch's student Trygve Haavelmo (1940, 319) observed that the impulse component of error terms could be neglected in step-ahead conditional forecasts, as it was likely to be small. Over time, however, the impulses were critical to the ability of the model to generate cycles. Whereas measurement errors tend to cancel out when averaged, impulses tend to cumulate. Haavelmo (1940, esp. figs. 1 and 2) constructed a dynamic model that mimicked the business cycle in a manner similar to Frisch's (1933) simulation but which, unlike Frisch's model, contained no intrinsic cycle in the deterministic part—the cycle arising strictly from the cumulation of random impulses in the manner of Slutsky ([1927] 1937). Because of their essential role in generating cycles, Haavelmo (1940, 313–14) argued that the error terms must be regarded as a fundamental part of the explanatory model on par with the deterministic components and not merely as a measure of the failure of the model to match reality.

While Haavelmo and Frisch emphasized the causal role of shocks and the need to distinguish them from errors of measurement, their focus was not on the shocks themselves. Frisch's approach to statistics and estimation was skeptical of probability theory (see Louçã 2007, chap. 8; Hendry and Morgan 1995, 40–41). In contrast, Haavelmo's dissertation, "The Probability Approach in Econometrics" (1944), was a milestone in the history of econometrics (see Morgan 1990, chap. 8). Haavelmo argued that economic data could be conceived as governed by a probability distribution characterized by a deterministic, structural, dynamic element and an unexplained random element (cf. Haavelmo 1940, 312). His innovation was the idea that, if the dynamic element were sufficiently accurately described—a job that he assigned to a priori economic theory—the error term would conform to a tractable probability distribution. Shocks, rather than treated as unmeasured data, were now treated as phenomena. Theory focuses not on their individual values (data) but on their probability distributions (phenomena). Although shocks were now phenomena, they were

3. The idea of measuring an economically important, but otherwise unobservable, quantity as the residual after accounting for causes is an old one in economics—see Hoover and Dowell 2002. Frisch (1939, 639) attributes the idea of measuring the impulse to a business cycle as the deviation from rational behavior to François Divisia.

essentially *secondary* phenomena—characterized mainly to justify their being ignored.

While Frisch and Haavelmo were principally concerned with methodological issues, Jan Tinbergen was taking the first steps toward practical macroeconometrics with, for the time, relatively large-scale structural models of the Dutch and the US economies (see Morgan 1990, chap. 4). Tinbergen's practical concerns and Haavelmo's probabilistic approach were effectively wedded in the Cowles Commission's program, guided initially by Jacob Marschak and later by Tjalling Koopmans (1950; Hood and Koopmans 1953). Although residual errors in systems of equations were characterized as phenomena obeying a probability law, they were not the phenomena that interested the Cowles Commission. Haavelmo (1940, 320–21; 1944, 54–55) had stressed the need to decompose data into "explained" structure and "unexplained" error to get the structure right, and he had pointed out the risk of getting it wrong if the standard of judgment were merely the *ex post* ability of an equation to mimic the time path of an observed variable. Taking that lesson on board, the Cowles Commission emphasized the conditions under which a priori knowledge would justify the *identification* of underlying economic structures from the data. Their focus was then on estimating the parameters of the structural model and on the information needed to lend credibility to the claim that they captured the true structure.

Shocks, as quantities of independent interest, were shunted aside. Though Haavelmo had added some precision to one concept of shocks, various meanings continued in common usage, even among econometricians. Tinbergen (1939, 193), for instance, referred to *exogenous shocks* "amongst which certain measures of policy are to be counted." The focus of macroeconometric modeling in the hands not only of Tinbergen but of Lawrence Klein and others from the 1940s through the 1960s was not on shocks but on estimating the structural parameters of the deterministic components of the models. Models were generally evaluated through their ability to track endogenous variables conditional on exogenous variables (cf. Klein and Burmeister 1976). Consistent with such a standard of assessment, the practical goal of macroeconometric modeling was counterfactual analysis in which the models provided forecasts of the paths of variables of interest conditional on exogenous policy actions. Having relegated shocks to the status of secondary phenomena, economists largely forgot about shocks as the causal drivers of business cycle phenomena.

But not completely. In a 1959 article, Irma and Frank Adelman simulated the Klein-Goldberger macroeconomic model of the United States to determine whether it could generate business cycle phenomena. They first showed that the deterministic part of the model would not generate cycles. They then showed that by drawing artificial errors from random distributions that matched those of the estimated error processes, the models did generate series that looked like business cycles identified according to the techniques of the National Bureau of Economic Research (a Turing test; see Boumans 2005, 93). While the Adelmans' test returned shocks to a central causal role in the business cycle, they focused not on individual shocks but instead on their probability distribution.

3. The New Classical Macroeconomics and the Rediscovery of Shocks

Although shock continues to be used with a wide range of meanings, after 1973 the idea of shocks as pure transients or random impulses conforming to a probability distribution or the same random impulses conforming to a time-series model independent of any further economic explanation became dominant. Why? Our thesis is that it was, first, the inexorable result of the rise of the new classical macroeconomics and one of its key features, the rational expectations hypothesis, originally due to John Muth (1961) but most notably promoted in the early macroeconomic work of Robert Lucas (e.g., Lucas 1972) and Thomas Sargent (1972); and second, that it was promoted by the increased role of shocks as a result of Christopher Sims's vector autoregression (VAR) econometric approach.

While rational expectations has been given various glosses (e.g., people use all the information available or people know the true model of the economy), the most relevant one is probably Muth's (1961, 315, 316) original statement: "[Rational] expectations . . . are essentially the same as the predictions of the relevant economic theory." Rational expectations on this view are essentially equilibrium or consistent expectations. A standard formulation of rational price expectations (e.g., in Hoover 1988, 187) is that $p_t^e = E(p_t|\Omega_{t-1})$, where p is the price level, Ω is *all* the information available in the model, t indicates the time period, e indicates an expectation, and E is the mathematical conditional expectations operator. The expected p_t^e can differ from the actual price p_t, but only by a mean-zero, independent, serially uncorrelated random error. The feature that makes the expectation an equilibrium value analogous to a market clearing price is that the content of the information set Ω_{t-1} includes the model itself, so that an expected price would not be consistent with the information if it differed from the best conditional forecast using the structure of the model, as well as the values of any exogenous variables known at time $t-1$.

The mathematical expectations operator reminds us that "to discuss rational expectations formation at all, some explicit stochastic description is clearly required" (Lucas 1973, 328–29 n. 5). Yet the need for a regular, stochastic characterization of the impulses to the economy places a premium on shocks with straightforward time-series representations, and this meaning of shock increasingly became the dominant one. The same pressure that led to the characterization of shocks as the products of regular, stochastic processes also suggested that government policy be characterized similarly—that is, by a policy rule with possibly random deviations. The economic, behavioral rationale was first, that policymakers, like other agents in the economy, do not take arbitrary actions but systematically pursue goals, and second, that other agents in the economy anticipate the actions of policymakers.

Sargent (1982, 383) relates the analysis of policy as rules under rational expectations to general equilibrium: "Since in general one agent's decision rule is another agent's constraint, a logical force is established toward the analysis of dynamic general equilibrium systems." Of course, this is a model-relative notion of general equilibrium (i.e., it is general only to the degree that the range of the conditioning of the expectations operator, $E(\cdot|\cdot)$, is unrestricted relative to the information set, Ω_{t-1}). Lucas took matters a step further in taking the new technology as an opportunity to integrate macroeconomics with a version of the more expansive Arrow-Debreu general equilibrium model. He noticed the equivalence between the intertemporal version of that model with contingent claims and one with rational expectations. In the version with rational expectations, it was relatively straightforward to characterize the shocks in a manner that reflected imperfect information—in contrast to the usual perfect-information framework of the Arrow-Debreu model—and generated more typically macroeconomic outcomes. Shocks were a centerpiece of his strategy:

> viewing a commodity as a function of stochastically determined shocks . . . in situations in which information differs in various ways among traders . . . permits one to use economic theory to make precise what one means by information, and to determine how it is valued economically. (Lucas 1980, 707)

His shock-oriented approach to general equilibrium models of business cycles was increasingly applied to different areas of macroeconomics.

Rational expectations, the focus on market-clearing, general equilibrium models, and the characterization of government policy as the execution of stable rules came together in Lucas's (1976) famous policy noninvariance argument (the "Lucas critique"): if macroeconometric models characterize the time-series behavior of variables without explicitly accounting for the underlying decision problems of the individual agents who make up the economy, then when the situations in which those agents find themselves change, their optimal decisions will change, as will the time-series behavior of the aggregate variables. The general lesson was that a macroeconometric model fit to aggregate data would not remain stable in the face of a shift in the policy rule and could not, therefore, be used to evaluate policy counterfactually.

In one sense, Lucas merely recapitulated and emphasized a worry that Haavelmo (1940) had already raised—namely, that a time-series characterization of macroeconomic behavior need not map onto a structural interpretation. But Haavelmo's (1944, chap. 2, sec. 8) notion of structure was more relativized than the one that Lucas appeared to advocate. Lucas (1980, esp. 702, 707) declared himself the enemy of "free parameters" and took the goal to be to articulate a complete general equilibrium model grounded in parameters governing "tastes and technology" and in exogenous stochastic shocks. Lucas's concept of structure leads naturally to the notion that what macroeconometrics requires is microfoundations—a grounding of macroeconomic relationships in microeconomic decision problems of individual agents (see Hoover 2012). The argument for microfoundations was barely articulated before Lucas (1980, 711) confronts its impracticality—analyzing the supposedly individual decision problems not in detail but through the instrument of "'representative' households and firms."

The Lucas critique stood at a crossroads in the history of empirical macroeconomics. Each macroeconometric methodology after the mid-1970s has been forced to confront the central issue that it raises. Within the new classical camp, there were essentially two initial responses to the Lucas critique—each in some measure recapitulating approaches from the 1930s through the 1950s.

Lars Hansen and Sargent's (1980) work on maximum-likelihood estimation of rational expectations models and subsequently Hansen's work on generalized method-of-moments estimators initiated (and exemplified) the first response (Hansen 1982; Hansen and Singleton 1982). Hansen and Sargent attempted to maintain the basic framework of the Cowles Commission's program of econometric identification (inspired by Haavelmo 1944) in which theory provided the deterministic structure that allowed the error to be characterized by manageable probability distributions and thus set aside. The target of explanation remained—as it had been for Frisch, Tinbergen, Klein, and the large-scale macroeconometric modelers—the conditional paths of aggregate variables. The structure was assumed to be known a priori, and measurement was directed to estimating parameters, now assumed to be "deep"—at least relative to the underlying representative agent model.

Finn Kydland and Edward Prescott, starting with their seminal real business cycle model in 1982, responded with a radical alternative to Hansen and Sargent. Instead of embracing the soundness of Haavelmo's division of labor between economic and statistical theories, they rejected it (see Kydland and Prescott 1990, 1991, esp. 164–67; Prescott 1986; Hoover 1995, 28–32).

Though neither Haavelmo nor his followers in the Cowles Commission clearly articulated either the fundamental nature of the a priori economic theory that was invoked to do so much work in supporting econometric identification or the ultimate sources of its credibility, Haavelmo's decomposition became the centerpiece of econometrics (being an unassailable dogma in some quarters).

Kydland and Prescott took the message from the Lucas critique that a workable model must be grounded in microeconomic optimization (or in as near to it as the representative agent model would allow). And they accepted Lucas's call for a macroeconomic theory based in general equilibrium with rational expectations. Though they held these theoretical presuppositions dogmatically—propositions that were stronger and more clearly articulated than any account of theory offered by Haavelmo or the Cowles Commission—they also held that models were at best workable approximations and not detailed, "realistic" recapitulations of the world. Thus they rejected the Cowles Commission's notion that the economy could be so finely recapitulated in a model that the errors could conform to a tractable probability law and that its true parameters could be the objects of observation or direct measurement.

Having rejected Haavelmo's "probability approach," Kydland and Prescott embraced Lucas's conception of models as simulacra:

> A "theory" is . . . an explicit set of instructions for building a parallel or analogue system—a mechanical, imitation economy. A "good" model, from this point of view, will not be exactly more "real" than a poor one, but will provide better imitations.

> Our task . . . is to write a FORTRAN program that will accept specific economic policy rules as "input" and will generate as "output" statistics describing the operating characteristics of time series we care about, which are predicted to result from these policies. (Lucas 1980, 697, 709–10)

On Lucas's view, a model needed to be realistic only to the degree that it captured some set of key elements of the problem to be analyzed and successfully mimicked economic behavior on those limited dimensions. Given the preference for general equilibrium models with few free parameters, shocks in Lucas's (1980, 697) framework became the essential driver and the basis on which models could be assessed: "We need to test [models] as useful imitations of reality by subjecting them to shocks for which we are fairly certain how actual economies, or parts of economies, would react."

Kydland and Prescott, starting with their first real business cycle model (1982), adopted Lucas's framework. Real (technology) shocks were treated as the main driver of their model, and its ability to mimic business cycle phenomena when shocked became the principal criterion for the empirical success (Prescott 1986; Kydland and Prescott 1990, 1991; and Kehoe and Prescott 1995). Shocks in Lucas's and Kydland and Prescott's framework assumed a new and now central crucial task: they became the instrument through which the real business cycle modeler would select the appropriate artificial economy to assess policy prescriptions. For this, it is necessary to identify correctly substantive shocks—that is, the ones the effect of which on the actual economy could be mapped with some degree of confidence. Kydland and Prescott's translation of Lucas's conception of modeling into the real business cycle model generated a large literature.

Both Kydland and Prescott's earliest business cycle models as well as their successors, the so-called dynamic stochastic general equilibrium (DSGE) models, were developed explicitly within Lucas's conceptual framework, though they subsequently were adopted by economists with quite different methodological orientations. Kydland and Prescott (1982) presented a tightly specified, representative-agent, general equilibrium model in which the parameters were calibrated. They rejected statistical estimation because it penalized models for not matching reality on dimensions that in fact were unrelated to "the operating characteristics of time series we care about." *Calibration* involves drawing parameter values from general economic considerations: both long-run unconditional moments of the data and facts about national-income accounting, as well as evidence from independent sources, such as microeconomic studies (Kydland and Prescott 1996, 74).

To evaluate their model, Kydland and Prescott (1982) adopt the "test of the Adelmans": would a business cycle analyst be unable to distinguish the artificial output of a model from the data on the actual economy (Kydland and Prescott 1990, 6; see also Lucas 1977, 219, 234)?[4] Kydland and Prescott's main criterion is how well the unconditional second moments of the simulated data matched the same moments in the real-world data. To generate the simulation, they simply drew shocks from a probability distribution whose parameters were chosen to ensure that the variance of output produced in the model matched exactly the corresponding value for the actual US economy (Kydland and Prescott 1982, 1362). This, of course, was a violation of Lucas's maxim: do not rely on free parameters. Given that shocks were not, like other variables, supplied in government statistics, their solution in later work was to take the "Solow residual" as the measure of technology shocks. In effect, they used the production function as an instrument to measure technology shocks (Prescott 1986, 14–16).

Kydland and Prescott treated the technology shocks measured by the Solow residual as data in Bogen and Woodward's sense. As with price indices, certain theoretical commitments were involved. Prescott (1986, 16–17) discussed various ways in which the Solow residual may fail to measure true technology shocks accurately, but concluded that, for the purpose at hand, that they would serve adequately. The key point at this stage is that—in keeping with Bogen and Woodward's distinction—Kydland and Prescott were not interested in the shocks per se but in what might be termed "the technology-shock phenomenon." The Solow residual is serially correlated. Prescott (1986, 7n5) treated it as governed by a time-series process. He claimed that very similar simulations and measures of business cycle phenomena (i.e., of the cross-correlations of current GDP with various variables at different lags) would result whether the

4. The phrase "test of the Adelmans'" was coined by King and Plosser (1994) and refers to Adelman and Adelman 1959.

shocks were modeled as nonstationary or as stationary but highly persistent (see also Kydland and Prescott 1990).

Kydland and Prescott's analysis was based not on direct observation of technology shocks (i.e., on the Solow residual) but on the statistical characterization of those shocks (the technology-shock phenomenon). The earlier simulation studies of Adelman and Adelman (1959) had been concerned not with the shocks but with the time paths of variables: the shock phenomenon was thus *secondary*. But for Kydland and Prescott, who focused on the covariation of the variables rather than their time paths, technology-shock phenomenon was *primary*.

In contrast with the Adelmans, whose measures of shocks depended on the whole structure of the model, Kydland and Prescott's technology shocks were measured by just one element of the model, the Cobb-Douglas production function. Measured this way, technology shocks on Kydland and Prescott's view have a degree of model-independence and an integrity that allows them to be transferred between modeling contexts.

Although real business cycle modelers typically use technology shocks to characterize the shock process, the technology-shock phenomenon, they have from time to time treated them as direct inputs into their models (essentially as observed data). Hansen and Prescott (1993) fed technology shocks directly into a real business cycle model to simulate the time path of US GDP over the 1990–91 recession.[5]

4. The Identification of Shocks

Whereas Kydland and Prescott had attacked Haavelmo's and the Cowles Commission's assumption that models define a tractable probability distribution, Christopher Sims (1980, 1, 2, 14, 33) attacked the credibility of the a priori assumptions that they used to identify the models. Nonetheless, it is the positive contribution of Sims's approach that bears most strongly on our story. Sims asks—to quote the title of Sargent and Sims's (1977) earlier paper—what can be learned about business cycles "without pretending to have too much *a priori* economic theory"?

---

5. The major reason for the focus of the real business cycle (RBC) literature on comparing unconditional moments is the way it characterized cycles as recurrent fluctuations in economic activity, going back to Burns and Mitchell 1946 through Lucas's equilibrium approach (Cooley and Prescott 1995, 26; Kydland and Prescott 1982, 1359–60). Robert King, Charles Plosser, and Sergio Rebelo (1988) provide an early example of a calibrated RBC model looking at time paths, while Christiano (1988) develops an estimated RBC model that compares theoretical and observed time paths.

Sims (1980) took general equilibrium, in one sense, more seriously than did the Cowles Commission in that he treated all the independently measured economic variables as endogenous. Although, as with Haavelmo, Sims divided the model into a deterministic and an indeterministic part, he rejected the notion that the deterministic part was structural. He regarded his system of equations—the *vector autoregression* (VAR) model—as a reduced form in which the random residuals were now the *only* drivers of the dynamics of the model and hence considerably more important than they had been in the Cowles Commission's approach. Sims referred to these residuals as "innovations," which stressed the fact that they were independent random shocks without their own time-series dynamics. Since the deterministic part of the model was not structural, all time-series behavior could be impounded there, so the shocks are now pure transients.

Sims used his VAR model to characterize dynamic phenomena through variance decomposition analysis and impulse-response functions. Variance decomposition is an accounting exercise that determines the proportion of the variability of each variable that is ultimately attributable to the exogenous shocks to each variable. The impulse-response function traces the effect on the time series for a variable from a known shock to itself or to another variable. Particular shocks need not be measured or observed in order to conduct either of these exercises; nonetheless, they must be characterized. The dynamics of the data must be cleanly divided between the deterministic part and the independent random shocks. The difficulty, however, is that, in general, there is no reason that the residuals to an estimated VAR ought to have the characteristic of independent random shocks—in particular, they will generally be correlated among themselves.

To deal with the problem of intercorrelated residuals, Sims assumed that the variables in his VAR could be ordered recursively (e.g., in a *Wold causal chain* via Cholesky decompositions), in which a shock to a given variable immediately affects that same variable and all those lower in the system. The coefficients on the contemporaneous variables are selected so that the shocks are orthogonal to each other.

Sims (1980, 2) admitted that individual equations of the model are not structural, and he suggested that "nobody is disturbed by this situation of multiple possible normalizations." In fact, given N variables, there are $N!$ possible normalizations (e.g., for $N = 6$, there are 720 normalizations). And far from nobody being disturbed, critics immediately pointed out that first, the variance decompositions and the impulse-response functions were, in general, not robust to the choice of normalization, and second, policy analysis required not just one of the possible renormalizations but the right one. Sims (1982, 1986) rapidly conceded the point. The VAR approach did not eliminate the need for identifying assumptions. Yet Sims had nevertheless changed the game.

The Cowles Commission had sought to measure the values of structural parameters by imposing identifying assumptions strong enough to recover them all. Sims had shown that, if the focus of attention was on identifying the shocks themselves, then the necessary identifying assumptions were weaker: with a *structural VAR* (SVAR)—that is, a VAR with orthogonalized shocks—one needs to know only the recursive order or, more generally, the causal structure of the *contemporaneous* variables. The parameters of the lagged variables in the dynamic system need not be structural, so that the SVAR is a quasi-reduced form, and less is taken on faith than in the Cowles Commission's or calibrationist frameworks.

The SVAR put shocks front and center, not because shocks could not have been identified in the Cowles Commission's framework or because shocks are automatically interesting in themselves but because their time-series properties are essential to the identification strategy. Variance-decomposition exercises and impulse-response functions do not necessarily consider measured shocks, but rather ask a simple counterfactual question, "What would be the effect of a generic shock u of size v to variable x on variables x, y, and z?" The situation is essentially no different than that of technology shocks measured using the Solow residual. The SVAR, like a production function used to measure technology shocks, can be used as a measuring instrument to observe shocks to each variable in the VAR system. Just as the real business cycle modeler may be more interested in the generic business cycle phenomena, so the SVAR modeler may be more interested in generic dynamic phenomena. But equally the SVAR modeler can use the particular observed shocks to the whole system of equations to generate specific historical time paths for variables or to conduct counterfactual experiments (e.g., Sims 1999).

There are, however, key differences with the calibrationist approach. Calibrationists make very strong identifying assumptions with respect to structure. Essentially, they claim to know not only the mathematical form of the economic relationships but their parameterization as well. The cost is that they give up on the notion that residuals will conform to tractable probability distributions. In contrast, the SVAR modeler makes minimal structural assumptions and specifies nothing about the values of the parameters other than that they must deliver orthogonal shocks. Whereas typical real business cycles are driven by technology shocks only, SVAR models necessarily observe shocks for each variable in the system.

5. Coming Full Circle: Estimation
by Impulse-Response Matching

Although starting from very different critical stances, both Sims's SVAR approach and the new classicals' calibrationist approach elevated shocks to a starring role. Shocks had become the targets of measurement; models or parts of models had become the measuring instruments. In short, shocks were observable data in Bogen and Woodward's sense. Still, economists were frequently more interested in the phenomena that shocks generated—how the economy reacted generically to a particular type of shock—rather than in the particular shock to a particular variable on a particular date (although sometimes they were interested in shocks as data). Yet the observability of shocks was sine qua non of identifying these phenomena in the first place.

Whether because of the similarity in their views of shocks or, perhaps, for the more mundane sociological reason that economists, like other scientists, cannot resist trying to make sense of each other's work and often seek out common ground, the 1990s witnessed a rapprochement between the DSGE and SVAR programs. Any DSGE model has a reduced-form representation, which can be seen as a special case of a more general VAR, and it also has a contemporaneous causal ordering of its variables that provides a basis for converting the VAR into an SVAR. A calibrated or estimated DSGE model, therefore, can generate variance decompositions and impulse-response functions, which may, in their turns, be compared directly with their counterparts generated from estimated SVARs in which DSGE models are nested. Such comparisons are methodologically equivalent to Kydland and Prescott's strategy of attempting to match the second moments of calibrated models to the equivalent statistics for actual data; they just use different target phenomena.

By the early 1990s the terms of the debate in macroeconomics had shifted from one between monetarists, such as Milton Friedman, and old Keynesians in the macroeconometric tradition, such as James Tobin and Lawrence Klein, or one between the old Keynesians and the new classicals, to one between the new Keynesians and the new classicals (Hoover 1988, 1992). The new Keynesians essentially adopted the technical paradigms of the new classicals, typically including the rational expectations hypothesis, but rejected the notion of perfect competition with continuous market clearing as a sound basis for macroeconomic models, which opened the door for activist policies to improve welfare. Sims (1989, 1992) regarded the debate between the new classicals—especially, the real business cycle modelers—and the new Keynesians as having reached an impasse. In his view, real business cycle modelers assessed their models with an impoverished information set (unconditional moments). Sims (1992, 980) argued that the debate between the monetarists and the old Keynesians had reached a similar impasse, which a focus on time-series information (mainly responses to innovations and Granger causality) had helped resolve by establishing that monetary policy has substantial effects on real output. Analogously, Sims (1992, 980) suggested that real business cycle modelers should consider the richer set of time-series information. He urged them to confront their models with "the documented impulse response facts about interactions of monetary and real variables" (980).

Sims wanted to reestablish the relevance of estimation methods in an area of research that had become dominated by calibration techniques, and he sought common ground in what amounted to adopting Lucas's views on modeling: to select a substantive shock and compare models by the implied dynamic responses to it; a good model is one in which the impulse-response function of the model matches the impulse-response function of the data, as determined through the instrumentality of the SVAR (see also Christiano 1988 and Singleton 1988). Once again, shocks (via impulse-response functions) were data used to characterize phenomena, and models were judged by their ability to reproduce those phenomena.

Sims's proposal must be distinguished from merely matching historical performance in the manner of Hansen and Prescott (1993). The interactions of the different elements are too complex to connect, for example, policy actions to particular outcomes (Leeper, Sims, and Zha 1996, 2). Lawrence Christiano, Martin Eichenbaum, and Charles Evans (1999, 68) argued that the comovements among aggregate variables cannot be interpreted as evidence for or against the neutrality of money, since a "given policy action and the economic events that follow it reflect the effects of *all* the shocks to the economy." Sims's proposal, following Lucas, amounted to a highly restricted counterfactual experiment in which the effects of an isolated shock can be traced out in the economy (i.e., in the SVAR) and compared with the analogous effects in a model. The goal was precisely analogous to experimental controls in a laboratory in which the effect of a single modification is sought against a stable background.

Much of the research in this vein focused on monetary shocks—that is, shocks to short-term interest rates. The short-term interest rate was regarded as the central bank's policy instrument and assumed in the theoretical models to be governed by a policy rule—the central bank's *reaction function* (usually a "Taylor rule"). Monetary policy was, of course, an intrinsically interesting and important area of research. It also held out the promise of clearer discrimination among theoretical models "because different models respond very differently to monetary policy shocks" (Christiano, Eichenbaum, and Evans 1999, 67).

A case that well illustrates Sims's strategy is the so-called price puzzle (see Eichenbaum's 1992 comments on Sims 1992). Simple textbook models suggest that tighter monetary policy should reduce the rate of inflation and the price level. One might expect, therefore, that an exogenous positive shock to the short-term interest rate would result in a declining impulse-response function for prices. In fact, Sims and most subsequent researchers found that the impulse-response function for prices in an SVAR tends to rise for some time before falling. The quest for a theoretical model that accounts for this robust pattern has generated a large literature (see Demiralp, Hoover, and Perez 2010).

Sims's (1992) call for macroeconomists to focus on time-series evidence was taken into consideration subsequently. Whereas in his 1992 article he reported several point-estimate impulse-response functions obtained from alternative VARs for data from different countries, Eric Leeper, Sims, and Tao Zha (1996) focused on the US data and used sophisticated VAR methods to characterize features of aggregate time-series data. Here, in contrast to Sims (1992), the authors present confidence intervals for the estimated impulse-response functions (cf. Christiano, Eichenbaum, and Evans 1996, 1999).

Parallel to characterizing dynamic responses to shocks in the data through VARs, there was the effort to build artificial economies, small-scale dynamic general equilibrium monetary models, to explain the business cycle phenomena and to derive policy implications of them. Sims himself joined this enterprise with Leeper (Leeper and Sims 1994; see also Christiano and Eichenbaum 1995, Yun 1996, and Christiano, Eichenbaum, and Evans 1997). Here the parameters either were estimated with methods such as maximum likelihood or general methods of moments, or were calibrated. Once the parameters were assigned numerical values, one can derive the theoretical impulse-response functions to a monetary shock. However, the closeness of the match between the model-based and the SVAR-based impulse-response functions is usually judged in a rough-and-ready fashion—the same ocular standard applied in matching unconditional moments in the real business cycle literature.

Rotemberg and Woodford 1997 and the literature that derived from this work took impulse-response matching one step farther. Setting aside some of the fine details, the essence of Rotemberg and Woodford's approach was to select the parameterization of the theoretical model to mimimize the distance between the impulse-response functions of the model and those of the SVAR, which became a standard approach in DSGE macroeconomics (only parameters that were identifiable were estimated, the others were calibrated). But their model failed to deliver the slow responses ("inertia") observed in impulse-response functions generated from SVARs. Other economists took on the task of building DSGE models and estimating them by impulse-response matching that captured the inertia of the impulse-response functions (Christiano, Eichenbaum, and Evans 2005; Smets and Wouters 2007; see Duarte 2011).

Rotemberg and Woodford's method, in effect, treated the impulse-response functions of the SVAR as data in their own right—data that could be used as an input to the estimator. Where previously the shock could be regarded as data and the impulse-response functions as phenomena, the shocks were now moved down a level. They stood in the same relationship to those functions as the raw prices of individual goods did to the price index. And the focus of the technique shifted from the isolation of shocks and mimicking of dynamic phenomena back, as it had in the post–Cowles Commission macroeconometric program, to the measurement of structural parameters.

6. Shocks, Macroeconometrics, and Observability

We have explored the question of how economists observe the business cycle phenomena by treating shocks sometimes as data and other times as phenomena. We have thus addressed three main questions in this essay. Two were explicit: What is the relationship of shocks to observation? Why did the uses of the language of shocks explode after the early 1970s? And one question was only implicit: What lessons does the history of shocks provide to philosophers of science or economic methodologists? The answers to these three questions are deeply entangled in our narrative.

In the earliest days of modern econometrics in the 1930s, estimated equations were conceived of as having unobservable error terms. Yet these systems of equations, which had their own deterministic dynamics, were also thought of as being perturbed by actual disturbances, so that the error terms were—to use Frisch's terminology—a mixture of stimuli and aberration. Business cycle theory was principally interested in the stimuli. Business cycle theory gave way after World War II to a theory of macroeconomic policy that aimed to avoid cycles in the first place. Attention thus shifted to the deterministic parts of structural models and, notwithstanding Haavelmo's characterization of shocks as well-behaved phenomena with a regular probabilistic structure, shocks became of secondary interest.

Shocks returned to center stage only when the introduction of the rational expectations hypothesis compelled economists to treat the stochastic specification of a model as a fundamental element rather than as a largely ignorable supplement, and economists began to notice that models could be treated as measuring instruments through which shocks became observable. Rational expectations compel at least a relative-to-modeled-information general equilibrium approach to modeling. Thoroughly done, such an approach—whether theoretically, as in a real business cycle model, or econometrically, as in an SVAR—endogenizes every variable except the shocks. Shocks are then elevated to be the sole drivers of economic dynamics, and their observability, if not their particular values, becomes the sine qua non of a properly specified model. It is, therefore, hardly surprising that a vast rise in the usage of shock occurs after 1973, since shocks are central to a fundamental reconceptualization of macroeconomic theory that, to be sure, began with Frisch forty years earlier, but did not sweep the boards until the rise of the new classical macroeconomics.

We have used Bogen and Woodward's distinction between observable data and inferred phenomena to provide an organizing framework for our discussion. Although it may prove useful as a rough-and-ready contrast, it appears not to draw a bedrock distinction: at some points shocks could be best regarded as phenomena, inferred from observable data, and at other points as data observed using models as measuring instruments, or as the raw material from which data were constructed and which were then used as an input to generate further phenomena or as the basis for higher-order inference. Economics, even in its deepest reaches, is about relationships. What the history of shocks shows is that when we give up the rather tenuous grounding of observability in human senses, then the distinctions between observable and inferrable and between data and phenomena are, at best, relative ones that depend on our principal interests and our targets of explanation, on our presuppositions, explicitly theoretical or merely implicit, and on the modeling tools we have at our disposal—which emphasizes the role of models as measuring instrument (Boumans 2005, esp. 16–17) that integrate a range of ingredients coming from disparate sources, and as autonomous agents that mediate theories and the real world (Morgan and Morrison 1999). Philosophers of science would do well to consider such cases.

References

Adelman, Irma, and Frank L. Adelman. 1959. "The Dynamic Properties of the Klein-Goldberger Model." *Econometrica* 27 (4): 596–625.

Bogen, James, and James Woodward. 1988. "Saving the Phenomena." *Philosophical Review* 97 (3): 303–52.

Boumans, Marcel. 2005. *How Economists Model the World into Numbers.* London: Routledge.

Burns, Arthur F., and Wesley Clair Mitchell. 1946. *Measuring Business Cycles.* New York: National Bureau of Economic Research.

Christiano, Lawrence J. 1988. "Why Does Inventory Investment Fluctuate So Much?" *Journal of Monetary Economics* 21 (2–3): 247–80.

Christiano, Lawrence J., and Martin Eichenbaum. 1995. "Liquidity Effects, Monetary Policy, and the Business Cycle." *Journal of Money, Credit, and Banking* 27 (4): 1113–36.

Christiano, Lawrence J., Martin Eichenbaum, and Charles L. Evans. 1996. "The Effects of Monetary Policy Shocks: Evidence from the Flow of Funds." *Review of Economics and Statistics* 78 (1): 16–34.

———. 1997. "Sticky Price and Limited Participation Models of Money: A Comparison." *European Economic Review* 41 (6): 1201–49.

———. 1999. "Monetary Policy Shocks: What Have We Learned and to What End?" In *Handbook of Macroeconomics*, edited by John Taylor and Michael Woodford, 65–148. Amsterdam: North-Holland.

———. 2005. "Nominal Rigidities and the Dynamic Effects of a Shock to Monetary Policy." *Journal of Political Economy* 113 (1): 1–45.

Cooley, Thomas F., and Edward C. Prescott. 1995. "Economic Growth and Business Cycles." In *Frontiers of Business Cycle Research*, edited by Thomas F. Cooley and Edward C. Prescott. Princeton: Princeton University Press.

Demiralp, Selva, Kevin D. Hoover, and Stephen J. Perez. 2010. "Still Puzzling: Evaluating the Price Puzzle in an Empirically Identified Structural Vector Autoregression." Unpublished working paper, Duke University.

Duarte, Pedro Garcia. 2011. "Recent Developments in Macroeconomics: The DSGE Approach to Business Cycles in Perspective." In *The Elgar Companion to*

Recent Economic Methodology, edited by Wade Hands and John Davis. Cheltenham: Elgar.

Eichenbaum, Martin. 1992. "Comments 'Interpreting the Macroeconomic Time Series Facts: The Effects of Monetary Policy.'" *European Economic Review* 36 (5): 1001–11.

Frisch, Ragnar. 1933. "Propagation Problems and Impulse Problems in Dynamic Economics." In *Economic Essays in Honor of Gustav Cassel*, 171–205. London: Allen and Unwin.

———. (1938) 1948. "Statistical versus Theoretical Relations in Economic Macrodynamics." Reproduced with comments by Jan Tinbergen. University of Oslo.

———. 1939. "A Note on Errors in Time Series." *Quarterly Journal of Economics* 53 (4): 639–40.

Haavelmo, Trygve. 1940. "The Inadequacy of Testing Dynamic Theory by Comparing Theoretical Solutions and Observed Cycles." *Econometrica* 8 (4): 312–21.

———. 1944. "The Probability Approach in Econometrics." *Econometrica* 12 (supplement), July: iii–vi, 1–115.

Hansen, Gary D., and Edward C. Prescott. 1993. "Did Technology Shocks Cause the 1990–1991 Recession?" *American Economic Review* 83 (2): 280–86.

Hansen, Lars Peter. 1982. "Large Sample Properties of Generalized Method of Moments Estimators." *Econometrica* 50 (4): 1029–54.

Hansen, Lars Peter, and Thomas J. Sargent. 1980. "Formulating and Estimating Dynamic Linear Rational Expectations Models." In *Rational Expectations and Econometric Practice*, edited by Robert E. Lucas Jr. and Thomas J. Sargent, 91–126. London: Allen and Unwin.

Hansen, Lars Peter, and Kenneth J. Singleton. 1982. "Generalized Instrumental Variables Estimation of Nonlinear Rational Expectations Models." *Econometrica* 50 (5): 1269–86.

Hendry, David F., and Mary S. Morgan, eds. 1995. *The Foundations of Econometric Analysis*. Cambridge: Cambridge University Press.

Hood, W. C., and T. C. Koopmans, eds. 1953. *Studies in Econometric Method*. New York: Wiley.

Hoover, Kevin D. 1988. *The New Classical Macroeconomics: A Sceptical Inquiry*. Oxford: Blackwell.

———. 1992. "The Rational Expectations Revolution." *Cato Journal* 12 (1): 81–106.

———. 1995. "Facts and Artifacts: Calibration and the Empirical Assessment of Real-Business-Cycle Models." *Oxford Economic Papers* 47 (1): 24–44.

———. 2012. "Microfoundational Programs." In *Microfoundations Reconsidered: The Relationship of Micro and Macroeconomics in Historical Perspective*, edited by Pedro Garcia Duarte and Gilberto Tadeu Lima, 19–61. Cheltenham: Elgar.

Hoover, Kevin D., and Michael E. Dowell. 2001. "Measuring Causes: Episodes in the Quantitative Assessment of the Value of Money." *HOPE* 33 (supplement): 137–61.

Kehoe, Timothy J., and Edward C. Prescott. 1995. "Introduction to the Symposium: The Discipline of Applied General Equilibrium." *Economic Theory* 6 (1): 1–11.

King, Robert G., and Charles I. Plosser. 1994. "Real Business Cycles and the Test of the Adelmans." *Journal of Monetary Economics* 33 (2): 405–38.

King, Robert G., Charles I. Plosser, and Sergio Rebelo. 1988. "Production, Growth, and Business Cycles: I. The Basic Neoclassical Model." *Journal of Monetary Economics* 27 (2–3): 195–232.

Klein, Lawrence R., and Edwin E. Burmeister, eds. 1976. *Econometric Model Performance*. Philadelphia: University of Pennsylvania Press.

Koopmans, Tjalling C. 1950. *Statistical Inference in Dynamic Economic Models*. New York: Wiley.

Kydland, Finn E., and Edward C. Prescott. 1982. "Time to Build and Aggregate Fluctuations." *Econometrica* 50 (6): 1345–70.

———. 1990. "Business Cycles: Real Facts and a Monetary Myth." *Federal Reserve Bank of Minneapolis Quarterly Review* 14 (2): 3–18.

———. 1991. "The Econometrics of the General Equilibrium Approach to Business Cycles." *Scandinavian Journal of Economics* 93 (2): 161–78.

———. 1996. "The Computational Experiment: An Econometric Tool." *Journal of Economic Perspectives* 10 (1): 69–85.

Leeper, Eric, and Christopher A. Sims. 1994. "Toward a Modern Macroeconomic Model Usable for Policy Analysis." *NBER Macroeconomics Annual* 9:81–118.

Leeper, Eric M., Christopher A. Sims, and Tao Zha. 1996. "What Does Monetary Policy Do? *Brookings Papers on Economic Activity*, no. 2:1–78.

Louçã, Francisco. 2007. *The Years of High Econometrics: A Short History of the Generation That Reinvented Economics*. London: Routledge.

Lucas, Robert E., Jr. 1972. "Econometric Testing of the Natural Rate Hypothesis." Reprinted in Lucas 1981, 90–103.

———. 1973. "Some International Evidence on Output-Inflation Tradeoffs." *American Economic Review* 63 (3): 326–34.

———. 1976. "Econometric Policy Evaluation: A Critique." Reprinted in Lucas 1981, 104–30.

———. 1977. "Understanding Business Cycles." Reprinted in Lucas 1981, 215–40.

———. 1980. "Methods and Problems in Business Cycle Theory." *Journal of Money, Credit, and Banking* 12 (4, pt. 2): 696–715.

———. 1981. *Studies in Business Cycle Theory*. Oxford: Blackwell.

Morgan, Mary S. 1990. *The History of Econometric Ideas*. Cambridge: Cambridge University Press.

Morgan, Mary S., and Margaret Morrison. 1999. "Models as Mediating Instruments." In *Models as Mediators*, edited by Mary S. Morgan and Margaret Morrison, 10–37. Cambridge: Cambridge University Press.

Muth, John F. 1961. "Rational Expectations and the Theory of Price Movements." *Econometrica* 29 (3): 315–35.

Prescott, Edward C. 1986. "Theory Ahead of Business Cycle Measurement." *Federal Reserve Bank of Minneapolis Quarterly Review* 10 (4): 9–22.

Qin, Duo, and Christopher L. Gilbert. 2001. "The Error Term in the History of Time Series Econometrics." *Econometric Theory* 17 (2): 424–50.

Rotemberg, Julio, and Michael Woodford. 1997. "An Optimization-Based Econometric Framework for the Evaluation of Monetary Policy." *NBER Macroeconomics Annual* 12:297–346.

Sargent, Thomas J. 1972. "Rational Expectations and the Term Structure of Interest Rates." *Journal of Money, Credit, and Banking* 4 (1, pt. 1): 74–97.

———. 1982. "Beyond Demand and Supply Curves in Macroeconomics." *American Economic Review* 72 (2): 382–89.

Sargent, Thomas J., and Christopher A. Sims. 1977. "Business Cycle Modeling without Pretending to Have Too Much *A-priori* Economic Theory." In *New Methods in Business Cycle Research*, edited by Christopher A. Sims, 45–109. Minneapolis: Federal Reserve Bank of Minneapolis.

Sims, Christopher A. 1980. "Macroeconomics and Reality." *Econometrica* 48 (1): 1–48.

———. 1982. "Policy Analysis with Econometric Models." *Brookings Papers on Economic Activity* 13 (1): 107–52.

———. 1986. "Are Forecasting Models Usable for Policy Analysis?" *Federal Reserve Bank of Minneapolis Quarterly Review* 10:2–15.

———. 1989. "Models and Their Uses." *American Journal of Agricultural Economics* 71 (2): 489–94.

———. 1992. "Interpreting the Macroeconomic Time Series Facts—the Effects of Monetary Policy." *European Economic Review* 36 (5): 975–1000.

———. 1999. "The Role of Interest Rate Policy in the Generation and Propagation of Business Cycles: What Has Changed Since the '30s?" In *Beyond Shocks: What Causes Business Cycles*, edited by Jeffrey C. Fuhrer and Scott Schuh, 121–60. Federal Reserve Bank of Boston Conference Series, no. 42. Boston: Federal Reserve Bank of Boston.

Singleton, Kenneth J. 1988. "Econometric Issues in the Analysis of Equilibrium Business Cycle Models." *Journal of Monetary Economics* 21 (2–3): 361–86.

Slutsky, Eugen. (1927) 1937. "The Summation of Random Causes as the Source of Cyclic Processes." *Econometrica* 5 (2): 105–46. [Originally published in Russian by the Conjuncture Institute of Moscow.]

Smets, Frank, and Raf Wouters. 2007. "Shocks and Frictions in US Business Cycles: A Bayesian DSGE Approach." *American Economic Review* 97 (3): 586–606.

Tinbergen, Jan. 1935. "Annual Survey: Suggestions on Quantitative Business Cycle Theory." *Econometrica* 3 (3): 241–308.

———. 1939. *Business Cycles in the United States of America: 1919–32*. Geneva: League of Nations.

Wicksell, Knut. 1907. "Krisernas Gåta." *Statsøkonomisk tidsskrift* 21 (4): 255–86.

Yun, Tack. 1996. "Nominal Price Rigidity, Money Supply Endogeneity, and Business Cycles." *Journal of Monetary Economics* 37 (2): 345–70.

Contributors

Vincent Barnett is an independent researcher with interests in Russian history, the history of economic thought, and the economic history of the film industry. He has previously held Research Fellow posts in the UK at Birmingham University, Cardiff Business School, Oxford University, and Bedfordshire University. His first book was titled *Kondratiev and the Dynamics of Economic Development* (1998) and his most recent is *E. E. Slutsky as Economist and Mathematician* (2011). He is currently preparing the volume on John Maynard Keynes in the Routledge Historical Biography series.

Marcel Boumans is associate professor of history and methodology of economics at the University of Amsterdam and at the Erasmus University Rotterdam. He is, with Evelyn Forget, coeditor of the *Journal of the History of Economic Thought*. His main research focus is understanding empirical research practices from (combined) historical and philosophical perspectives. His current research project is on science outside the laboratory. On these topics he has published a monograph, *How Economists Model the World into Numbers* (2005), and edited *Measurement in Economics: A Handbook* (2007). Most recently, he wrote, with John Davis, a textbook, *Economic Methodology: Understanding Economics as a Science* (2010).

Loïc Charles is professor of economics at the University of Reims and researcher at INED and EconomiX. His interest is in history of economics thought, economic history, and early modern history. He has published in the *European Journal of the History of Economic Thought*, *HOPE*, and *Revue d'histoire moderne et contemporaine* and has a forthcoming article in *Past and Present*. He is preparing a book with Christine Théré on François Quesnay and physiocracy.

Emmanuel Didier is a permanent research fellow at the Groupe de sociologie politique et morale (CNRS-EHESS). He has been trained as a statistician and practices quantitative sociology, but he mainly studies statistics as a sociological object. His latest book is *En quoi consiste l'Amérique: Les statistiques, le New Deal, et la démocratie* (2009), and his forthcoming one, *Benchmarking*, with I. Bruno and J. Prévieux, is a critique of management by numbers that penetrates public administrations nowadays.

Federico D'Onofrio is a PhD student at the University of Utrecht in the history of economics. He is writing his dissertation on the history of agricultural statistics.

Pedro Garcia Duarte is associate professor of economics at the University of São Paulo (FEA-USP), Brazil. His research interests are the history of postwar economics, in particular macro and monetary economics, with an emphasis on how modeling strategies and techniques had their use stabilized over time. He has published articles on this subject in leading journals and has recently coedited the volume *Microfoundations Reconsidered: The Relationship of Micro and Macroeconomics in Historical Perspective*, published by Edward Elgar in 2012.

José M. Edwards is assistant professor of economics at the School of Government of the Universidad Adolfo Ibáñez (Chile). His research focuses on the academic production and analysis of self-reports, and more generally on the history and methodology of recent economics.

Craufurd D. Goodwin is James B. Duke Professor of Economics at Duke University, where he has served as department chair, vice provost, and dean of the Graduate School. He was editor of *HOPE* from 1969 to 2010 and is editor of the book series Historical Perspectives on Modern Economics (Cambridge University Press). A long-standing interest of his has been the Bloomsbury group; among his publications on Bloomsbury are *Art and the Market: Roger Fry on Commerce in Art* (1998), "Economic Man in the Garden of Eden" (2000), and "The Bloomsbury Group as Creative Community" (2011). His most recent research has been on the American journalist Walter Lippmann.

Kevin D. Hoover is professor of economics and philosophy at Duke University. He has written extensively on macroeconomics, monetary economics, econometrics, the history of economics, and economic methodology and philosophy. He is editor of *HOPE* and past editor of the *Journal of Economic Methodology*.

Harro Maas is associate professor at Utrecht University. He has published widely in the history of economics, especially the Victorian period. His book *William Stanley Jevons and the Making of Modern Economics* (2005) was awarded the Joseph J. Spengler best book award by the History of Economics Society. At present he directs a research project, funded by the Netherlands Organisation for Scientific Research, on the history of observation that takes three sites of observation as its starting point: the observatory, the laboratory, and the armchair.

Mary S. Morgan is professor of history and philosophy of economics at the London School of Economics and the University of Amsterdam. She has published on a range of topics from statistics to experiments, narrative and observation, and from nineteenth-century Social Darwinism to game theory in the Cold War. Her main books include *The History of Econometric Ideas* (1990); *Models as Mediators* (1999; with Margaret Morrison); *How Well Do Facts Travel?* (2011; with Peter Howlett); and *The World in the Model* (2012). She is currently a British Academy–Wolfson Research Professor and, in that capacity, is working under a grant titled "Re-thinking Case Studies across the Social Sciences."

Malcolm Rutherford is professor of economics at the University of Victoria, Canada. He has published widely on the topic of institutional economics in *HOPE*, the *Journal of the History of Economic Thought*, the *European Journal of the History of Economic Thought*, the *Journal of Economic Issues*, *Labor History*, and the *Journal of Economic Perspectives*. He is author of *Institutions in Economics: The Old and the New Institutionalism* (1994) and *The Institutionalist Movement in American Economics, 1918–1947: Science and Social Control* (2011).

Thomas A. Stapleford is associate professor in the Program of Liberal Studies at the University of Notre Dame, where he also teaches in the graduate program in History and Philosophy of Science. His dissertation, revised and published as *The Cost of Living in America: A Political History of Economic Statistics, 1880–2000* (2009), won the Joseph Dorfman Best Dissertation Award from the History of Economics Society in 2004. He has published articles on economic statistics and political economy in a variety of journals and is working on a history of family economics, the first effort by economists to make empirical studies of household life.

Christine Théré is a researcher at the National Institute of Demographic Studies (INED) in Paris. She specializes in the history of French political economy and its authors before 1789. She coedited *Oeuvres économiques complètes et autres textes de François Quesnay* (2005) with Loïc Charles and Jean-Claude Perrot. She is preparing a book with Loïc Charles on François Quesnay and physiocracy.

Index